D1553781

The Scottish Reformation

By the same author

Blast and Counterblast
The Parishes of Medieval Scotland
The Enigma of Mary Stuart
Medieval Religious Houses, Scotland
The Scottish Covenanters, 1660–1688
Regional Aspects of the Scottish Reformation

The Scottish Reformation

Church and Society in sixteenth century Scotland

Ian B. Cowan

ST. MARTIN'S PRESS
New York

St. Martin's Press, Inc., 175 Fifth Avenue, New York, NY 10010
Printed in Great Britain
First published in the United States of America in 1982

ISBN 0-312-70519-0

Library of Congress Cataloging in Publication Data

Cowan, Ian Borthwick.
The Scottish Reformation.

Bibliography: p.
Includes index.
1. Reformation - Scotland. 2. Scotland - Church history - 16th century. I. Title.
BR385.C76 1982 274.11'06 82-5834
ISBN 0-312-70519-0 AACR2

To Ingrid

Contents

Preface

Views about the Scottish Reformation have changed dramatically in the last twenty years. Until then, partisanship, rather than scholarship, had often prevailed in accounts of the events of 1559–60. The appearance some four hundred years after the Reformation of Gordon Donaldson's volume entitled *The Scottish Reformation*, and some two years later of the collection, *Essays on the Scottish Reformation* (ed. D. McRoberts, 1962) by a group of largely Catholic historians, produced a new professedly non-partisan dimension in studies of the Scottish Reformation. Since that date many other volumes have examined different aspects of the Reformation in Scotland. Few, if any, of them have remained totally free of bias, and most have chosen to concentrate on one particular aspect of the religious upheaval. In this respect, the organization of the church, both before and after the Reformation, has attracted more attention than has its spiritual impact upon society. The present study, of which Chapter Five is an amended and expanded version of the thesis advanced in my Historical Association pamphlet on *Regional Aspects of the Scottish Reformation* (1978), not only attempts to rectify that defect, but also provides a personal interpretation of the more recent views on the causation and emergence of the Reformation in Scotland. The two maps included in this volume are reproduced from that pamphlet, by kind permission of The Historical Association.

My interest in this subject was first stimulated by my former teacher and colleague, Professor Gordon Donaldson, historiographer royal for Scotland, and has benefited much from the advice of my friends and colleagues in the University of Glasgow: Dr Jenny Wormald, Dr James Kirk, and Dr John Durkan. My thanks are also due to Mr Donald Withrington of the University of Aberdeen who kindly read and commented upon my typescript. If faults and bias remain, the responsibility is mine. I also wish to record my appreciation for the help of Mrs Alison Mason who so ungrudgingly prepared my somewhat illegible manuscript for the publisher, and my thanks to my daughter Susan-Jane who prepared the index.

Ian B. Cowan
University of Glasgow

1
Religious and Secular Influences in Pre-Reformation Scotland

By the sixteenth century the church in Scotland had a well-defined organization governed by a hierarchy that included two archbishops and eleven bishops. Under their authority, or in the case of the religious orders, that of their superiors, a host of well-organized clerics, both regular and secular, numbering in total some 3,000 in a population of about 800,000 or 900,000, purported to serve the religious needs of the nation. On the organizational side so much is clear and well attested. What is less certain, however, is how the church affected men's lives. In theory church and society were seen acting in concert. Nevertheless, while at certain levels it can be demonstrated that there was no sharp division between the workings of the church on one hand and the social and economic life of the laity on the other, this identity of interest could be minimal. Lay participation in the working of the church was only evident in a few peripheral areas: the occasional clerk or lawyer might appear in his professional capacity in synods or other ecclesiastical bodies; parish clerks might be elected by local landowners; and the exercise of lay patronage, which was in itself restricted, might give to the laity some voice in appointment to benefices. The church for its part, however, claimed a much wider jurisdiction over the lives of the laity.[1]

In essence this claim stemmed from the fundamental duty of the church to act as the custodian of the nation's spiritual welfare. In this respect the church fulfilled its role in a variety of ways. Services could be magnificent occasions, and the Aberdeen breviary compiled under the supervision of William Elphinstone, bishop of Aberdeen (1483–1514), not only gives an indication of the complicated nature of certain services and of the wide variety of saints who were honoured, but also illustrates that music was an integral part of such services. Of the various service books used in church, the most important were the missal and the breviary. The *Missale* was strictly a book of public worship and contained the service of the mass; along with the ordinary and the canon, or the fixed and invariable part of every mass, daily recited, were a number of *Missae* or Offices, with collects, epistles, gospels, graduals and sequences, proper to each Sunday or solemn feast and other special occasions. The Breviary was a work of more general complexion and excepting the daily service of the mass contained the entire offices throughout the year. It had been compiled in the eleventh century from several books of divine offices – the *Psalterium*, *Antiphonarium*, *Hymnarium* and *Martyrologium* – and contained the canonical hours, the prayers, hymns and lessons ordained to be sung at certain hours of the day and night. For convenience it was frequently divided into two parts, the one for the summer and the other for the winter half of the year. Unlike the canon of the mass, which was carefully protected from alterations, additions and omissions, the breviary, in virtue of the power vested in every diocesan bishop to accommodate the rites of the church to their particular needs, incorporated a variety of usages. Distinctive versions that had adapted the arrangement of the psalms, a selection of lessons and the reading of the gospels to local festivals were in use at cathedrals such as York, Hereford and Lincoln. The Scots had chosen to follow the custom of Sarum or Salisbury with perhaps one or two saints added to adapt the books to some restricted locality. The Aberdeen Breviary, however, changed the situation vastly. More than seventy Scottish saints, drawn from every district of Scotland, and all provided with historical lessons and their own feast days, appear. This was clearly meant to supplant the Sarum use in Scotland and appeal directly to the people as a national liturgy. Any doubts on this score were removed by an edict of James IV in 1507. He not only recommended that books of devotion should henceforward be 'eftir our awin Scottis use and with legendis of Scottis sanctis' but positively ordered that 'na maner of sic bukis of Salusbury use be brocht to be sauld within our realme in tym cuming'.[2]

Only cathedrals, collegiate churches and large burgh churches had the resources for the most impressive services, the most solemn of which were marked by the lighting of extra candles in the church. The day's liturgy began with 'morrow mass' and thereafter mass might be celebrated hourly up to the time of the 'high mass' which was a sung mass with organ, celebrated by the parish priest and attended by all the chaplains of the choir and of the nave. Vespers were said or sung, possibly with organ, some time in the afternoon between two and five o'clock, and were followed by compline.[3]

Spiritual services were not confined to the saying of the mass, however. The sacraments that accompanied birth, marriage and death were all of extreme importance, as was the hearing of confession and the granting of dispensations of all kinds. Baptism was normally carried out in the parish church. The font, made of wood or stone with an inset basin of lead, usually stood at the door. The child was often immersed; the priest held it with its face towards the east and dipped it first on the right side, then on the left and then face downwards. After baptism the child was lifted from the font by one of the sponsors. In Scotland this was known as 'heaving' and there are a number of references to James IV 'heving' infants at the font. Baptism by affusion of water also seems to have been practised and in this instance a sponsor often held the child during the ceremony. Either way priesthood and laity were united in their participation in this ceremony.

Marriage, if accompanied by the sacrament, was likewise held in church after the calling of the banns on three separate occasions in the parish churches of both parties. The regularization of situations that might otherwise have prevented the solemnization of marriage might also be the feature of a pre-nuptial ceremony. An example of the latter process occurred in St Michael's, Dumfries, on 6 August 1550, where Herbert Maxwell of Kirkconnell and his wife Janet, daughter of George Maxwell, burgess of Dumfries, delivered to William Gordon, dean of Dunblane, letters executorial dated Rome, 28 November 1549, under the seal of the penitentiary, giving communion to absolve and dispense the petitioners for marrying within the fourth degree of affinity and kinship and legitimizing any children. Absolution was duly given whereupon the couple took legal instruments to protect their further interests. Such dispensations could be expensive and it is clear from a somewhat earlier agreement that the cost of obtaining the necessary dispensation might be shared between the groom and his prospective father-in-law. Formal betrothal often preceded marriage by many years but could in some instances be agreed a relatively short time beforehand. The betrothal of David Bothwell and Janet Hamilton, daughter of the late James, earl of Arran, which took place before the parish priest of Linlithgow at 8 a.m. on 13 February 1532 to be followed by the marriage at 4 a.m. on the following day was, however, clearly irregular in so far as the banns had not been read on the requisite number of occasions. This ceremony, unlike many Scottish weddings in the middle ages, was at least in church, for in many instances before the Reformation a simple affirmation of marriage between the contracting parties was all that was legally required. Death was another matter and the solemn dirge was constantly being celebrated in parish churches. On the vigil of a requiem mass, the common bellman would traverse a burgh calling out the names of the departed and exhorting the faithful to pray for their souls and requesting them to attend the solemn dirge the following afternoon. This memorial service - the Placebo and Dirge - consisted of vespers and matins for the dead and was performed when the body was brought to the church and placed before the altar. Burials of the more socially important were carried out in the church, the most popular spot being within the choir as near the high altar as possible.[4]

Every effort was made to maintain the sanctity of the churchyard, but it is obvious that as a public meeting place it might be used for markets and fairs, bear-baiting and wrestling. Such abuses inevitably reflected on the parish priest. He might already be the subject of criticism as a pluralist, for many of the 1,100 odd parishes in the country were held by non-residents who might engage underpaid curates to carry out parochial functions. These weaknesses may, however, have been more than offset by frequent contact between layman and priest. The rural priest who farmed his glebe would be integrated both socially and economically with the populace which he served; the chaplin who served in a lord's chapel might also act as tutor to his children; likewise in urban areas the clergy and in particular chaplains in burgh churches maintained a close relationship with the guilds and fraternities whose altars they served. Increased rapacity by both vicars and curates may have jeopardized this relationship in the sixteenth century, but in many instances the priesthood was still admirably placed to serve the society in which its members lived and worked.

The impact of the church depended, however, upon its own vitality as an institution and as the immediate post-Reformation period has frequently been treated as a period of decline in the

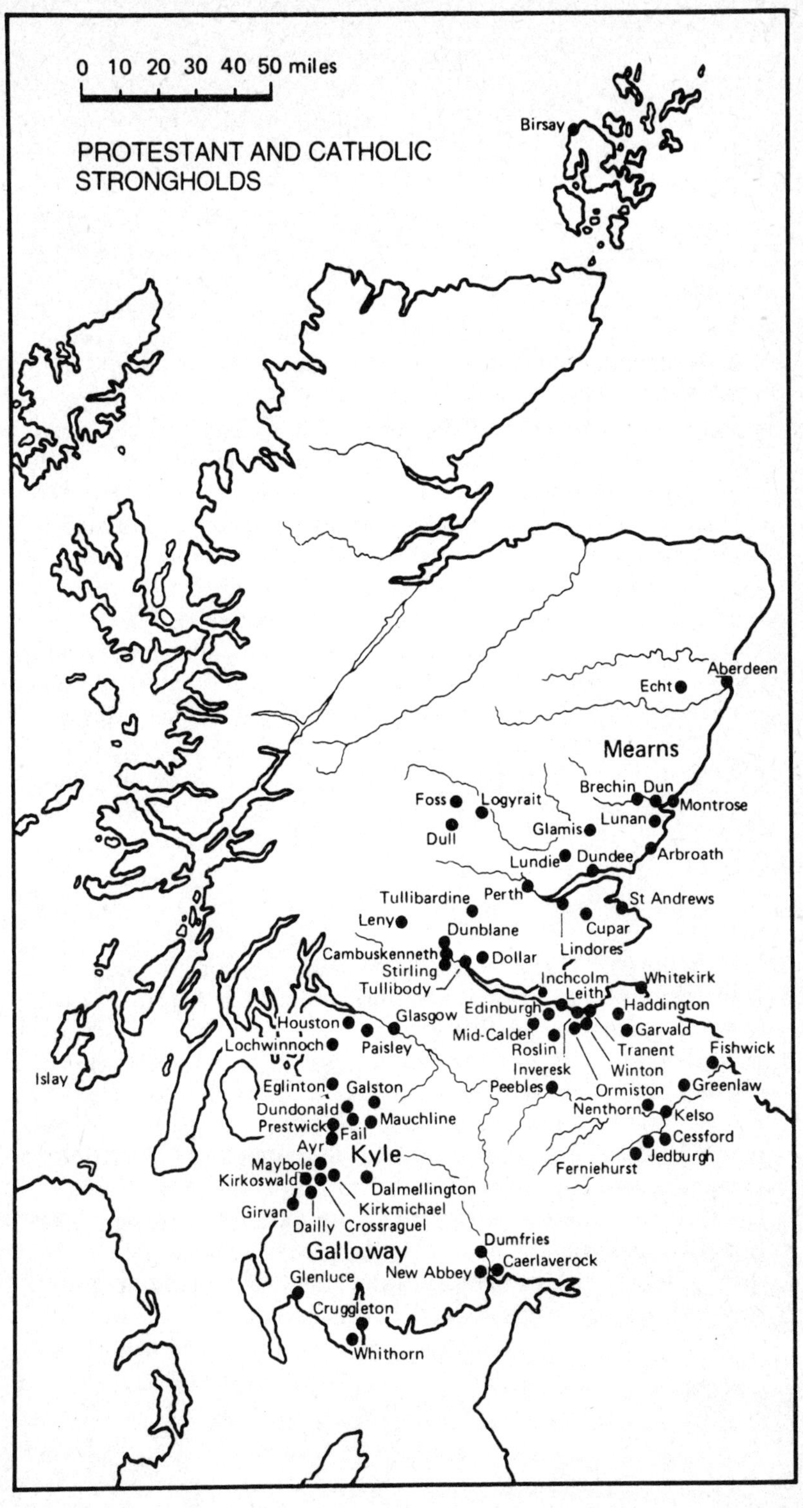
0 10 20 30 40 50 miles
PROTESTANT AND CATHOLIC STRONGHOLDS
Birsay
Aberdeen
Echt
Mearns
Brechin
Dun
Montrose
Lunan
Foss
Logyrait
Glamis
Dull
Arbroath
Lundie
Dundee
Perth
Tullibardine
St Andrews
Leny
Cupar
Dunblane
Lindores
Cambuskenneth
Dollar
Stirling
Tullibody
Inchcolm
Whitekirk
Leith
Edinburgh
Haddington
Houston
Glasgow
Mid-Calder
Garvald
Lochwinnoch
Paisley
Roslin
Tranent
Fishwick
Inveresk
Winton
Islay
Eglinton
Galston
Peebles
Ormiston
Greenlaw
Dundonald
Nenthorn
Kelso
Prestwick
Mauchline
Fail
Cessford
Ayr
Kyle
Jedburgh
Maybole
Ferniehurst
Kirkoswald
Dalmellington
Kirkmichael
Girvan
Dailly
Crossraguel
Dumfries
Galloway
Caerlaverock
New Abbey
Glenluce
Cruggleton
Whithorn

fortunes of the Scottish church, the continuing contributions of the church have often been overlooked. The vitality inherent in both monastic and secular clergy was not inconsiderable and this was manifest not only in the continuing organization of the church but in the role that the church still played in the life of medieval society. This duality was present in the religious processions and the other holy day celebrations held in honour of the particular patron saint of a craft guild within a burgh. These were specially associated with the religious life of the citizens, but the secular side was also provided for by the holding of *Wappinschaws* (weapon displays) and sports. The major processions took place at Candlemas and Corpus Christi and both at Aberdeen, where all the guilds of the town went in procession before the blessed sacrament, and at Edinburgh, where a band of musicians led the way, the spectacle must have been imposing. Religious objects or relics were frequently carried on such occasions and at Edinburgh on 1 September each year, St Giles day, a statue of the saint led by 'tabors and trumpets, banners and bagpipes' was borne through the burgh. How far such manifestations encouraged popular religious fervour is uncertain, but the efforts made later by the reformed church to ensure their suppression would indicate that the enthusiasm engendered was not inconsiderable. Closely associated with these processions were the plays and pageants; little is known about them but they represented in dramatic form a variety of spiritual subjects which were first acted in churches and afterwards in the streets on a moveable stage. In addition there were playfields (open spaces for the public performance of plays) attached to all the leading burghs. Taking themes such as the creation and the fall of man, these plays were enacted annually at Perth from the late fifteenth century to the Reformation. At Aberdeen the first association of the crafts with the Corpus Christi celebrations occurs in a statute of 1513 ordaining the provision of torches for religious processions. It is not, however, until 1530 that pageants were maintained in connection with the Corpus Christi procession. Further enactments show that such pageants were strictly regulated by the bailies and that the crafts jealously guarded their respective positions or 'roumes' in the procession before the sacrament. The deacons or masters of the crafts were held responsible for furnishing the pageants in the years between 1530 and 1551; a defaulting craft was liable to a fine. This, coupled with a reenactment in 1531 of a statute of 1510, calling on all the crafts to maintain the processions and prescribing fines and even banishment for failure to do so, suggests that resistance to such occasions was not unknown, but whether on religious or financial grounds cannot be ascertained. The uncertain relationship between such pageants and devotion is also to be seen at Haddington, for although there are references to a cycle of craft pageants between 1530 and 1552, the town council in 1537 ordered the crafts to play their pageant for that year on Midsummer Day instead of at Corpus Christi. Changes are also evident at Edinburgh where the play produced by the hammermen for over a decade after 1505 had King Herod as its subject, but by 1553 reference is made to municipal plays. These were mostly of an allegorical nature and could not be compared with the older dramas founded on religious themes. Financial and secular considerations had become paramount and their religious impact considerably less.[5]

Pilgrimages, which had figured equally prominently as an outward expression of popular piety, also became less common in the sixteenth century. Changing religious attitudes may have hastened this decline, but political and later religious upheavals in various parts of Europe undoubtedly also played a part. Nevertheless, Scottish pilgrims continued to visit Compostella, Rome and the Holy Land. A departing pilgrim wearing his pilgrim's badge, cloak and cap and bearing his pilgrim's staff and wallet was still not an unknown sight. One of the more illustrious Scottish pilgrims of the early sixteenth century was Archbishop Blacader of Glasgow who, having already journeyed to Rome in 1504, set out once again in 1508 bound on this occasion for the Holy Land. Blacader left Scotland in early February intending in the manner of many pilgrims before and since to spend Easter in Rome. By mid-May he was in Venice where on 1 June 1508 he took part in the traditional ceremony of blessing the sea and, having remained there until later that month, he embarked on a ship for the long sail to Jaffa. Like so many pilgrims before him, he failed to survive the journey, dying en route on 28 July. Of the thirty-six companions with whom he had set out from Venice, only nine survived. Whether better fortune attended a more humble pilgrim, Patrik Gilleis of Glenkirk, bailie of Peebles who received a royal letter of protection before setting out on his pilgrimage to Jerusalem in the following year cannot be ascertained. In the years thereafter Scottish pilgrims to the Holy Land grew fewer and fewer, but the hermit John Scott who was living near Jedburgh, *c.* 1535 had pilgrimaged there and had returned with 'some date-tree leaves and a pocke full of stones which he fained were taken out of the piller to which Christ was bound when he was scourged'. In 1550 a lay-brother called Thomas, a Scotsman by birth, was reported in Brussels to have spent many years in Jerusalem. Contact between Scotland and the east was far from extinguished in the sixteenth century and in 1520 a monk of St Catherine's monastery of Mount Sinai actually visited Edinburgh to enrol the faithful in the confraternity of St Catherine and receive from them alms for the up-keep of her shrine.[6]

Other pilgrims were less adventuresome and visited pilgrimage centres nearer home; Sir James Sandilands was licensed in 1526 to pass to Rome in penance for the crime of murder and John Erskine of Dun, who had killed a priest in the belfry of the parish church of Montrose, was licensed in 1537 to pass to France. If overseas pilgrimages diminished in importance, Scottish devotional centres remained in vogue. Among the most popular of the Scottish shrines were those at Tain, Whithorn, St Andrews and Glasgow, whose cathedral was described in 1449 as 'the most stately among cathedrals in Scotland in which the bodies of many saints especially St Kentigern repose'. Traditionally, however, 'the four heid pilgrimages of Scotland' were Paisley, Melrose, Scone and Dundee. Smaller pilgrimage centres were no less favoured; James IV, a frequent pilgrim to Tain and Whithorn, also visited the relics at Kilwinning in Ayrshire in 1508, and paid several visits to the shrine of St Adrian on the Isle of May where seafowl shooting provided an additional attraction. In August 1536, James V made a pilgrimage on foot from Stirling castle to the Loretto chapel in Musselburgh after the failure of his first attempt to sail to France for his marriage to the daughter of the French king. This chapel, which stemmed from increased devotion for Marian shrines, was founded in 1534, some six years after the inception of a similar shrine at Perth. Not everyone approved of such pilgrimages and undoubtedly the crowds of genuine pilgrims attracted not only many undesirables, but also encouraged the fabrication of false relics and bogus miracles. Sir David Lindsay in his *Dialog betuix Experience and ane Courtear*' writes:

I have sene pass one mervellous multytude
   Young men and women, flyngand on ther feit,
Under the forme of feyrit sanctytude,
   For tyll adore one image in Loreit

Quhy thole ye under your dominioun
   Ane craftye preist or fenyeit fals armeit
Abuse the people of this regioun
   Onely for thare particular profeit
   And speciallye that Heremeit of Lawreit
He pat the comoun peeple in beleve
   That Blynd gat seycht and crukit gat thare feit
The quhilk that palyard ne way can appreve.

Nevertheless, if the relics exhibited at some of these shrines were less than authentic few of the more blatant frauds which were perpetuated both in England and continental Europe appear to have been attempted in Scotland. The pardoner with his collection of false relics so vividly portrayed by Sir David Lindsay in the *Satire of the Three Estates* is not entirely a literary fiction, but in general, it is significant that protestant historians like Knox who would almost certainly have seized upon such activities with relish, are remarkably silent on the subject.[7]

If the church could not satisfy popular religious aspirations by encouraging pilgrimages and pageants, it might still hope to do so by enabling its adherents to worship in surroundings that encouraged genuine devotion. In this respect churches were not only to be functional but also beautiful and meaningful. This was achieved by the encouragement of the arts of stone-carving, wood-carving and painting, the major inspiration for which was undoubtedly of French and Flemish origin. Even though there was an unquestionable deterioration of style in ecclesiastical architecture during the first half of the sixteenth century, constructions such as that of the east end or choir of the parish church of Stirling were completed during this period. The initiative was taken by the town council which declared in 1507 that they had 'takin apon hand to big and compleitlie edifye, and end ane gud and sufficient queyr conformand to the body of the peroch kirk of the said burgt' and entered into an agreement to this effect with the abbey of Dunfermline to which the church was appropriated. A service was held in the reconstructed choir in 1520, but it does not seem to have been completed at that date and payment for timber for the choir was still being made in 1523. The building of collegiate churches also continued. At Biggar, which was cruciform in plan, the work commenced by the founder in 1545/6 was continued by his son until the intervention of the Reformation; while at Seton which had become collegiate in 1493 the widow of George, third lord Seton who was killed at Flodden:

> Biggit the northomoss yll of the College kirk of Seton and took down the yll biggit be Dame Katherine Sinclair on the south side of it, the said college kirk, because the syde of it stood to the syde of the kirk, to mack it a parfacte and a proper cornet and cross kirk and biggit up the steeple as ye see it now to one grit high swa that it wants little of compleiting.

Stone carving exemplified infinite attention to detail and in this respect elaborately carved sacrament houses not only illustrate the intricacies of the craft but also illustrate the same intense popular devotion to the Blessed Sacrament that was widespread in the Low Countries and Germany. Wood-carving was an equally important outlet for religious expression, but the surviving examples such as the Ochiltree Stalls in Dunblane cathedral and the rood screen with its magnificent oak door in the parish church of Foulis-Easter are of late fifteenth rather than of sixteenth century origin. So too with religious paintings, of which the best Scottish examples are four large pre-Reformation paintings on oak panels at Foulis Easter and the superb panels, attributed to the Flemish artist Hugo van der Goes, which were painted for the collegiate church of the Holy Trinity Edinburgh shortly after 1469. Similar paintings must have been evident in other large Scottish churches and one of immediate pre-Reformation provenance that was hung above the altar of the incorporation of glovers in the parish church of Perth depicts their patron, St Bartholomew, holding a flaying knife.[8]

Of all the arts fostered by the church, the music that formed an integral part of its devotions was one of the most favoured and the flowering of the art of composition following the erection of the Chapel Royal at Stirling in 1501 owed much to religious inspiration. Little of the repertoire survived the Reformation but there is enough extant to prove that a rich store of polyphonic music existed in Scotland before that event. Most of the surviving pieces are by sixteenth-century composers and are included in three main collections, all of ecclesiastical origin: the Scone Antiphonary, the Dunkeld Music Book and the St Andrews Music Books. The latter collection appears to be the earliest of the three and its pieces may not be of Scottish composition. The Dunkeld collection on the other hand, which contains motets and antiphons but only one complete mass for five parts, undoubtedly contains some compositions of Scottish origin although others are Flemish. So too in the Scone Antiphonary in which, however, at least seven works – five masses and two motets – are attributable to Robert Carver, canon of Scone. Born in 1487, Carver entered religious life in 1503 and was composing by the age of twenty-two. His nineteen-part motet for four sopranos, two altos, ten tenors and three basses has led to his description as a 'composer gifted with a high degree of musical imagination and sensitivity'. An experienced and competent choir would have been required to perform such a work and it may be doubted whether the abbey of Scone, which only possessed about sixteen canons in the period of the Reformation, could have provided the expertise required for its performance. Nevertheless, the foundation of collegiate churches and the song schools associated with them undoubtedly stimulated musical studies.

At the cathedrals too, music was encouraged and provision for choristers was a significant feature in most constitutions. At Kirkwall Bishop Reid, in reviewing the statutes in 1544, provided that the chanter who was to be instructed in at least the Gregorian chant should be bound to raise and terminate the singing in the choir, to regulate the singers and the celebration of divine service on Sundays and to admit boys to the choir. His deputy the subchanter was to be well instructed in both kinds of song, and was especially to be a skilled player upon the organ. Every Sunday and feast days during the first and second vespers, high mass, and in the time of the more solemn feasts he was obliged to play upon the organ the *Te Deum Laudamus* and the *Benedictus*. Provision was also made for six choristers who were to be candle-bearers and were to sing the responses and versicles and other things, as dictated by custom in the choir. At Aberdeen, Bishop Elphinstone's statutes of 1506 decreed that the cathedral should support eleven boy choristers and twenty singing priests, while at Dunkeld the endowment of four additional vicars' choral in 1446 and the institution shortly after that date of six choir boys appears to have had the desired effect; in the early sixteenth century members of the choir could be described in one case as 'highly trained in the theory of music as well as the art of singing', in another as 'steady in the chant', and in yet another as 'sublime in musical theory and in organ playing'. This latter accomplishment was very important as the organ occupied a central part in church music, and masses and motets frequently incorporated a solo part for the organ which in turn blended with the singers. Organs were being installed in all major churches by the early sixteenth century; a canon of Holyrood was paid seven pounds in 1506 for repairing the 'organis in Strivelin' and in 1511 one 'Gilleam' described as 'organist makar of the kingis' was given eight pounds three shillings 'for expensis maid be him on the said organis in gait skynnis and parchment for the bellis [bellows], in nailles and sprentis of irne, in glew, papir, candill. . . .' A monk of Kilwinning built the organ in the parish church of Ayr in 1536 and became responsible for its maintenance thereafter. Town councils in particular were especially attentive to the standard of music attained; chaplains whom they employed were expected not only to be 'plain' singers, that is, to sing a Gregorian melody in unison, but also to be able to sing 'pricket' song, that is to sing one of the countermelodies pricked or set down against a Gregorian melody. At Holy Trinity, St Andrews, an agreement was reached in 1527 that no priest was to be granted an altar in the church unless competent in 'playnsong pricket song and descant'. Standards were rigorously maintained and at Aberdeen in 1540 the magistrates dismissed the entire choir, with the exception of one old man, and enrolled a new one. The mastership of the burgh song school was an important post and in this respect councils vied with one another to engage the finest musicians. The services of John Fethy, one of the most accomplished musicians of his day, who was responsible for introducing into Scotland 'the curius new fingering and playing on organs' – a technique involving the use of the thumbs as well as the fingers – were much sought after. Fethy, who had studied in Flanders, served in turn as organist at Dundee in 1531, St Nicholas, Aberdeen, in 1544 and in Edinburgh where he was allowed twenty shillings on appointment for 'tonying of the organis' from 1551. He was also an accomplished composer, although only one of his works, a setting of 'O God Above' survives in the Scottish Psalter of 1566.[9]

Most Scottish musicians had been trained in Flanders. Fethy and his fellow composer Thomas Inglis both left Scotland in 1498 to study music there. In 1512 'foure scolaris, menstrallis' were sent to Flanders at the king's command to buy musical instruments, and in 1553, Edinburgh town council allowed a chaplain of St Giles a year's leave of absence to visit England and France to 'get better eruditioun in musik and playing' on the organs.[10]

In its encouragement of music and the visual arts the church was fulfilling both the spiritual and temporal aspirations of contemporary society. This is also evident in the church's interest in education, where theoretical concern for knowledge in its own right is matched with the very practical need for an educated priesthood. Education was primarily the concern of the church. Universities were founded by bishops and, if by the sixteenth century secular interest was more apparent and the foundation and patronage of schools was no longer an exclusively ecclesiastical function, teachers almost without exception were churchmen. Schools fell into two categories; at an elementary level the song schools and reading schools, which can be corporately termed little schools, and at a more advanced level grammar or high schools. In theory there should have been a song school in every parish but in practice provision tended to be restricted to cathedrals and other important churches including invariably those with collegiate status. Authority over song schools in a diocese was nominally vested in the chapter or precentor of the cathedral, but in practice this dignitary did not exercise jurisdiction outside his own cathedral. The principal concern of song schools attached to institutions was to train choristers in music and at least the rudiments of Latin in order that the services of the choir could be fittingly maintained. The main grammar school aim was the acquisition of Latin and it was through study in both schools, coupled with practical service in the church, that young clerics studied for promotion to the priesthood. In Aberdeen in 1503 a choir boy appointed one of his fellow choristers who had already qualified in the song school to deputize for him in the choir while he studied in the little school and the grammar school. In 1531 the provost and town council engaged another chorister to sing in the choir until he was promoted to the order of priesthood.[11]

At some centres, however, the education provided by such schools reached a wider circle of pupils and even though many of those students may have been destined for an ecclesiastical career, others were not. At Kirkwall, the cathedral school founded by Bishop Reid in 1544 had two chaplains attached to it. One was to teach in the song school and was to be a doctor in both kinds of song and the other, who was to teach in the grammar school, was to be a master of arts and an erudite grammarian. These two masters were not only to teach all the boys of the choir, but also any poor people who were willing to be taught. The cathedral school founded at Elgin by the chapter in 1489 was also a 'general school' for the burgh and was to provide instruction in music and reading to all who came to it. Such steps were not uncommon for by this period many of the schools that had originated as church schools had become the concern of the burgh. Thus at Linlithgow the bailies appointed a chaplain to teach in the song school and 'leir all bairnis that will cum thereto'. In 1539 at Inverness, the clerk presented by the town council to the bishop was 'to rule the school, to instruct and teach the chaplains and scholars coming thereto in the art of music, not only in chant but in organ playing'. At Ayr in 1551, the parish clerk was licensed by the burgh to hold a song school for the neighbour's children. Most teachers were churchmen and although a few married men are occasionally found as schoolmasters, theoretically all teachers were clerics. In practice most were chaplains who were hoping for further preferment in the church. Appointments were usually of a temporary nature and the rapid turnover in schoolmasters underlines the point that those men were generally poorly-paid hirelings who, but for the addition of a chaplaincy or some other living, such as that of parish clerk, could not have subsisted. Lack of a schoolhouse and accommodation for the master was another problem which may have encouraged mobility and for this reason the schoolmaster was often chaplain of a hospital. At Glasgow, the schoolmaster was also chaplain of the leper hospital of St Ninian beyond Glasgow bridge. He lived at the hospital and so also did twenty-four poor scholars. Provision for poor scholars was fairly common; a minimum of fifteen was thought desirable at Old Aberdeen in 1544, but how far such schemes were put into effect is more difficult to judge. In theory at any rate no-one was to be denied an opportunity of serving in the church because of poverty.[12]

Such schooling was essentially urban. Little is known of rural education and the only positive provision for it on record appears to be the endowment of a chaplaincy at Carmyllie in Angus in

1500, where in addition to the normal religious stipulations the chaplain was instructed to hold at the chapel 'a school for the instruction of the young'. There are some indications that this was not unique. In one unidentified parish in St Andrews diocese the parishioners expressed a desire to found a chaplaincy of the Holy Rood at which the chaplain was to be obliged to hold a public song school in the church for the teaching of scholars in Gregorian chant, the organ and descant. Such developments, however, by their very nature must have been extremely limited, and it seems much more likely that such pupils were educated either by boarding them in burgh grammar schools, a practice for which there is ample evidence in the early sixteenth century, or by utilizing the services of the many private chaplains attached to even the smallest households. The results of such an education might go no further than acquiring the ability to read and write, but the large number of well educated notaries who came from remote country areas and had presumably obtained their education in this manner, would argue for the efficiency of the system. A growing tendency to board pupils in burgh grammar schools may have achieved more in this respect than the Education Act of 1496 which ordained that all barons and householders should send their eldest sons to grammar schools at eight or nine years of age and to keep them there till they have 'perfyte latyne'. Insofar as the intention behind this act was to serve the ends of justice it was perhaps doomed to failure; education in sixteenth-century Scotland was still fostered by the church to subserve the church's ends. Nevertheless, involvement of the municipalities ensured that some of the benefits were increasingly conveyed to other sections of society and this in turn found expression in the provision of a higher form of education through the universities.[13]

No fewer than three Scottish universities – St Andrews in 1412, Glasgow in 1451 and Aberdeen in 1495 – were founded in the course of the fifteenth century when the intellectual stimulation brought about by the revival of learning was reflected in the foundation of many European universities. Each of the universities attempted to strengthen its organization during the following century. A refoundation at King's College, Aberdeen on 17 September 1505, proposed a college of thirty-six persons. Less success attended efforts at Glasgow to make the original college fully collegiate but major developments were recorded at St Andrews.

Attempts to reorganize the Pedagogy and St Johns College which was virtually annexed to it failed in 1512, thwarted by the foundation in the same year of the college of St Leonard by Alexander Stewart, archbishop of St Andrews and John Hepburn, prior of St Andrews, who elevated the hospital and church of St Leonard into 'the college of poor clerks of the church of St Andrews'. Attempts to reorganize the Pedagogy were revived in 1523, but not brought to fruition until 12 February 1537/8 when a scheme of 1525 to found a college under the patronage of St Mary of the Assumption to teach theology, canon and civil law, physics, medicine and the other liberal disciplines was revived. This more than absorbed all the Pedagogy area schools; and the ancient church of St John was to be absorbed, re-dedicated and given collegiate standing. If Archbishop Beaton hoped for royal confirmation for his foundations, personal difficulties with James v and not merely episcopal procrastination held it up. Beaton later revived the scheme, the bull of foundation being dated 12 February 1537/8. The 'New College' was placed in the Old Pedagogy and the assimilation of that institution was completed on 7 February 1538/9 when the principal of the Pedagogy became first principal of St Mary's. There is, however, evidence of some continuing uncertainty on Beaton's part in documents issued within a few days of each other in February 1538/9. Following a further petition from John Hamilton, archbishop of St Andrews, on 26 August 1552, a further revision of the constitution was approved, and this was completed by the issue of a new charter in 1554.[14]

In these ways the church through its teaching (and all university teachers were churchmen) proposed to provide a service for the community at large. In practice, however, the return to society was less than it might have been. Arts alone of all the faculties consistently attempted to fulfil its obligations in all three universities. The provision of a grammarian for the teaching of Latin at Aberdeen was undoubtedly an attempt to raise standards, and it was paralleled at St Andrews in 1495 and 1516 when the Faculty of Arts raised its entrance requirements in grammar. In terms of university teaching no statutes relating to grammar have survived for St Salvator's, but in the case of St Leonard's it was stipulated that 'thrice in the week after dinner a competent lesson should be held in Grammar, Verse, Rhetoric or out of the books of Solomon'. It was also laid down that scholars who presented themselves between Easter and the end of September in any year should become grammar students in preparation for the following session. The appointment of a grammarian at St Mary's College provided for further instruction in grammar; teaching would have been based on the standard texts, such as the 'Old Grammar' of Donatus or the 'New Grammar' of Alexandre Villedieu, in both of which the lessons were graded to the age and talents of the pupils.[15]

A similar trend is discernible at Glasgow, where the appointment in 1501 of a chaplain, with the duty of residing daily in the Pedagogy and teaching grammar to the students every day, marks a distinct attempt to improve the standard of university Latin. The masters of the city grammar school were closely associated with the university from the early sixteenth century to the Reformation and this may have been reflected in higher standards. Efforts in this direction also involved giving more status to rhetoric as a university subject, a measure that seems to have met no objections from scholastic logicians unless it threatened the basic philosophical character of the university course. Such attempts to raise the standard of arts courses were not, however, too successful. Part of the difficulty stemmed from the limitation of the arts curriculum, which resulted in the arts courses being viewed either as a preliminary to further vocational study or as an extension of a general education which might be terminated long before graduation. This latter category of short-time students included the sons of magnates, lairds and burgesses who, at St Andrews in particular, attended in small but increasing numbers during the first half of the sixteenth century. These few may not have quite measured up to the hopes of the 1496 act which stated that the eldest sons of barons and freeholders having mastered Latin at their grammar school should be sent to study arts and law at the university, but it no doubt ensured a higher measure of efficiency in some local courts and in a few instances may also have promoted the growth of commercial enterprise.[16]

Thus through the arts the church served the needs of the community; and in theory at least the other university faculties strove to do the same. In reality the situation was, however, very different. Medicine if it was taught at all before the appointment of a mediciner at Aberdeen shortly after 1505 was not regarded as a serious vocational study, and even there it appears to have been short lived. At St Andrews, William Manderston, doctor of medicine, was incorporated in the university in 1528; a graduate in medicine from Paris, he was rector of the university in 1530 when Patrick Arbuthnot, master of arts and medicine, and royal physician, was incorporated in the university. On 28 February 1535/6 he is described as one of the 'maisters and actuall lectourers' and three years later he was commended as one of the 'daly teachers' who worked for the 'commoun weill'. The inclusion of a mediciner in one of Archbishop Beaton's proposed curricula for St Mary's College in 1537/8 may reflect Arbuthnot's influence, and also explain the disappearance of these proposals from the revised constitution of 1554. By this date Glasgow too seems to have been devoid of medicinal teaching for although an ex-Carthusian Englishman could write in 1536 'I am now in Skotland, in a lytle unyversyte or study named Glasgo, wher I study and practyse Physyk ... for the sustentacyn and my lyvyng', there appears to be little substance to his claim. Exponents of civil law may have been received from time to time in very much the same manner, but in neither of the two older universities is there much indication of the teaching of civil law. At Glasgow a succession of possible teachers of civil law can be established only as far as 1472. A movement towards a revival of civil law at St Andrews followed the education act of 1496, but efforts towards this end were not too successful and if in practice the dividing line between canon and civil law was frequently overstepped, it was not until the foundation of St Mary's College that provision was formally made for the teaching of canon and civil law and degrees were awarded in each category in the 1540s. The appointment of a civilist and a canonist at Aberdeen in terms of the constitution of 1505 might have anticipated this development, but whatever the immediate effect of the proposals, neither of these teachers were present during the course of a rectorial visitation of 1549 which seems to suggest that the faculty of law was moribund.

The scarcity of theology students is more explicable. Stress was laid upon theological studies in the foundation of St Salvator's College and at Glasgow, but as the requirements for even the baccalaureate in theology were stringent in terms of both age of the entrant and the years of study required, only advanced scholars of considerable ability were likely to embark on such a course. Consequently while there was some theological teaching at Glasgow, students were few and far between. In 1507 it is noted:

> Master Patrick Coventry, henceforward bachelor in the Bible, having previously finished the requisite lectures and disputations according to the use and custom of our university, under the presidency of the distinguished man, Mr. William Cadzow, professor of sacred theology, was, in the presence of several prelates, lords and masters, in our greater schools, lawfully pronounced bachelor of sacred theology by the said Mr William and acquired justly and lawfully confirmation of the said degree of bachelor as aforesaid

but little development appears to have taken place thereafter until the arrival of John Mair as principal in 1518. His policy appears to have been to promote the study of theology at the expense of canon law and to this end he sought the collaboration of Aberdeen-trained friars to help its revival. Some success seems to have attended his efforts; a few monks appear to have studied theology at this time and at least two secular priests appear to have continued their studies during the period of Mair's principalship. Thereafter theological studies languished and although John Davidson who became principal in 1556 was a trained theologian and may have been anxious to promote such studies, his arrival came too late to make any discernible impact. So too at Aberdeen, for although theology figured prominently in the 1505 constitution and the principal in 1531 was expected to lecture on the subject daily, a report of 1549 claimed that the students in theology were not working, were failing to take holy orders and were improperly dressed, sporting long hair and beards. No such charges arise at St Andrews where the faculties of arts and theology appear to have been closely connected, but the emphasis must always have been on quality rather than quantity and many of the students appear to have come from religious houses, including the Augustinian priory of St Andrews, which in turn also provided many of the teachers.

In career terms, theology was not the most important subject an ambitious secular clerk could pursue; canon law provided a much more attractive prospect and this may explain why, of all the faculties other than arts, that of canon law proved initially to be the most successful. At Glasgow, however, early success proved transitory and the buildings in which canon law was taught were in disrepair by 1483 and few graduates appeared thereafter. When the principal John Mair supported the abolition of courses in canon law in order to promote the study of theology, the subject received a blow from which it apparently never recovered. So too at Aberdeen in which law students were few and the canonist absent in 1549. But at St Andrews where practical training in the courts seems to have been given greater weight than theory canon law did flourish. The foundation charters of St Salvators made no provision for a lawyer, but a chaplaincy was established in 1500 in favour of a bachelor of canon law who should lecture three times a week. A similar trend is seen at St Leonard's College where, although founded expressly for the study of arts and theology, six years later two of its leading theologians were described as 'professors of canon law in the Church of St Andrews'. With the recognition of the teaching of civil and canon law at St Mary's college in 1537/8, the process of encouraging legal studies was complete. The reward to society was impressive and many of the earliest senators of the College of Justice including from the clergy Gavin Dunbar, archbishop of Glasgow, and Alexander Durie, bishop of Galloway, and from the laity Henry Balnaves of Halhill and James McGill of Rankeillor, were law graduates of St Andrews.[17]

With a sufficient body of qualified lawyers within its ranks, it is clear that one of the major services that the church could offer to the community at large was its legal expertise. As an institution the church's jurisdiction covered many fields. As a body responsible for faith and morals the competence of its courts covered a variety of matrimonial cases including actions over legitimacy, dowries and actions for annulment. Transactions made under oath, whether secular or spiritual, fell under its control as did the confirmation of testaments. Disputes concerning churchmen alone, especially relating to the acquisition of benefices and their fruits, were dealt with by church courts, but the laity also frequently preferred to have their cases heard before ecclesiastical courts which were often deemed more efficient than corresponding civil courts. The constitution of such courts varied. On occasion the pope might appoint judges delegate, usually three in number, to hear appeals and cases in the first instance. Most cases, by virtue of the ecclesiastical jurisdiction vested in a bishop were, however, heard by his principal judicial officer called the official who by the sixteenth century usually had lesser officials under him. By that time, moreover, commissaries of varying nomenclatures and competence began to appear with their courts which possessed co-extensive jurisdiction with the existing diocesan courts.[18]

The type of cases heard before the courts varied greatly and the extant sixteenth-century records suggest that executry cases, followed by cases arising from failure to honour contracts under oath together with actions over the payment of teinds (tithes) and other ecclesiastical dues, predominated over a lesser volume of business relating to matrimony, defamation and benefice disputes. Most such disputes, however, went to Rome before one of the supreme tribunals of the church – the Sacred Roman Rota – sometimes an appeal but more often as a case of first instance and in this respect the number of cases heard in Scotland was only a fraction of the total. The bulk of actions before the Rota were of a beneficial nature, but a few cases relating to matrimonial affairs also found their way to Rome. Such cases only touched a minority of the population, but at a lower level every diocesan archdeacon possessed his court to deal with breaches of discipline by clergy and laity alike. These could also be dealt with by the dean of Christianity who could also confirm minor testaments of less than £40 value. No records of such courts are extant, but glimpses of the quality of justice exercised in ecclesiastical courts are seen in Myln's description of his diocesan colleagues at Dunkeld in the early sixteenth century, in which he notes of Walter Brown, official of Dunkeld in the late fifteenth century, and for whom Myln acted as clerk and notary for three years, that he possessed a 'remarkable knowledge of canon law and a strong sense of justice'.[19]

Because of their training such priests were able to perform a variety of legal functions, one of the most important of these being that of notary public, a position initially held only by priests – it was not until the 1540s that the lay notary began to appear. Notaries, who usually held a chaplaincy or some other ecclesiastical benefice in addition to their legal office, were enrolled by a protonotary apostolic and were then authorized to authenticate legal acts. Such acts were engrossed in their protocol books, or register of deeds, by the addition of their docquet and sign manual (endorsement and signature). Notaries made out instruments on marriage, admissions of parish clergy and registered protests against various actions. Such duties performed by a priest for members of the laity cemented the bond between them, and this affinity was frequently strengthened by the clergy acting as agents in a burgh court, witnessing laymen's wills and acting as their scribes. The vast majority of their deeds were, however, evidence of title, many of them recording the leasing and feuing of church lands, a process illustrating the non-religious side of the relationship between laymen and the clergy.[20]

For many people the most important aspect of this relationship was on an economic plane. This was evident at two levels; the legal obligation of all landowners and their tenants to pay teind and the requirement of all tenants to pay rent. In the matter of the first it is clear that by the early sixteenth century many parishioners resented paying teind. Litigation over the non-payment of teind became a standard feature of processes in the civil courts during this period and did much to cause friction between churchmen and the laity. On the other hand it is equally evident that arrears of rent were uncommon, not only because the consequences of non-payment might mean eviction, but also because the church as landlord appears to have acted fairly towards its tenants. Leases were sometimes granted for life and were nearly always of at least five years' duration. Evictions at the end of such a period were uncommon, the tenants themselves frequently changing their lands not under pressure, but of their own free will. Relations between tenants and the laymen appointed by ecclesiastical superiors as bailies and chamberlains appear to have been harmonious and created a measure of continuous lay participation in the temporal affairs of the church. Nevertheless, the characteristic continuity of tenure and security of tenure of the many thousands of tenants who lived on the ecclesiastical estates was under threat in the early sixteenth century, not only through the appointment of lay commendators, but also through the growing proprietary attitude of churchmen. In consequence the close links that had existed between ecclesiastical superiors and their tenants came increasingly under threat. If the actual negotiations with tenants remained in the hands of officers and sergeants appointed by the bailies and chamberlains, the frequent absence of commendators from their benefices meant that chapters no longer played a part in decision making, but were expected to rubber-stamp decisions made by the commendators and their deputies. Changes of commendator also tended to be more disruptive than that occasioned by the appointment of a new abbot and might lead in turn to a struggle over the appointment of deputies. At one stage no fewer than three separate rental books for Melrose were said to be in existence; one in the possession of the chapter, another, compiled by a former chamberlain, was in unknown hands and a third had been retained by a relation of the previous commendator. In such circumstances friction between tenants and their superior was almost inevitable.[21]

If goodwill between kirkmen and their tenants was slowly being eroded in this period, the interaction that had previously characterized their relationship was not entirely at an end. The commendator of Kilwinning personally wrote out a tenant's rental; Bishop George Browne of Dunkeld listened to tenants' complaints as he inspected his episcopal estates and David Beaton as commendator of Arbroath presided over regality courts in the 1520s. Though gradually such occurrences became more rare, the compensating factor for many tenants was the fact that secular and financial considerations encouraged most commendators to feu rather than lease the land at their disposal. In consequence the influence of the church diminished even further, while the spread of feu-ferme tenure brought for some new and probably more exacting landlords, and for others a heritable tenure of their holding. Those fortunate enough to receive feus emerged from the turmoil in a position of economic strength but those who remained as tenants had reason to mourn the passing of the old order, as the new lay landlords upset the existing pattern of leaseholding and insisted upon short leases which could be revised to their own advantage at regular intervals.[22]

Tenants and others caught at a disadvantage amid the economic upheavals of the period might suffer social distress and in this respect the sixteenth-century church could still demonstrate its concern. Some of the social services provided by the church were institutionalized, others of a more individual nature. Of the former, hospitals, which could often be more accurately described as almshouses, even though founded in many cases by laymen, were ecclesiastical institutions. Many of the earlier foundations had certainly fallen into decay or were on their way to becoming secularized. Others were burned during the English invasions of the 1540s and were apparently never rebuilt. Concern for the poor was by no means at an end, however, and at least twelve new hospitals were founded before the Reformation while many others appear on record for the first time. A few of those were in rural areas; a new almshouse was founded at Biggar in 1546; the provost of the collegiate church of Methven founded a hospital there for five sick and aged poor in 1549/50 and, at North Berwick, a hospital was established for poor brethren in 1541/2. The majority of the new foundations were, however, in burghs: thus at Aberdeen, a hospital was founded for twelve old men in 1531/2; a hospital attached to the collegiate church of Kirk o' Field, Edinburgh, was instituted *c.* 1510, but a more prestigious hospital was founded there in 1541 for two chaplains and seven bedesmen. The hospital suffered severe damage shortly after its foundation as all the manses and chambers founded near the monastery were destroyed by the English in 1544 and it was not until 1558 that repairs were being contemplated. A much more ambitious seven-year project for a hospital in the burgh with a priest, mediciner and forty beds was planned in 1552, but as finance for this was to be obtained from a levy on householders, it came to nought. More success attended the establishment of a hospital for seamen by the corporation of the shipmasters and mariners of Leith in 1555. Wayfarers were also catered for at Perth with the erection of a hospital for poor travellers. Little information is forthcoming about the running of such hospitals, but some details are recorded about the day-to-day life of the hospital founded near the Stablegreen of Glasgow in 1524/5 by Roland Blacader, sub-dean of the cathedral. This hospital was to have six beds and was to be looked after by a keeper and his wife chosen by the chaplain. Provision for the care of the poor is carefully stipulated; the six beds were to be furnished with coverlets and pillows and the diet of the poor is equally explicitly stated. Vegetables and herbs supplied from the keeper's garden were to be supplemented by lentils to the value of forty shillings bought in winter by the chaplain and the keeper between the feasts of saints Martin and Andrew. These were to be cooked with green vegetables and herbs every evening for the feeding and nourishment of the poor; and when herbs failed, the keeper was to cook white gruel from the lentils, properly prepared, for the hospital's inmates. For fear of misappropriation the lentils were to be kept in a locked chest and only issued by the chaplain as and when required. The chaplain was also to provide an iron pot of two quarts capacity for cooking gruel and vegetables and a cauldron of the same capacity for washing the feet of the poor.

For their comfort in winter the chaplain was also to supply an iron grate for making a fireplace and to buy three pounds worth of coal which was to be stored in the 'coyl hows'. Similar provision was also made for the keeper and his wife who were to have bedding and a fire provided; the chaplain too was to be allowed twenty shillings for coals to be bought for himself.[23]

Such provision was simple but by the standards of the day adequate for those fortunate enough to obtain shelter in such institutions. Overall provision was, however, far from satisfactory. The northern dioceses of Argyll, Caithness, Dunkeld, Moray, Ross and the Isles, all of which lay either wholly or partly in the Highland area, possessed at best five small hospitals in the sixteenth century and most of these had only a shadowy existence. Inadequate endowment meant they were always subject to decay and although Bishop Browne of Dunkeld (1484-1515) revived and augmented an earlier foundation, the hospital of St George providing only for a master and only seven poor folk, served to highlight the inadequacy of institutional care for the poor within this area. The bonds of kinship may have provided an adequate substitute, and individual churchmen were certainly not unmindful of their obligations in this direction as exemplified by George Hepburn, dean of Dunkeld (1497-1527), who not only provided a weekly 'boll of meal for certain decrepit poor folk in the city', but also ordered porridge to be supplied every day when there was a dearth in the country.[24]

Outdoor relief of this kind was provided by both the church and burgh authorities, but the conscientiousness of both in this respect is debatable. At Perth, even after the Reformation, alms were only dispensed to those 'that held the Holy Lamb, the tounis mark and takin on their breistis'; the friaries for their part appear to have reduced their charity to a routine in which 'one penny or one piece of breade anis in the oulk [week]' was deemed sufficient concern for the poor. From time to time, however, outside relief of another kind was available through the good offices of the church. Requiem masses were one of the most constant features of the day to day round in any parish church and the founders of such masses, in order to ensure the attendance of some participants, were frequently prepared to pay for the privilege. In founding his hospital near the Stablegreen at Glasgow, Roland Blacader also made arrangements for his own obit (memorial service) and that of his parents; he instructed the chaplain to choose sixty honest poor people possessing hearth, house and home in the city of Glasgow who should attend church at the time of the celebration of his obits and pray for his soul, and the souls of his parents and of all the faithful dead. On the morning after these ceremonies eight pennies were to be paid to each of them; in this act of charity religious observance and social welfare imperceptibly merged.[25]

Even by this date, however, the church's role in society was under challenge; education and provision for the poor were being increasingly sustained by town councils and although priests might still teach in schools and oversee almshouses, the church had no longer the dominant voice in such appointments. The institutionalization of the Court of Session as the College of Justice in 1532 and the provision of more efficient royal courts attracted a growing number of lay advocates and after 1540 lay notaries also became more numerous. Even culturally the church's role as patron of the arts was being successfully challenged by a development of secular architecture patronized by crown and magistrates. Faced with this challenge to its role in society the church's answer should have lain in its religious ministrations. Unfortunately for the future welfare of the church, however, the service which had been increasingly overlooked amid its myriad interests was the administration of the sacraments and the promotion of vernacular preaching as a means of explaining the Christian message to an increasingly literate populace. The church in the early sixteenth century was aware of its dilemma, but resolution of its problem depended upon the ability of the church, both monastic and secular, to meet the challenge of the changing circumstances of the times.[26]

2
The Monastic Ideal

The impact of the church upon society was dependent upon its own vitality as an institution. In this respect the fifteenth century has frequently been treated as a period of decline in the fortunes of the Scottish church, and failure to arrest this decline led inexorably and inevitably to the demise of that church and all it stood for at the Scottish Reformation of 1559/60. It is, however, open to question whether the church in this period was faltering in its purpose. It was clearly not without faults, but their magnitude and the part that they played in the making of the Reformation in Scotland can only be assessed when ranged alongside its continuing and not inconsiderable contribution to Scottish life and society.

Monasticism was apparently out of favour, and several of the smaller houses such as Saddell in Kintyre, which was suppressed in the early sixteenth century, and Urquhart in Moray which was united to Pluscardine in 1454, were in very serious difficulties. At the larger houses the situation was not much more promising, but the number of religious appears to have been stable and much rebuilding took place at many sites. At Cambuskenneth an extensive scheme of reconstruction which led to a rededication of the church, buildings and burial ground on 11 July 1521 seems to have been carried out in late medieval times and a new abbot's hall is mentioned in 1520. At a somewhat earlier date reconstruction work at the abbey of Melrose which probably commenced shortly after its destruction in 1385 proceeded for much of the following century and entailed a complete alteration in the character of the lay-out. The impoverishment of the community in the early sixteenth century may have prevented its completion according to original plans, but the rebuilt abbey church with its rich carvings detail is quite exceptional by Scottish standards. Elsewhere rebuilding was of a more traditional nature, but remains of late medieval work at Paisley, Crossraguel, Iona and Arbroath all testify to considerable activity. At Jedburgh, which had been burnt in 1464 and where the south presbytery chapel as well as both transepts and the crossing tower had to be rebuilt, armorial bearings testify that work continued under three successive abbots between 1468 and 1503. Major rebuilding of this nature required considerable financial resources and while some of this was no doubt supplied by the houses themselves from their own not inconsiderable revenues, the possibility of aid from other wealthy patrons should not be precluded.[1]

The spiritual vitality of Scottish monasticism cannot, however, be judged in mortar and stone; the life-style of the monks and canons who constituted the community can alone attest to the maintenance of the religious ideal. In this respect there was graver cause for concern as corporate life had undoubtedly been weakened by the allocation of individual portions and private quarters to monks and canons. This was not an entirely new problem as two visitation reports made by the bishop of St Andrews on conditions at the abbey of Scone as early as 1365 and 1369 clearly reveal. In the first instance, reference is made to the 'diminution of divine service and of regular observance' and it is recommended that 'divine service, both matins and the [regular] hours and vespers, be not performed perfunctorily, that is negligently; nor rapidly nor hastily, but distinctly and devoutely sung and said, even as holy priests of old were accustomed to perform this at the proper hours: also the bells must ring for the said services after usual custom and at the proper hours.' The same observations were more or less repeated in 1369 and it was additionally stressed that all canons who were priests were to say their masses as often as they could and were in no instance to defer celebration beyond three days. In defence of the communal life in 1365 it was decreed that young canons who had duties outside the monastery were not to ride abroad except in company of men chosen by the abbot and prior, and no matter how late they might return they were to repair to the dormitory and sleep in common with their brethren. In particular they were not to wander about the towns of Scone or Perth, nor haunt taverns or booths, except for some reasonable and necessary cause, and by leave of their superiors. Fear of scandal is also reflected in the recommendation that 'women must not dwell henceforth within the precincts of the monastery', but while irregularities may have taken place from time to time, few charges of sexual immorality seem to have been levied against the inmates of male monastic houses.[2]

If some monks and canons enjoyed a worldly life within the security of the cloisters, others remained equally faithful to their vocation; thus the plea of one canon of Holyrood to be allowed to return from serving an appropriated parish church in Galloway because he could not live there as a good catholic and religious man could have been echoed by others. Many monasteries apparently had adequate libraries and the *scriptorium* at Culross was capable of producing a very fine psalter in the second half of the fifteenth century. If in these respects Scottish monasteries retained their traditional characteristics throughout the fifteenth century, far-reaching changes in their administration were also under way.[3]

The character of headship of most religious houses altered during this period. Until mid-century most abbots and priors had belonged before their elevation to the monastic order that their house observed; thereafter the nature of appointments began to change and headship was more often bestowed upon members of the secular clergy who only entered their respective orders after their appointment. Such appointees frequently belonged to local families and their attitude towards monastic life was not unnaturally affected by this fact. Family interests were frequently furthered by the appointment of another member of the kin to look after the secular interests of the monastery and this, which invariably led to a diversion of some revenues in the direction of the laity, may be regarded as a half-way step towards a further acquisition of assets by the appointment of a head who would no longer enter orders but would be content, despite a promise of entering the order, to act as a commendator for life. The opportunities for acquiring such a position were extended by the grant of a papal indult (licence) in 1487. This concession accorded to James III by Pope Innocent VIII stipulated that on the occurrence of vacancies in benefices in cathedral churches and monasteries worth more than two hundred florins gold, the pope would postpone provision for eight months and during that period await supplications from the king and his successors so that 'on receiving intimation, we may the better be able to proceed to the provisions, as we should think expedient'.[4]

This undertaking, which stemmed directly from a conflict

following papal provisions in 1483 to the bishoprics of Dunkeld and Glasgow which had not been in accord with royal wishes, was not perpetual, but Innocent urged his successors 'that in such provisions they take equal care to observe our practice'. More often than not this advice was followed, but in the confused situation following the battle of Flodden, Pope Leo x, who eventually confirmed the Indult in January 1518/19, seized the initiative and provided without awaiting intercession to several consistorial benefices. In taking this step, Leo was assisted by internal political rivalries in Scotland between supporters and opponents of the queen mother, Margaret Tudor. Such squabbles were not infrequent during the troubled royal minorities of the first half of the sixteenth century and provided the opportunity for successive popes, even within the terms of the Indult, to support a rival candidate, or on occasion to provide nominees of their own choosing. English intervention likewise allowed the papacy a certain manœuvrability and it appears to have been the rejection, at the instance of Henry VIII, of presentations made by the governor, the Duke of Albany, to the abbacy of Melrose and bishopric of Moray that led to an act of November 1526 in which the Scottish parliament claimed that 'quhen prelacyis sic as bisheprykis or abbacys hapnis to vaik the nominacioun thairof pertens to our soverane lord and the provision of the sammyn to our haly fader the paip'. This royal right of nomination was expressly admitted by Pope Paul III who at the same time extended the supplication period to twelve months. Nonetheless, while this further concession may have compromised more independent action by the papacy, counter-provisions brought about by political uncertainty in Scotland remained a feature of the system.[5]

This fear of intrusion by other candidates had certainly not been allayed by the Indult and, even before disaster at Flodden gave Leo x an opportunity to reassert papal authority, controversies were raging over the headship of several religious houses. The *cause célèbre* was a dispute over Melrose which raged for twenty years and more after the Indult between David Brown and Bernard Bell. In order to resolve the difficulty on 1 October 1506 James IV nominated Robert Beaton, abbot of Glenluce, as abbot and asked for the claims of William Turnbull (in whose favour Bell had resigned at the turn of the century) and Brown to be extinguished. This was not easily achieved; Turnbull was placated by translation to Coupar-Angus, but Brown did not resign his claim until the grant of a pension in 1510.[6]

The progress of events at other monasteries was not markedly different and could lead to unedifying scenes. At Kilwinning in 1512/13 the last Tironensian abbot William Bunche who had withdrawn an intimation of his intention to resign was assaulted in the abbey church by the earls of Glencairn and Angus in an attempt to force him to resign in favour of John Forman, precentor of Glasgow, on whose behalf James IV had also petitioned the pope. The scene that ensued vividly illustrates the changed circumstances in which monastic houses found themselves for Glencairn.

> seized the abbot (who resisted and after called out, and earnestly entreated to be set at liberty) with force and violence of arms, throwing off his sword and shield and giving them to one of his followers; and while the armed men surrounded him, sometimes threatening, sometimes fawning upon him, to make himself submit to the pleasure of Mr John Forman, the pretended abbot of Kilwinning, and open the gates of the abbey to the King's herald and others of the same opinion standing without the gates, held him long in his embrace, until induced by the persuasion of Alexander Scott, prior of Kilwinning, and some of the armed men, he let him go, panting for breath and calling out 'Suffer me to sit here, and cut off my head, because, while I live, I shall never agree to what you propose.'

Despite this treatment, for which the crown must bear some responsibility, William Bunche was to die with the king at Flodden in 1513. Even before his death, however, he appears to have bowed to the inevitable and surrendered his rights, not to Forman but to James Beaton, archbishop of Glasgow. The struggles over the commendatorship were punctuated by even more bitter controversies over the bailieship of Kilwinning between the Hamiltons and the Montgomerys of Eglinton which illustrate the problems that might occur when bailies did not achieve commendatorships. The *infeftment* (the investment with legal possession of heritable property) of Hugh, second earl of Eglinton, as heir to his grandfather as bailie led to a two-year struggle with the commendator Alexander Hamilton who refused to recognize Eglinton's hereditary title to the office. Eglinton's claim in this respect read to the monks by the curate of Kilwinning and the acceptance of his right by episcopal commissioners in April 1545 was only grudgingly accepted by the commendator and an action before the Lords of Council and Session was required before the final instrument of *sasine* (the act of procedure of giving possession of feudal property) was produced in August 1547. With the revival of the Hamilton interest after the appointment of Gavin Hamilton as commendator in 1550, the third earl of Eglinton, who had acted as bailie since September 1546, insisted upon new charters confirming him in office but echoes of the dispute continued for the rest of the century.[7]

If other controversies lacked the complications evident at Kilwinning, the search for lucrative commendatorships resulted in an abundance of disputed cases in the period after Flodden. At Glenluce, the pope ignored a crown request to confer the commendatorship of the abbey upon David Hamilton, bishop of Lismore, and provided instead the Cardinal of St Eusebius. The cardinal in turn resigned but decided in so doing to back the claims of Alexander Cunyngham who had been elected by the monks and confirmed in his appointment by the father abbot of the Cistercian order. The ensuing controversy was long and litigious and was resolved only by the seizure and imprisonment of Cunyngham who was eventually prevailed upon to surrender his rights on 7 June 1516, although litigation continued thereafter. In this case local interests obviously played a major part in the dispute for Cunyngham was a cousin of the earl of Glencairn who actively supported his cause. Further controversies between 1544 and 1547 characterize the history of this house and other monasteries in Ayrshire and the south-west such as Crossraguel, Kilwinning and Soulseat which suffered similar problems from time to time. At Tongland, likewise, various proposals were made in 1529 for the disposition of the abbey until annexation to the bishopric of Galloway was finally adopted as a solution to the problem. At Whithorn too difficulties had arisen at an earlier date because Leo x had provided Silvio, cardinal of Cortona in opposition to the crown's nominee, Alexander Stewart, Albany's natural brother. Although the governor took a strong line and informed the pope that Scottish interests would not let him have the priory even if he won his case in Rome, Silvio maintained his right and eventually ceded to Ninian Fleming, then a boy of fifteen, on 19 May 1525. In the event some compromise seems to have been reached because on 8 July 1525, following the resignation of Silvio, Gavin Dunbar was provided, but on Dunbar's provision to the see of Glasgow in 1533, Ninian Fleming was then nominated as commendator in July or August of that year. By this stage, however, another contender had appeared in the person of Abraham Vaus, provided on 26 July 1532. His efforts to obtain the priory brought bitter complaints from James v, and Fleming's claims to the priory were eventually recognized.[8]

Such disputes appear to have punctuated the history of most Scottish abbeys during the first half of the sixteenth century. Political rivalries continued to ferment discontent, for example at Paisley in 1548/9 when the Angus faction attempted to prevent Claud Hamilton succeeding his uncle as commendator, but on other occasions sheer opportunism on the part of petitioners seems to have been the motivating force. The suit of David Douglas, who was provided to Holyrood on 15 July 1530, was clearly of this nature but he sustained litigation against Robert Cairncross, whom he claimed was the intruder, for at least a year, without any apparent success. Papal intervention seems to have diminished thereafter although in 1539 Pope Paul III made a determined effort to obtain the wealthy abbey at Dryburgh for the blind archbishop of Armagh and distinguished theologian, Robert Wauchope. He was provided by the pope on 8 November 1539, one day after James v nominated Thomas Erskine, but protests by the king on 22 February and 4 May 1541 led to provision for the royal candidate on 5 May. Nevertheless, Wauchope continued the struggle until at least 1544. Such challenges to royal authority ensured that the maintenance of the Indult depended upon the eternal vigilance of the crown.[9]

If disputes over the headship of major monastic foundations were not entirely eliminated in terms of the Indult, the situation at lesser religious houses, especially priories, remained even more uncertain. A controversy raged at Monymusk in 1524 and no fewer than three rival candidates were seeking Restennet in the early 1530s. In the same period Pittenweem was in dispute between Adam Blackadder and John Roull who had attempted to exchange the priories of Coldingham and Pittenweem only to be thwarted by James v's refusal to accept Roull as prior of Coldingham. The extent to which such disputes continued in the years preceding the Reformation must await a full analysis of the Vatican records, but rival petitions for the priories of Monymusk and St Mary's Isle in

1558 appear to suggest that controversy over these lesser religious houses continued unabated.[10]

The consequence of many such struggles was the ultimate appointment of lay commendators, who at best may have satisfied their consciences by entering minor orders. By the time of the Reformation only a handful of genuine choir monks were still in office as heads of Scottish religious houses; the prior of the Charterhouse at Perth; Donald Campbell, abbot of Coupar Angus and John Philp abbot of Lindores were almost sole representatives of a rapidly disappearing breed, who increasingly in the early sixteenth century had set about the task of setting their affairs in order.[11]

At Kinloss, the succession of Thomas Crystall to the abbey in 1504 ushered in a new era in the abbey's history. In a series of lawsuits a number of endowments pertaining to the abbey were recovered from various expropriators. His contribution to the temporal welfare of the monastery was, however, secondary to his efforts to rescue the decayed and irreligious state into which the abbey had fallen. Physical repairs to the monastery's fabric also characterized his abbotship; the chapel of St Jerome was repaired and two clocks placed on the church, the smaller of which was used as an alarm in rousing the brethren to say lauds. Spiritual services were certainly not neglected and the monks possessed a well-thumbed copy of Cistercian usages.[12]

Crystall's resignation on 4 July 1528 in favour of Robert Reid, sub-dean of Moray, who only professed as a monk on 11 July 1529, might have proved disastrous for the monastery, but in fact Reid proved to be an exemplary abbot. Although his presence at the abbey must have been infrequent, he maintained the tenor of Crystall's reforms. He promoted the building of a fireproof library in 1538 and in the same year invited the celebrated painter Andrew Bairhum to paint altar pieces for three of the chapels. Whether his example would have been followed by his nephew Walter, who succeeded him in 1553, is imponderable, but the monastery was clearly in good shape spiritually and physically at the period of the Reformation.[13]

Most commendators felt no such responsibility for the welfare of the monasteries of which they were nominally heads. A handful of ecclesiastical commendators may have proved the exception to this rule and this is certainly true at Beauly to which Robert Reid, abbot of Kinloss, and later bishop of Orkney, was provided on 1 November 1531. At Beauly, which had been repaired in the fifteenth century, a decay of monastic discipline had apparently preceded his appointment and the monastery cannot have been unaffected by unsettled political conditions in the north in the latter part of that century. A bull of excommunication issued on 4 July 1506 against plunderers who had stolen and concealed the possessions of the abbot was not promulgated until 1514, and difficulties at this time may have influenced the decision to extinguish the order of the Vallis Caulium and institute the Cistercian order, a transformation which was finally effected by a papal bull of 10 May 1510. Thereafter the monastery appears to have recovered some of its lost vitality. The recovery of land and fishing rights were among the tasks which faced Reid, but his chief benefaction lay in the re-building of the nave and the restoration of the bell tower which had been destroyed by lightning. Four years later, in 1544, he erected a new prior's house to replace the existing ruinous structure. The monks themselves were not forgotten and five junior monks were reputedly seconded to Kinloss for three years for instruction under the Italian scholar Ferrario. The number of monks involved is questionable as the community always appears to have been small, but there were eight monks in 1560, each of whom received forty shillings per year, for their 'habit silver' and had for their 'flesh iid in the day, for their fish ilk day iid'.[14]

Such obligations fell lightly on the shoulders of secular commendators. A letter from the archbishop of Glasgow in 1559 commanding that the commendators of Jedburgh and Melrose be ordered to repair their ruined and dilapidated buildings suggests that buildings were neglected, but whatever the truth of the assertion, it is clear that much of the damage was done by successive English armies. In 1523 damage was done by English armies to the border abbeys of Kelso, Jedburgh and Dryburgh, and the last was to suffer again in 1542. But between 1544, when Hertford began his operations in Scotland, and 1549 the havoc wrought by the invaders was systematic and widespread. The abbeys, nunneries, friaries and hospitals of the Borders, Lothian and Merse underwent terrible destruction and the invaders carried their forays to the Firth of Tay, burning the abbey of Balmerino, the nunnery of Elcho and the friaries of Dundee. From these devastations the religious houses had little chance of recovering. Nevertheless, repairs had been set in motion at most of them and even at Jedburgh which had suffered more than most the abbey church was used for the ordination of clergy in 1550.

Commendators, less in deference to the laws of the church than to the need to safeguard their positions, remained unmarried, but were not celibate. Mistresses and numerous children on whom they bestowed some of the wealth of their ill-gotten benefices became a marked feature of the system. Whenever possible the alienation of monastic lands, mainly by feuing, continued apace and while socially and economically this process may have possessed beneficial results for the many small tenants who obtained such feus, the effect of such transactions must have had a detrimental effect on monastic finances in the long run. In time some of the smaller houses would have become totally secularized, but the larger houses clearly had greater resilience and may even have benefited from the emergence of a clearer distinction between their temporal and spiritual responsibilities.[15]

What of the internal life of the monasteries in this period of exploitation? Some commentators have seen it as a period of inevitable decadence; others have argued that the dominant feature of a sixteenth-century monastery was its position as a property-owning corporation. However, it can be argued that as the feuing of monastic lands escalated and effective control of monastic property finally passed from the hands of the communities in which it had rested since their foundation, the monks and canons were freed from many of their former responsibilities. In such circumstances monastic converts could settle, if they so desired, for a life of leisure and comfort based upon the security of their individual portions. Some clearly did so and well-dressed Augustinians in furs whose main concern after vespers was eating and drinking were a feature of the system.[16]

Be this as it may, not all religious were so minded and, where abuses had crept in, serious attempts to eradicate them are a feature of sixteenth-century monasticism. In this respect James V ostensibly promoted monastic reform; in 1530/1 he requested the abbot of Citeaux and the *diffinitores* (those delegated to carry out the decisions) of the General Chapter, in view of the shortcomings of the order in Scotland, to provide an abbot to visit and reform houses in his kingdom. In 1532 James promised his support to the abbot of Soulseat, commissioned by the Premonstratensian General Chapter to visit the monasteries of that order. In view of James' unprincipled use of the Indult, his sincerity in making these offers may be doubted but the visits did take place and were not entirely without effect. At first glance the visit of the abbot of Chaalis who came to reform Cistercian houses in 1531 appears to have raised more problems than it solved. This was perhaps only to be expected for the abbot's major concern was not to change the religious character of the monks, but rather to end the vice of private ownership, a habit which was so deeply engrained that resistance was inevitable. James V himself hastened to the defence of the Cistercian houses and informed the father abbot of Citeaux that the abbot had 'failed to ask himself whether he was dealing a blow at country and custom by his expedients hastily imposed to alter the immemorial manner of monkish life'. The king's main concern, however, seems to have been to free the Scottish Cistercians from the ecclesiastical censures imposed and so allow the monks to carry on their divine offices, although he promised no more in return than that the monks would observe the abbot's constitutions 'as far as country and custom permit'.[17]

Similar lack of success appears to have attended the proposed visit to Premonstratensian houses by the abbot of Soulseat who applied to the crown for 'supply, help, maintenance and assistance' because he feared that the abbots 'would nocht obey, bot be the contrary resist and withstand to the sammyne'. However, the abbot's apprehensions may have arisen from the refusal of the abbot of Dryburgh and prior of Whithorn to recognize his primacy rather than from a fear that the prospect of reform would in itself promote resistance. No further information is available about these proposals, but the abbots of Coupar Angus and Glenluce ignored the king's defence of the *status quo* and returned to the attack in 1534 when they censured the abbot of Melrose. It appears that the monks of Melrose and those of its daughter-houses, Balmerino and Newbattle, had been cultivating private gardens, selling their produce in local markets, treating their portions as individual possessions and receiving sums of money for the purchase of clothing and other necessities. The monks of the houses in question opposed the removal of their privileges on the grounds that Scotland was less fertile and less abundant than France and other countries and that their predecessors had enjoyed these privileges.

James once again rushed to the defence of the threatened houses, pointing out that the obstacles to reform were the geographical position of the country and the customs which the Scottish Cistercians had always observed; he requested the primate of the Cistercians in 1534 or 1535 to permit 'what the old superiors of the order observed without sacrificing its weal'. Royal intervention on behalf of the monks seems to have prevented the implementation of the measures from which the monks of Deer obtained a specific relaxation in 1537. Nevertheless, in that very year the abbot and convent of Deer made a compact that they should thenceforth lead a regular and reformed life and, after providing for the brethren and officers of the abbey, hold its fruits and rents in common. A similar agreement is recorded in 1553 when a promise by the community of Coupar Angus 'to lead a regular life' and order their manners 'according to the reforms of the Cistercian order', was coupled to the resolve that the abbot and convent should possess and use in common the fruits and income of the monastery. In a further enactment of the same date, the convent made nominations to the various offices in the abbey, including the priorship which had been for some time vacant. As a genuine monk, the abbot, Donald Campbell may have been influenced by reforms emanating from the Council of Trent, but if this was the case he appears to have been unable to eliminate the system of portions which still pertained there at the Reformation.[18]

Although these efforts to end personal portions were mostly unsuccessful, there is little evidence, beyond the archbishop of Glasgow's command to the commendators of Jedburgh and Melrose to 'maintain in these places, proportionate with their revenues, a sufficient number of religious', to support the view that 'preoccupation with the size of portions led to a deliberate policy of restricting entry'. Novices are to the fore in several Scottish abbeys in the immediate pre-Reformation period. At Kinloss, in an attempt to rescue the abbey from the decayed and irreligious state into which it had fallen, Abbot Crystall increased the number of monks, which had dropped to fourteen to more than twenty (a figure which squares with contemporary evidence). Under his successor, Robert Reid, Ferrario not only taught monks of Kinloss but also novices from Beauly. Similar concern was exhibited at Cambuskenneth by Abbot Alexander Myln who in 1522 proposed sending his novices to the abbey of St Victor at Paris. In 1539 a Paisley novice in rather different circumstances was granted a licence to visit 'apostolic thresholds' because of 'great matters moving his conscience'. Of a community there of nineteen, four were novices in 1543.[19]

The steady influx of novices helped to maintain numbers in the community in many religious houses, some of which retained a remarkable stability in this respect over the centuries. At Lindores where twenty-six monks are recorded in 1219, there was only one less in 1532, and nineteen or twenty in 1558 when at least five other novices should possibly be added to those recorded. At Kinloss an abbot and twenty-four monks are noted in 1229; the minimum present in 1560 is an abbot and at least eighteen monks. If some communities such as that at Culross seem to have declined before the Reformation, other major abbeys north of the Forth seem to have remained stable in their composition. The border abbeys which suffered the effects of war and invasion inevitably appear to have declined in numbers. At Melrose twenty-nine monks, including the abbot and sub-prior, subscribed a charter in April 1536, but at least three other monks can be identified at that time. After the destruction of 1545, numbers seem to have fallen and the convent seems to have numbered no more than seventeen at the Reformation. At Newbattle the abbot and twenty-four monks appear in 1528, but numbers had decreased to about fifteen at the Reformation. At Kelso too the ravages of war had taken their effect; a detailed description of the buildings and possessions of the monastery in 1517 states that in peaceful times there were thirty-six to forty monks besides the abbot and the prior. A petition of 1462 had made a similar declaration, but put the actual size of the community at seventeen or eighteen. The fact that there were at least twenty-one monks besides the commendator in 1539/40 may indicate an increase from the earlier figure rather than a decline from the possible total. Nevertheless by 1566 the number of monks had evidently been reduced to twelve.[20]

Smaller houses and those in remote areas were also at risk, but once again the decline when evident does seem to have occurred before the middle of the fifteenth century and then to have levelled off. No canons existed at Blantyre by 1476 and Monymusk, which only contained two canons in 1450, had actually become a community with a prior and four canons in 1549/50. Some attempts at reform were apparently made there in the sixteenth century but ended in a dispute between the community and the prior who ordered one of the canons 'to keip his chalmer in the dormitour and pass nocht furth of it bot *ad necessaria*'. Even in the Highland area small religious houses (with the exception of Saddell) clung tenaciously to their existence. The Premonstratensian abbey of Fearn situated near Tain was being rebuilt throughout the fifteenth century, but in a letter of James V to Pope Paul III of 9 March 1541, the house is described as ruinous and neglected. If true this might be attributed to a series of commendators who, commencing with Andrew Stewart, bishop of Caithness, held the abbey from 1508. Nevertheless, the convent appears to have consisted of five or more canons at the Reformation. Ardchattan was similarly placed with six monks recorded in 1538 and at least three or four at the Reformation.[21]

If any conclusions can be drawn from this rather disparate evidence it would appear to be that commendation was not necessarily the development which threatened the Scottish monasteries. On the border warfare with England was the chief threat to the continuance of the monastic life; elsewhere a serious decline seems to have taken place in some of the smaller houses during the course of the fifteenth century. This had resulted in the demise of some communities, but those that had survived seemed to be in better shape in the sixteenth century than in the previous one. Larger monasteries, once removed from political and military conflict, appear to have remained remarkably stable in their composition.[22]

Numbers alone, however, do not justify the existence of a religious community; how far did viable monasteries continue to maintain observance of their rule? On one issue the consensus of opinion seems to be that in male houses at least the rule of chastity appears to have been observed. Nunneries seem to have been more questionable in this respect and the general breakdown in discipline seems to have been so complete that with the exception of St Katherine of Siena, founded in Edinburgh in 1517, most female houses appear to have been on the point of dissolution on the eve of the Reformation. At male houses, abbots or rather commendators are castigated by contemporary satirists but with the exception of Sir David Lindsay's gibe in *The Three Estates*:

> Speir at the monks of Bamirrinoch
> Gif lecherie be sin

there is little hint of immorality and legitimations of offspring of monks or canons are very difficult to locate, although at Pittenweem in 1549 it was stressed that women were to be excluded from the dormitory and also from the canon's little houses in the priory garden. Their venal sin was not lechery but gluttony and accusations of this and criticisms of the life of ease and comfort which some of the monks apparently enjoyed are the most prevalent in relation to monastic morality. At Pittenweem, no member of the community was to leave the priory bounds without permission of the sub-prior or without a companion; no-one was to spend the night in town or make a habit of obtaining special permission to do so – an echo of the 1365 injunction which forbade canons of Scone to wander about towns, or haunt booths or taverns.[23]

Attributes on the credit side are much more discernible: many monks and canons were not only literate but on occasions remarkably well-educated. At Arbroath a monk who was a master of arts taught not only the novices but also the children of lay people who had letters of confraternity. In the sixteenth century determined efforts were made to further improve the educational standard of the religious and to this end the more important monastic communities were ordered in 1549 by a provincial council of the Scottish church to send some of their members to universities to pursue literary studies in theology and scripture. Similar injunctions in 1552 and 1559 reveal that this programme was never fully implemented, but even before 1549, plans towards this end had been fulfilled in at least a handful of monasteries. At Kinloss, Abbot Crystall sent two monks for instruction with the Blackfriars of Aberdeen and on their return one became chanter and the other taught the younger brethren scholastic questions. At Glenluce a slightly different approach was adopted when Abbot Walter Malin introduced a graduate of theology from Newbattle to educate his young monks. Various monks from Kilwinning in Ayrshire attended Glasgow university from its foundation in 1451 and so anticipated the decrees of the council by almost a century; the admission of Dene Charles Stuyle to Glasgow in 1519 indicates that this tradition of university education was still alive in the sixteenth century.[24]

Most monks and canons, nevertheless, lacked a formal university education, but their literacy at least could be turned to account in various activities. The existence of a *scriptorium* at Culross is apparent not only in the late fifteenth century psalter, but in numerous entries in the *Treasurers Accounts* between 1502 and 1539 which record payments by the king for antiphonallis and other service books for the use of the Greyfriars and Chapel Royal at Stirling. Elsewhere monks at Kinloss and Dunfermline acted as copyists as did Alexander Scot, a monk of Newbattle who transcribed the Cistercian *Institutions* in 1528; the visitation to the priory of Pittenweem in 1549 recommended that members of the community should be kept busy as scribes when not at divine service. Illumination appears to have been less developed, but the beautiful floral designs in the Cambuskenneth cartulary serve as a reminder that this art was not unknown. Book-binding and repairing were further activities to which the religious devoted their attention and a few even engaged in literary pursuits. At Kinloss, John Smyth wrote a short but interesting chronicle while at St Andrews a more substantial piece was produced in the early sixteenth century by John Law. If monks like Robert Wedale of Culross who acted as master of works at the palace of Linlithgow and Thomas Brown of Kilwinning who repaired the mass books and built an organ in the parish church of Ayr, for which he was paid five pounds by the town council, occasionally deserted their cloisters to use their particular skills, the latter at least demonstrates the place which music played in the services of the church. Several of the religious proved to be skilled musicians and Robert Carver, one of the canons of Scone, displayed exceptional talents as a composer. His nineteen-part mass cannot have been readily sung at his own abbey, but its composition nevertheless underlines the importance still placed upon the sung mass, a fact confirmed by his fellow Augustinian Robert Richardson. As a devotee of the Gregorian plain chant Richardson condemned singing in unison which he claimed prolonged the mass and left less time for study; nevertheless he still held it in high regard.[25]

The frequency of such masses is central to any discussion of the vitality remaining in Scottish religious houses during the early sixteenth century. The 1549 report on the visitation to the priory of Pittenweem not only indicates what is desirable in this respect, but by implication also reveals some of the imperfections. In summer matins should be recited chorally at six, in winter at seven; in addition the need for audibility is stressed. To stir up popular devotion, lauds were to be sung on solemn feasts; then the bell would ring for the holy mass, after which the brethren should celebrate masses in turn until the time for the community high mass. In many respects the recommendations echo the reports of the Scone visitations of 1365 and 1369 but, while it is clear that services may not have measured up to the desired standard, they were, nevertheless, being maintained. Belief in the piety of the monks of Crossraguel is reflected in the bestowal of twenty pounds by Egidia Blair, Lady Row of Baltersan who died in 1530, on condition that her body be buried in St Mary's aisle of the abbey, while similar faith in the efficacy of the devotions of the monks of Kilwinning is expressed in the will of the first earl of Eglinton made on 28 September 1545, in terms of which an obit for his soul was to be said in the abbey kirk. Indeed the tradition of the choir service was so ingrained amongst most monastic communities that at Crossraguel, Kilwinning and New Abbey it continued for several years after the Reformation. Nevertheless, it has been claimed that 'the most damning fact about the monks is simply that they played hardly any part in the Reformation on either side'. But could they be expected to do so? Their cloistered life and theological training unfitted the majority of them both for service in the reformed church and from acting as spear-heads of counter-reformation. Open resistance to the reformed faith could only be expressed by the saying of their offices and, unless effectively prevented from exercising this option, a passive refusal to conform was their only means of protest against the changes of which few approved. That the community at large respected these attitudes may be inferred from the concessions which allowed them to retain their portions and chambers until their deaths and also from the infrequency of attacks upon the fabric of the buildings they continued to occupy. In this respect no distinction should perhaps be drawn between monks and canons regular, for if the latter found it easier to conform and serve in the reformed church, the decision to do so stemmed not so much from a sense of hostility to the order which they had served until the Reformation but had now elected to leave, but in the hope that the new reformed church would provide more meaningful spiritual ministrations.[26]

All in all monasticism in Scotland on the eve of the Reformation was in a better shape than has sometimes been allowed. Left to their own devices several of the smaller houses and possibly some of the larger war-ravaged abbeys would have disappeared. In a considerable number of the larger houses, monks and canons were, however, still engaged in their traditional devotions and pursuits under the supervision of the priors who in the absence of the lay commendators had assumed spiritual headship. Reforms were being contemplated and in some cases fulfilled and, but for the intervention of the Reformation (in the making of which the monasteries appear to have played little part), reformed monasteries bereft of many of their former endowments, but spiritually more alive, might have emerged.

In these developments, popular opinion had played little part and the reformers for their part also chose to ignore a monastic revival which constituted no threat to their own programme for reform. But they could not ignore the friaries, which were still actively pursuing many of their original ideals. Some of the Dominican houses seem to have fallen into disarray during the fourteenth and early fifteenth centuries. However, the establishment of a Scottish province in 1481 and the appointment of John Adamson as provincial in 1511 initiated a new regime. With the support of the bishops and other influential figures, in 1519 he closed the friaries at Cupar and St Monans which had each maintained only two friars, and transferred their endowments to the friary of St Andrews. Consolidation had, however, been preceded by plans to found a new friary at Dundee and, following a petition in 1517, this was achieved through the generosity of one of the burgesses before March 1521. The Franciscans likewise tried to promote reform but, although the friars minor remained active their numbers seem to have diminished during the course of the sixteenth century. However, the vitality which characterized the Observant branch of the Franciscans more than counterbalanced any loss in this respect. From their introduction into Scotland in 1463 the number of their houses steadily increased and four friaries were already in existence before 1479, while during the reign of James IV, five further houses were established. Though plans by that king to found houses of Augustinian friars did not materialize, the Carmelite friars achieved modest success with new houses founded at Kingussie before 1501 and at Edinburgh where the town council granted a site to the friars of Queensferry in 1520, although final possession of the site and its Rood chapel was not effected until five years later.[27]

The fervour of the friars was also recognized in terms of increased endowments. Hugh, first earl of Eglinton left ten pounds to the Grey friars of Ayr to pray for him and his late wife for three years and ten merks to the Dominicans to pray for them for one year. The Carmelites of Irvine received five pounds for similar services. The register of the Ayr Dominican friary is full of donations of property to the friars and in 1531 the burgh of Ayr granted the Dominicans the use of a piece of common land at the mill with fishing rights on the river. Gifts of arable or grazing land were particularly welcome and Edinburgh may not have been the only Observantine friary to derive profit from agricultural pursuits. The Dominicans of Perth cultivated their lands and crofts, owned their privilege of mills and sold their crops and hides but at least part of the profit was set aside for charity. Produce from their glebe also provided the friars with much of their sustenance. At Lanark in 1546 the friars got compensation 'for their kaill destroyit and dountrod by mennis feit'. Herbs which would be used for culinary and healing purposes were also grown while an orchard was a distinctive feature of the friaries at Dumfries and Jedburgh. Some changes are, however, discernible in the Reformation era for although the Franciscans of Haddington and Dundee still cultivated their own crops, other friaries such as Dumfries and Kirkcudbright had abandoned cultivation by 1550, receiving rents from their tenants in lieu.[28]

Rents or ground annuals were also acquired by gift and testamentary legacy and formed a substantial part of the income of many friaries, other than those of the Observantine rule who were forbidden to accept such endowments. Accounts for 1561–2 reveal that the Perth Dominicans possessed annual rents producing £60 yearly, but nothing of this nature was owned by the Observantine friary. This appears to be true elsewhere and while small testamentary gifts of money were sometimes accepted by the Observantines, donations continued to be preferred in kind. Whereas royal alms were invariably received by the conventional Franciscans and Dominicans in money, similar gifts to the Observantines with the exception of a small annual donation to each house usually took the form of chalders of barley and wheat, barrels of salmon and herring and similar commodities.[29]

Gifts whether in rents or kind were dictated by piety and in this respect it is possible that in the years immediately before the

Reformation something of the lay generosity previously exhibited towards other ranks of the clergy had been transferred to the friars. Their prayers were certainly regarded as more efficacious than those of the secular clergy, and a papal edict engrossed in the register of the Ayr Dominicans in 1518 seeks to defend the friars against the resentment of the secular clergy who saw them as rivals for popular favour and generosity. In the same way, secular priests objected to requests for burials in friary churches and objected to the fact that parishioners, including James IV when resident at Stirling, often preferred to attend the friars' mass and confession.[30]

In many respects the friary church also represented the business life of the local community. Fiduciary trust in the Observantine friars of Stirling was expressed by Sir John Stirling of Keir who in 1533 placed in their safe keeping funds for the endowment of a daily service at the high altar in Dunblane cathedral after his death. In the previous year the rents accruing to a chaplaincy to be founded in the parish church of Falkirk were similarly to be placed in a box entrusted to the friars during the donor's lifetime. Friary churches were often the centre for legal business. It was general practice to arrange and execute contracts, deeds of agreement, conveyances of land and writs of every description within friaries, either within the church itself or possibly in the chapter house, the cemetery and even in the street outside. Such a transaction was concluded 'in the public street of Aberdeen at the Place of the Friars Minor' in 1551, but most occasions were more formal. At Dumfries a commissary sat in judgment in the friary church in August 1534 'in presence of the official of Nyth' and a contract registered there on 18 June 1543 was entered in the records of the local consistory court. The religious activity of the friary was not neglected and donations received in the course of the sixteenth century attest to the friars' zeal. Some of these gifts took the form of alms from the crown, but private benefactors were also evident. Thus in 1520 the vicar of Colvend granted the gift of an annual rent of five merks from a tenement in the Vennelheid in return for which the friars undertook to celebrate mass annually for his soul at their altar of St Salvator 'within the church beside the altar of the Blessed Virgin without the choir'. A religious fervour combined with business acumen is shown in the delivery at the tolbooth of Dumfries on 6 April 1536 of a new bell for the friary, which their guardian refused to accept until the bell was examined by skilled men.[31]

In terms of their community service, it is clear that preaching was the friars' chief attribute. This task was even accomplished in Gaelic and George Browne, bishop of Dunkeld, arranged that both friars minor and friars preacher well acquainted with the Irish tongue should preach at least once a year in the upper parts of his diocese and hear confessions. Other bishops followed suit and, when provincial councils speak of preaching by religious, they probably had the friars in mind. Their very vitality, however, meant that the intellectual tensions among friars was very great. Many friars had contact with the universities and their own libraries were well stocked. At Aberdeen, William Ogilvy, chancellor of Brechin left many books to the library at his death in 1480 and this gift was supplemented fifteen years later by James Lindsay, archdeacon of Aberdeen who added a further seventy volumes. As printed books became more readily available their libraries appear to have expanded and allowed friars to participate to the full in the intellectual ferment of the early sixteenth century. Their very intellectuality could, however, take them in the direction of heretical opinion. In this respect it is not surprising that two black friars and one grey friar were burnt as heretics in 1539 and in the year that followed one died in escaping from prison and several others fled to England. Of those who did so, several had been outspoken critics of the establishment. One had informed a bishop that his duty was to be a preacher or 'els he was a dumme dog and fed not his flock but his awin bellye', while another had preached in Dundee 'moir liberallie against the licentious lyifes of the bishop nor ther could weall beir'. Such outspoken criticism was frequently directed to furthering the cause of reform from within, but other friars were equally staunch in their defence of the establishment and figured prominently in several trials for heresy.[32]

It does seem, however, that much of the solicitude of the friars for the welfare of the church may have been directed towards the more prosperous merchants, craftsmen and small landed proprietors, from whose ranks they drew their own recruits. In this respect while the friars may not have been particularly wealthy, their relative prosperity and apparent disregard for the poor may have alienated them from some classes of society. The increasing worldliness of the friars and their persistent litigation over their annual rents may also have led to a degree of alienation amongst their middle-class supporters. Nevertheless, it was to the masses that the friars could be more readily represented as greedy defrauders of the poor, although on this score the Observants who did not possess annuals were less open to criticism. Such attacks were in fact a testimony to the importance of the friars and their continued vitality. Their apparent wealth is illustrated in the disturbances of 1543 when the broth pot of the Blackfriars of Perth was paraded through the streets; it again comes to the fore in Knox's description of the Greyfriars of Perth whose 'scheittis, blancattis, beddis and covertouris wir suche, as no Erle in Scotland hath the bettir'. This message was repeated in the Beggar's Summons which ordered the friars to demit their houses in favour of the poor by 12 May 1559. The friars so castigated were not particularly wealthy but their revenues made them vulnerable. The reformers exploited this weakness to crush the preaching orders which in many ways were best adapted to meeting the new faith on its own terms. In short the friars constituted a much greater danger to the reformed faith than the monks and canons who may have possessed an inward strength, but had little contact with the outside world. The destruction of the friaries in 1559/60 was a calculated act, but while this in itself was significant it could not finally have dictated the course of reformation. In this respect the role of the secular clergy was to be decisive.[33]

3
The Secular Clergy

The state of the secular clergy on the eve of the Reformation was closely tied, like that of the religious, to the effect of the Indult of 1487 on the higher officers of the church. In terms of the crown's right to delay nominations to bishoprics for eight months after the death or resignation of a former incumbent, no set pattern is discernible. The nominations of both Stewart archbishops of St Andrews were withheld for some four to five months, but William Stewart was nominated to the see of Aberdeen only twelve days after the death of his predecessor. Though the provision of Andrew Stewart to Caithness was delayed for some eight months after the death of John Sinclair in 1501, two subsequent Stewart holders of this bishopric were appointed with only a month's delay at each vacancy. A speedy appointment frequently arose from a resignation in favour or the appointment of a co-adjutor, both effected during the previous bishop's lifetime. The succession between 1487 and 1569 of the Chisholms at Dunblane, without any apparent intervention from the crown, owed its success to both these devices. The appointment of co-adjutors, in this instance by the crown, seems to have ensured continuity of succession in the bishopric of Orkney between 1498 and 1526 and royal nominations thereafter appear to have been made with the minimum of delay. This was also the case in the Isles before 1514 and although the complexities of the succession after that date render the situation obscure, crown presentations were not unduly delayed if two or three months is taken as the norm. So it was in most other dioceses. The pattern of nomination in the bishopric of Ross reveals a situation in which little over a month separates one bishop from his predecessor, and in Galloway too the succession was equally stable until the eve of the Reformation. Likewise at Aberdeen where a three to four month interval between the death of Alexander Gordon and the nomination of Gavin Dunbar appears to have been the longest hiatus.[1]

The last three sees were also remarkably free of succession disputes, but this may have been a matter of chance as none of these bishoprics fell vacant during the political struggles that were most often the cause of delays in appointment. In Moray which, despite apparent difficulties with the appointment of Robert Shaw in 1525, had until then experienced vacancies of less than two months, a crisis arose following Shaw's death in 1527. The nomination of Archibald Douglas by the earl of Angus seems to have been postponed for several months and further delay was occasioned by the earl's fall from power. In consequence the provision of Robert Stewart, following upon the crown's nomination, did not take place until some two years after the death of his predecessor. Thereafter the normal pattern was resumed, Stewart's successor being nominated some two months after his death.[2]

At Glasgow and St Andrews, the situation was complicated by disputes of even greater political complexity. In the early sixteenth century, Glasgow presented few problems for, with the exception of a delay of three months in nominating Blackadder's successor which can be attributed to the circumstances of his death *en route* for the Holy Land, vacancies were of unexceptional length. But with the rejection of the nomination of James Hamilton in 1548, ostensibly because of his illegitimacy but in practice as part of the power struggle between the earl of Arran and Mary of Guise, uncertainty prevailed and some eighteen months elapsed before the nomination of James Beaton paved the way for his ultimate success. So it was too at St Andrews where the short delays in nominating James and Alexander Stewart were followed by a multi-sided contest in 1513/14 initiated by Leo X's provision of his nephew Innocenzo Cibo as administrator of the see, this being followed in turn by the nomination of other contestants supported on one hand by Margaret Tudor and on the other by the magnates who favoured Albany as governor. The ultimate triumph of Andrew Forman brought this contest to an end but, on his death in 1521, a further eight months were to elapse before the nomination of James Beaton as his successor. The appointment of his nephew David Beaton as co-adjutor avoided a similar problem on James's death in 1539 and, following upon David's own assassination in 1546, the almost immediate grant of the temporalities to

James Hamilton heralded a return to normality even though his actual appointment was not fully effective until June 1549.[3]

In both 1521 and 1549 the prolongation of the St Andrews vacancy may have been deliberate as no other circumstances seem to have intervened. In the dioceses of Argyll and Brechin too, long vacancies became commonplace. In Argyll, vacancies (apparently uncomplicated by the presence of other contestants) occurred in 1496, 1523 and 1538 and resulted in gaps of thirteen, twenty and five months respectively; only an exchange of benefices broke this pattern in 1553. The Brechin vacancies were of a less extreme nature, but in 1516 a vacancy of seven months occurred, followed by another of six months before the nomination in 1557 of Donald Campbell, who in the event never effectively held the bishopric.[4]

If the machinery of appointment worked reasonably well, the quality of bishops that it produced was not impressive. The nomination by James IV of his brother, James, duke of Ross to the bishopric of St Andrews in 1497, followed on his death by the placement of the king's illegitimate son, Alexander Stewart, then aged nine, set the pattern for appointments which persisted to the Reformation. The nominations of royal servants to Moray in 1501, to Ross in 1507 and to the Isles in 1511 were not novel in so far as they rewarded loyal servants of the crown, but were unusual in terms of their exclusiveness. Somewhat earlier, in 1506, the then royal treasurer James Beaton was recommended for Dunkeld as co-adjutor with right of succession, but when this failed to gain papal approval James recommended him first for the bishopric of Galloway and then for the archbishopric of Glasgow to which he was ordained and consecrated on 15 April 1509. It is little wonder that one contemporary source comments that James IV 'gav all the benefices that vaikit in his time to his familiaris ... whereof came great skaith [harm] to his realm'. Nevertheless, those bishops appointed before 1513 do appear to have taken their episcopal duties fairly seriously but succeeding appointments were much more questionable. In the period after Flodden in particular, the bishoprics fell prey to the magnates. The earl of Huntly obtained the bishopric of Aberdeen for his cousin; the earl of Angus procured Dunkeld for his son; the brother of the earl of Atholl was elected to Dunkeld but settled for Caithness and John Hepburn, son of the first earl of Bothwell, was appointed to Brechin. If nominations made by the Duke of Albany between 1518 and 1524 conformed once again to the policy of using bishoprics as rewards for crown servants, the personal rule of James v brought appointments which were made initially to further political support for the earl of Angus who controlled the young king and later, by James himself as a means of exploiting the wealth of the church. Little attention was paid to the clerical qualities of the candidates proposed and the nominations to Moray and to Ross in 1538, followed by the promotion of David Beaton as co-adjutor to his uncle James at St Andrews quite ignored the immoral lives of the candidates. In 1526 the bishop of Dunblane resigned his see in favour of his brother and the bishop of Galloway likewise gave way to his nephew. Appointments to the bishoprics of Argyll and Caithness foisted the sons of magnates on these sees, neither of whom chose to be consecrated.[5] Among the episcopal appointments of the period, only the selection of Robert Reid, abbot of Kinloss, for the vacant bishopric of Orkney in 1541 stands up to scrutiny. Thus the early decades of the sixteenth century saw public appointments to the greatest benefices being increasingly filled by men who would certainly not enhance what popular respect was left for church dignitaries. And this trend continued, ever more obviously and damningly, until the 1560s.

With the death of James v in 1542 and the appointment of the earl of Arran as governor of Scotland, the pattern of episcopal appointment again changed. Hamilton family interests became one guiding factor in forwarding nominations to the pope and appeasement of political rivals was another. In the latter interest, the earl of Huntly's brother was unfruitfully provided to the bishopric of Caithness in 1544, and in the following year with somewhat more success Huntly's uncle was nominated to Aberdeen. The assassination of Cardinal Beaton on 29 May 1546 presented the ideal opportunity for Hamilton advancement and John Hamilton was admitted to the temporalities of the see only two days after the cardinal's murder, although his appointment did not become fully effective until June 1549; two years later Gavin Hamilton, then commendator of Kilwinning, was appointed co-adjutor. In the meantime, further attempts to advance the Hamilton family interest had led to the nomination of James Hamilton to the vacant archbishopric of Glasgow in 1547, but political intrigue meant a long delay and the provision by the pope of Alexander Gordon led to a compromise appointment in the person of James Beaton in 1550. By this date the queen mother, Mary of Guise, was already deeply involved in episcopal appointments and with her assumption to the regency in 1554 she was able to pursue her own policies more freely. In the main her nominations to bishoprics followed her policy of obtaining support for the Franco-Scottish alliance. To this end she nominated the abbot of Coupar to Brechin, but he failed to obtain provision; Alexander Gordon was nominated to Galloway, but again provision was not forthcoming; only her provision of Adam Bothwell to Orkney was fully successful. All three of her nominees joined the reformers and in this respect her selection of candidates seemed maladroit. From any other standpoint her appointments did not differ greatly from those of her predecessors. Though bishops like John Hamilton were not entirely devoid of quality and actually recognized the need for reform, their ineffectiveness stemmed in no small part from their own personal shortcomings, which were further revealed when the Reformation crisis finally broke, involving not only themselves but also their cathedral establishments.[6]

Scottish cathedral clergy might have been expected to have been a bastion of strength in the difficult times facing the church in the early sixteenth century. Cathedrals were important as pilgrimage centres and in terms of their personnel were not only effectively staffed but continued to expand in the course of the fifteenth and early sixteenth centuries. In the diocese of Argyll this appears to have been achieved by the creation of temporary prebends, created only for the lifetimes of their holders but, while this device was also favoured at other cathedrals new permanent prebends were also established. Such expansion was not without its difficulties, however, for at Dornoch the original cathedral constitution had utilized the teind of all existing parish churches whose revenues were not required for the upkeep of the bishop or the general funds of the cathedral chapter. However, even there further expansion did not take place at some point before the Reformation as the hospital at Helmsdale and the chaplaincy of Kinnald were utilized to endow two further prebends, making a final establishment of thirteen prebends in all.

Expansion on a similarly modest scale took place at Elgin where the establishment of twenty-three prebends before 1242 left little further scope for the erection of further canonries although from time to time prebends for life were created. Sixteenth-century developments saw the addition of two further prebends which raised the number of prebends to a final total of twenty-five. Such modest developments were overshadowed by the changes which took place at several other cathedrals in the century before the Reformation. At Dunkeld the state of the chapter in the century after 1274 appears to have remained static at twenty-two canons, but more prebends were to be added before the Reformation.[7]

Similar changes characterized developments at Rosemarkie, although insufficient evidence makes the exact extent of the fifteenth-century changes difficult to determine. Seven additional prebends appear in the fifteenth century, however, and yet another only materialized in 1560. At Dunblane a gradual build-up of the chapter occurred in the course of the fifteenth and early sixteenth centuries, with seven designated prebends appearing for the first time. More certainty exists at Aberdeen at which two prebends were erected in 1445 and another for a sub-chanter in the following century. At Brechin three new prebends were added in the fifteenth century although another became extinct, and the number of prebends stood thereafter at fourteen. There were no sixteenth-century creations at Glasgow, but this followed a spate of activity in the fifteenth century when no fewer than nine new prebends were founded. More progress in this respect was seen at Kirkwall in Orkney and in the Isles. At the former a reconstitution of the chapter took place in 1544 on the grounds 'that only six canons and as many chaplains ... were known hitherto to be erected in the same ... and what pertained by the foundation to each of them neither is known nor appears by writings'. Members of the old chapter continued in possession of their prebends, however, and the new constitution which allowed for fifteen canons ironically did not become fully operative until well after the Reformation. An attempted reform in Sodor or the Isles was similarly thwarted. There a mid-fifteenth-century attempt to provide the diocese with a chapter and a new cathedral had failed, and in these circumstances the clergy of the diocese in association with the archdeacon of Sodor, who was the only dignitary, may have been deemed the electors of the fifteenth-century bishops (who seemed to have lacked not only a chapter but also a cathedral). This at least is the substance of a plea made by the crown to the pope on 1 April 1498, which requested that Iona abbey should be erected as the see of the bishop of the Isles until 'his principall Kirk on the Isle of Man be recoverit from Inglismen'. Although successive bishops from 1499 held the abbey as commendators, and may have regarded the abbey church as their cathedral, there is no evidence that the Benedictine monks ever formed a cathedral chapter; indeed in the early sixteenth century an impressive augmentation of the bishopric revenues was under way and was apparently connected with the development of a cathedral chapter then in progress, as a chancellor appears in 1541 and a dean may also have been functioning before 1560.[8]

Well before this date other administrative reforms were under way in many Scottish dioceses that had not previously possessed those areas of limited territorial jurisdiction known as deaneries. Such units had existed since the thirteenth century in the dioceses of Aberdeen, Argyll, Galloway, Glasgow, Moray and St Andrews, but some of these deaneries may not have had a continuous existence. At Dunkeld they ceased to exist and in Moray, with the exception of a recognizable succession of deans in the deanery of Inverness, they are extremely elusive figures. Intermittent references to later deans and a dean of Angus within Dunkeld by 1479 may simply point towards spasmodic attempts to parallel the administrative framework achieved in larger lowland dioceses. In Argyll too, the reconstitution of earlier deaneries may have been associated with the fourteenth-century reorganization of the chapter; if so, this particular part of the exercise appears to have failed. The sixteenth century saw further efforts to achieve such administrative reforms and though the situation in Moray does not appear to have improved and Brechin and Caithness remained devoid of deaneries, a dean of Orkney appears in 1527 and a dean of Dingwall materializes in the diocese of Ross. In Argyll a further reconstitution seems to have taken place in the sixteenth century with the appearance of three deaneries; Kintyre which was recorded in 1520 and Lochaw and Morvern which appear for the first time in 1541 and 1545 respectively. The evidence is more specific at Dunkeld for there Bishop Browne's biographer, Alexander Myln, relates 'as the population grew, the bishop by his officials' advice divided the whole diocese into four deaneries'. Even in the Isles the appearance of a dean of Bute in 1514 and a dean of Mull who was also vicar of Iona, indicates an administrative sub-division of the diocese into deaneries, thus bringing Sodor into line with most other Scottish dioceses.[9]

A dean was responsible for the moral discipline of both clergy and laity and to this end held a court in the parish churches of his deanery to hear cases and complaints and determine whether parish clergy were fulfilling their duties. After suspending his parish clerk in 1535, the curate of Insch in Aberdeenshire laid his complaint before the dean of the Garioch. The dean also enquired whether services were properly conducted and whether the Eucharist was suitably reserved. Morality was also safeguarded and the dean dealt with cases of adultery, fornication and non-attendance at church. Gossiping might also be punished although one dean was prepared to hear the complaint of Bessie Moodie of Kilbarchan who alleged that a priest breakfasted on honey plums before saying mass. In Dunkeld diocese the dean of Atholl, who 'kept open house in Highland fashion' punished judiciously all public offenders, whether they were clergy or country folk, and had succeeded, it was claimed, 'in routing out abominable sins in Atholl and Drumalban'. Minor civil cases were also dealt with and one dean investigated the theft of nails in Lanark in 1514.[10]

Similar developments had also taken place in the judicial responsibilities of bishops and, with the exception of Argyll, jurisdiction exercised by the bishop's official in the ecclesiastical courts was supplemented by the appointment of commissaries. These officers with jurisdiction over the diocese had appeared in most dioceses by the mid-fifteenth century, although in Caithness the first commissary does not appear until 1522. Likewise the appointments of commissaries for Bute and Arran, Iona and Skye in the early sixteenth century not only indicate an expansion of judicial services in the Isles but also demonstrate a new vitality in the ecclesiastical organization of that diocese. The late fifteenth and early sixteenth centuries, moreover, saw the appearance in several dioceses of a number of commissaries whose authority was confined to a section of the diocese or a jurisdiction peculiar within it. One of particular interest in this respect is the diocese of Glasgow in which the dignitaries of the cathedral and several canons of the cathedral had the parishes of their prebendal churches provided with individual commissary courts. Such developments not only exhibit an expansion of judicial services, but also demonstrate a new vitality in the ecclesiastical organization of the dioceses concerned.[11]

Few records of these commissary courts still exist but some insight into their activities can be gained from a description of the career of the commissary general of Dunkeld at the end of the fifteenth century, who was said to be 'the first man who effectively punished the excesses and crimes of the highland folk'. This task was made no easier in so far 'as he came of a noble Highland house and persons guilty of incest, adultery and fornication summoned for correction presumed to call themselves kinsmen in expectation of indulgent dealing'. However, the commissary's response, it was said, was to aver that for this reason and for the good of their souls, correction would be even more severe.[12]

Many of the commissaries were also cathedral canons and for this reason were frequently absentees; indeed it is clear that at any given time few of them were present at services in the cathedral or even at chapter meetings. As early as 1262 it is recorded that 'certain of the canons of the cathedral of Glasgow are pleased to hear the name ... but they entirely neglect to perform the duties of their office'. In the early fifteenth century the same state of affairs prevailed and remedial statutes reveal the nature of the problem. The dean, chanter, chancellor, treasurer and sub-dean were bound to reside for six months each, while the other canons were to be in residence for a period of three months in the year, although these need not be continuous. The imposition of financial penalties enforcing such attendance had little effect, and in 1455 it was reported that 'few or none' of the canons made residence. At Glasgow in 1502 even the names of two of the canons were unknown. The position was similar elsewhere and at Aberdeen in 1448 the complaint was made that the canons' manses had fallen into disrepair. Even at these cathedrals, however, a select number of canons may have found it financially rewarding to remain in residence and with the dignitaries who appear to have been more frequently present, they constituted the core of the chapter resident at any given time. For most canons, clearly, the status and the emolument were the prime considerations. It was as much this desire as any wish to augment divine service that led to the creation of additional prebends during the course of the fifteenth and early sixteenth centuries.[13]

At some cathedrals the level of attendance does, however, seem to have been much better than in others. Alexander Myln, himself a canon of Dunkeld, writing of his fellow-canons in the early sixteenth century may not be entirely trustworthy but the general tenor of his account is convincing. The dean, he insists, despite appeals from his friends and kin 'exercises his office and does not leave the church of Dunkeld; every day of his residence he appears devoutly among his brethren at high mass: on other days he rules the choir at the three greater hours'. The precentor, who acted as the bishop's chamberlain, also resided at Dunkeld, but the chancellor who for a time acted in a similar capacity to the archbishop of St Andrews must of necessity have been more frequently absent. More frequent attendance at the cathedral is reflected in the building and renovation of manses. One canon, who also excelled in penmanship, had refurbished an old-fashioned highland house which served as his residence. A number of canons were credited with building their manses from their foundations while others are reported as effecting necessary repairs. Attendance at cathedral services are also credited to some of the canons, but this matter receives notably less emphasis than some others; one canon is noted as being rarely absent from matins and another, who is credited with often rising in the middle of the night to perform the office of Lauds, celebrated mass daily when morning began and, after hearing high mass later, devoted the rest of the day to judicial work, study and reading the law and theology. Even where this was not the case, it should not be thought that absentee canons were necessarily idle. Most were careerists and their proficiency in canon law in particular, in which many possessed qualifications, allowed them to act as judges in the ecclesiastical courts. Myln noted amongst such canons, in addition to the archdeacon who had his own court, a sub-dean who was commissary general and dean of the whole diocese; one prebendary who was 'a learned and excellent textualist', and was commissary of the official principal of St Andrews; another, also specially versed in canon law, who was to be appointed commissary general of the diocese and yet another who is praised for his remarkable knowledge of canon law who had also been official of Dunkeld. Other canons, particularly at Aberdeen and Glasgow, were prominent in the field of university education while others again used their talents as administrators in both royal and private service.[14]

Even if they fulfilled their statutory residential obligations cathedral canons formed, however, only a small part of the total establishment. Since they were normally absent from the cathedral for the greater part of the year, deputies known as stallars or vicars choral officiated for the canons. Such vicars frequently augmented their livings by seeking appointments as chaplains at the numerous altars situated within cathedrals. Care was taken that vicars-choral were competent in the various parts of the service and before appointment they were subjected to a careful examination of their ability to read and sing. They would be expected to interpret the musical notation of the Gregorian plain-song and render it vocally. At Aberdeen, even if they passed this test successfully, vicars were appointed subject to a year's probation in which they were expected to learn the three service books which contained the music of the choir services – the Psalter, Hymnary and Antiphonary. Initially each vicar may have lodged in the manse of the canon whose vicar he was, but eventually more adequate provision came to be made. At Aberdeen a separate vicars' residence, le Myddletron, housed these deputies and at Glasgow where from the mid-fifteenth century the vicars choral constituted a college in their own right, separate residences were provided.[15]

Vicars choral were maintained by the canons whom they represented. Of the thirty-two canons who eventually constituted the chapter at Glasgow, all but two were bound to pay for the upkeep of vicars; these two had to maintain six choir boys and a sacristan respectively. Such payments did pose difficulties and the niggardly stipend paid to the Glasgow vicars of the choir, who were leaving for more remunerative posts elsewhere, led in 1480 to the doubling of their salaries. A slightly different solution to this problem was achieved at Aberdeen for the revised statutes of 1506 stated that there was no longer to be a vicar choral for every canon. Instead, the sums assigned to be paid by each canon were paid into a common fund and from that twenty priests who were vicars received ten pounds each. Although the number of vicars choral had diminished, priest vicars were given a new security of tenure through their formal institution. These men, more than the canons, were at the very heart of cathedral life, both spiritually and socially. But who were they? A study of their equivalents at Dunkeld who by Myln's admission 'bear the burden and heat of the day' reveals in their ranks advocates, notaries and consistorial clerks. All are praised for their musical ability, one is 'steady in the chant', another is 'highly trained in the theory of music as well as in the art of singing', while others are described as having been accustomed from their youth to take their part in service and rule the choir. Such details are unfortunately lacking elsewhere and vicars choral generally remain shadowy figures. Not so the canons and dignitaries who emerge as a well-born elite, sometimes related to either the bishop or some other notable family who might hold the patronage of their prebend. Most were university educated, and well suited to their office if they cared to exercise it, but with the exception of some of the dignitaries and a few working canons, most were more concerned with their interests elsewhere.[16]

Many cathedral canons also held prebends in collegiate churches, in the foundation and endowment of which devotion found its most meaningful form of expression in late medieval Scotland. These prebends like those in cathedrals did not entail the cure of souls and, being free from the restriction placed by canon law on the holding of only one benefice to which the cure of souls was attached, were particularly attractive to pluralists. About eleven such colleges were founded for saying votive masses for the dead in Scotland between 1450 and 1500 and yet another thirteen were initiated before the Reformation. Two of these were founded by the crown, but the majority owed their creation to the piety of nobles, lairds and bishops. The zeal of the founders was, however, more considerable than their resources; even at Trinity College, founded by Mary of Gueldres, the choir and transepts were all that existed when building operations came to an end in 1531. Most frequently, however, the college was erected in an existing parish church or chapel which was thereafter reconstructed, although here again, as a Crichton where the nave was left unfinished, completion was seldom achieved. This did not inhibit further foundations and a college was founded in the parish church of Biggar in 1546 and plans for the endowment of yet another by the earl of Huntly were actively afoot in 1550. Rebuilding sometimes preceded collegiate status and the magnificent church of St Giles, Edinburgh, which was virtually rebuilt in the first quarter of the fifteenth century, did not achieve collegiate status until 1468 when the magistrates and community successfully revived an earlier proposal for the erection of their parish church. In other Scottish towns the same factors were at work, and there are many churches which became collegiate in the sixteenth century and which exhibit the same close links between the burgh church and the community.[17]

If collegiate influences reveal a continuing vitality in the church and apparently a continuing sense of community identity, it is equally important to note that their growth in status and wealth added little to the parochial services available. Although numerous altars and chaplaincies were founded both before and after attaining collegiate status, these were mainly devoted to the saying of masses for the dead and the parochial work and cure of souls was entrusted, in spite of the magnificence of such churches, to underpaid vicars pensioner. Moreover, as the foundation of such colleges meant an upsurge in the appropriation of parish churches, the revenues of which were diverted to the college from the parish which was thereafter invariably served by a vicar pensioner, the erection of a collegiate church could vitiate services over quite a considerable area. On the credit side all collegiate churches had their song schools and while the number of endowed lay choristers was small, other boys who were not endowed may have attended such schools. A few collegiate churches also possessed grammar schools. Restalrig had its own song and grammar school and at Semple the first and second parts of Alexandre de Villedieu's grammar was to be taught to the pupils.[18]

In other burghs in which the churches did not acquire collegiate status the same traits are discernible but their clergy were often more readily controlled by the burgh council. The town council of Linlithgow oversaw the duties of the chaplains in the parish church and not only approved the hours of services but also superintended minor details such as the number of lights on the altar and regulations for dress in the choir. In 1530, the town council of Arbroath complained to the bishop because the chaplains of the Lady Chapel had failed to perform the services for Holy Week. Concern for the upkeep of the fabric of the burgh church was equally a matter of concern and both at Dundee and St Andrews the town council assumed responsibility for repairs after agreements had been made with the abbey of Lindores and the priory of St Andrews, to which the parish churches were appropriated. At Dundee the council which employed the chaplains under contract also hired a kirkmaster to supervise church repairs. The severe damage inflicted on the parish church during the English invasion of 1548 was to test this policy to the utmost. Nevertheless around the year

1551 the kirkmaster was instructed to raise overdue church rents – Our Lady annuals – to help meet the cost of repairs. On 31 December 1551 the Dundee council met with the deacons of the crafts 'convenit in the provost's ludging touching the common weill of the burgh and the reparation and decoreing of thair mother Kirk'. Among the decisions taken was the renewed collection of payments for burial plots in the church and choir 'efter auld use and consuetude'. As for the actual work initiated on the project, timber for re-roofing St Mary's church was obtained from ships trading in the Baltic and on 10 October 1552 a contract for the re-roofing of 'Our Lady Kirk' was made between the kirkmaster and one 'Pottane Blak, wricht' and his helpers. By 31 January 1553 the payment of a bounty to those concerned would seem to indicate that work was proceeding satisfactorily, only six years before the full force of protestant zeal was to appear in Dundee. So too in 1554 at St Giles, Edinburgh, where Walter Bynning was engaged by the council to paint the panels of the new choir stalls. Equal attention was paid to the organs and in 1555 a fee of twenty-four shillings was paid 'to Sir Johne Fetie at the command of the Counsale for tonying of the organis at Sanct Geillis day'. The sums expended on the ornaments of the church are equally instructive. Burgh councils were still expending sums on such items on the very eve of the Reformation. As late as 1554/5 at Ayr the following expenditure is recorded: 3s. 8d. for strings for the censers; 10s for 4 ells of linen to cover the lecterns; 15s. 4d. for 'hallowing' the silver chalice; 6s. to the goldsmith for repairing two chalices and 10s. for a tin chalice.[19]

This kind of evidence which strongly suggests that the integrated social and religious life of the pre-Reformation Scottish burghs still centred on its parish church is also borne out by an examination of the relationship between the clergy and the burgesses whom they served. In this respect the role of the numerous chaplains to be found in most churches may have been more significant than that of the parish priest. The duties of such chaplains are listed in their deeds of institution. They included not only the saying of mass at the altars that they served, but also collectively in 'singing with the rest of the chaplains . . . on Sundays and all other festivals, at high mass, matins and vespers, and all other usual services performed in the said church by the said chaplains'. One chaplain indeed on his appointment bound himself to sing with the other chaplains and choristers in the choir of the church on all feast days.[20]

Some of these chaplains were maintained from the common good of the burgh, but many others had been endowed by private benefactors with whose descendants the patronage remained. One of these, Herbert Cunynghame, patron of the chaplaincy of the Holiblude in St Michaels church at Dumfries, went on 7 December 1550 to that altar and presented James Gladstanis for life 'to sing every Thursday ane Solemn mass of the body of Christ as his predecessors had been wont to do'. A few months later Gladstanis was also presented to the vacant chaplaincy of St Gregoris by its patron Mathew Gladstanis because 'it will not sustane ane chaplane of itself'. This act shows clearly that chaplaincies were frequently insufficiently endowed.[21]

The motivation to retain such altars was strong and, though their chaplaincies were often under-endowed, pious benefactors were still to the fore even on the eve of the Reformation. Thus when John Crosby resigned a tenement in favour of his daughter and son-in-law, he not only retained a life rent in the property, but also instructed his heirs to make a payment of sixteen shillings to the chaplains of the parish church of Dumfries 'to celebrate annually once on the day of their burial a Placebo, a dirge and a requiem mass for their souls in perpetuity, according to the tenor of the charter of infeftment given to the said chaplains'.[22]

Belief in the efficacy of such prayers can also be seen in an endowment made in 1542 by one of the burgesses of Newburgh who conveyed two roods of land to the bailies and burgesses 'patrons of the chaplaincy of St Kathrine founded by their predecessors within the new church of the burgh to Sir John Richardson, *alias* Cuk, chaplain and his successors', for augmentation of the stipend of the chaplaincy and 'for prayers on behalf of the souls of the founders of the monastery of Lundoris, superiors of the burgh of Newburgh, and for the souls of the venerable father John, the present abbot, and his successors in the monastery, and for the souls of his own father and mother, of his ancestors and descendents, and for the souls of all the faithful defunct for ever'. Most town councils were not only zealous in the maintenance of such agreements but also endeavoured to aid the chaplains in the fulfilment of their duties. An appointment to an altar in Elgin made by the town council in 1546 not only provided honest board in the houses of eight, and at the most fourteen, neighbours but stipulated that the chaplain was to 'say mass and sing devyn service within the said paroche kirk at all dais, houris and tymes he beis disposit thairto'. At Inverness on 29 April 1557 the town council with no thought of impending religious change 'for uphald of dale service into thare kyrk for the glore of God and honor thair kyrk' augmented 'Schir Andrew Brebner chapland to Sant Pettyr with fouvyr merkis yerle to be payit of the common gud of Innernes with the oblation and anwell of Sant Duthace altar'.[23]

Burgh churches such as these were only representative of a fairly small number of Scottish parish churches, but it is clear that even in rural parish churches the pattern of devotion was not markedly dissimilar. Belief in the efficacy of prayers for the dead and support for the church from local landowners in Dumfriesshire is seen in an agreement of 15 June 1547 in which Robert Maxwell, son and heir of John Maxwell of Kowhill, bound himself to pay five merks annually to the chaplain of the Lady Service of Holywode if he could obtain entry to certain lands at the Brigend of Dumfries following which he would make an endowment equal to that sum for 'suffrage and prayers yearly . . . at the parish altar of Holywode for the souls of the said John Maxwell of Kowhill, Gelis Heris, his wife' and others.[24]

Two years later on 15 July 1549 Janet Maxwell, Lady of Tynwald, spouse of Robert Maxwell of Kowhill bound herself and her heirs to pay and deliver to Sir John Wallace, younger, chaplain, and after his death to the chaplain chosen by Janet and her heirs, lairds of Tynwald; for which sum Sir John and his successors, chaplains, bound themselves to celebrate at an undesignated altar within the parish church of Tynwald every week, on Sunday, Wednesday and Friday, High Mass for the souls of the late Edward Maxwell, Lord of Tynwald, husband of Janet, and William Maxwell, his father, and of Janet, now Lady of Tynwald'.[25]

Altars and their attached chaplaincies provide an 'outward show' of devotion but do not reflect the extent of provision for the general cure of souls in Scottish parishes. The efficiency of the parochial organization was vitiated by a policy of appropriation which had resulted in the diversion of revenues from eighty-five per cent of the parishes; where parochial duties had to be performed by an underpaid vicar. Any study of the cure of souls in the medieval period must therefore be mainly concerned with the history of vicarages and their endowments. Vicarages did not, of course, constitute all the parochial cures in Scotland, and even at the Reformation 148 independent parsonages remained free from appropriation – yet these churches did not necessarily enjoy a better type of service than those which were appropriated. Few independent parsonages were served by their parsons as most such incumbents were pluralists who frequently used substitutes to serve their cures. In some such parishes there were properly ordained vicarages, and in these cases the vicars had the same advantages as vicars elsewhere – security of tenure and a fit portion of the fruits. In other cases the substitute was denied even these privileges, and the unsecured vicar, or more frequently curate, who was appointed at will by the parson, was equally easily removed and in return for his labours normally only received a small pension from the revenues of the church. Unappropriated churches might therefore exhibit all the evils of appropriated churches and could in addition add several undesirable variations.[26]

Unappropriated churches were especially attractive to pluralists and the unqualified. As far as the latter were concerned, one of the sternest critics of this practice, the Catholic reformer Quintin Kennedy, could write in the sixteenth century that a commonplace occurrence was to see 'ane bairne and ane babe, to quhame scarcelie wald thou geve ane fair apill to keip, get perchance fyve thousand soules to gyde: And all for avarice ... that thair parentis may get the proffect of the benefice ... and the pure simpyll bairne scarslie gett to bryng hym up vertuuslie'.[27]

Pluralism was not confined to unappropriated churches; careerists also ensured that both parsonages and vicarages were occupied by clergy who held other positions in the church, which, if they did not entail the cure of souls, could be held in conjunction with one another; absenteeism could be readily covered by the employment of substitutes. The pursuit of such benefices inevitably led to disputes between contending parties because of the complex rules governing patronage and papal rules of reservation, rights established in the course of the fourteenth century, which not only extended the papal claims to dispose such benefices, but also established a call on the payment of annates, or first fruits, of each benefice so reserved. The rules most likely to be invoked related to the death of benefice holder at or in the neighbourhood of the

Curia; the death of a papal chaplain at any time or place; or through death in one of the designated eight months; March, July, September and December being the only four months in which the benefice was still at the patron's free disposal.[28]

These papal rights remained unregulated after 1487. Yet it was perhaps these claims, rather than those of provision, which had lain behind James I's acts against barratry or unauthorized dealings at Rome. The rules of reservation which might apply to all non-elective benefices had led clerks to Rome in the hope that they would gain by litigation either the benefice or a substantial pension from its fruits and it was this practice that parliament in 1424 had attempted to curb by forbidding clerks to 'purches any pensions out of benefice secular or religious'. Only by special permission of the king, or in 1428 by leave of the diocesan bishop or royal chancellor, was an overseas journey to be undertaken on pain of various penalties for the crime of barratry. The provisions of this act were repeated in 1482 and 1484, but no mention of this particular grievance was found in the Indult. The practice continued unabated and legislation of 1496 not only indicated that elective benefices were still the object of unofficial petitions, but also referred to pleas for 'diverse utheris that mycht be gavin and providit within the realme'. Occasionally licences were sought and obtained to 'pas to the courts of Rome' or 'to impetrat a pensioun', but these were the exception rather than the rule; the tide of petitions could not be stemmed and supplications to the pope continued in undiminished numbers until the Reformation.[29]

Much of the litigation took place in Rome before the auditors of the Sacred Roman Rota, the records of which reveal a stream of petitioners and witnesses testifying to the cases before the court. Many of the disputes were, however, heard in Scotland. Thus, the vicar of Walston obtained a papal rescript ordering three judges delegate to hear a case between himself and another claimant to the vicarage. In another case, in a dispute over the vicarage of Bathgate, the litigant sought a copy of apostolic letters directed to judges delegate in 'a case moved against him'. An instance of such procedures in action is seen in the case of a chaplain called Romannos who had been provided in Rome to the parsonage of Lyne and who had attempted to claim possession on his return to Scotland. At the instance of Thomas Murhede, parson of Lyne, he was cited by one of the vicars-general of the archbishop of Glasgow but, having appeared in person, he had failed to produce 'the principal provision or collation' without which the vicar-general refused to admit him as parson.[30]

Such litigation was usually terminated by a resignation in favour of the successful party to the action; this was sometimes unconditional, sometimes with a right of regress attached and often after some form of pension arrangement. In this respect the device of '*resignatio in favorem*' has often been misrepresented, for in many cases the resignation was not by an incumbent but by a litigant who, if his claims or ultimate chance of success were slight might be only too happy to settle for monetary compensation; and for the actual possessors a pension on the fruits of their benefice might prove infinitely cheaper than the cost of litigation.[31]

Such a system was good neither for the clergy nor for the benefices they claimed to serve. Parochial service and the manner in which it was carried out lay at the root of many of the problems facing the church in sixteenth-century Scotland. Laxity in the means of serving appropriated churches had led in the thirteenth century to a systematic method of providing ministrations by 'a perpetual vicar canonically instituted who should have a fit portion of the profits of the church'. But the decree of 1215 that specified this merely canonized a system which had been slowly evolving; in Scotland the institution of perpetual vicars, as such incumbents came to be styled, was under way in the diocese of Glasgow by the end of the twelfth century. In consequence, vicarage settlements became so commonplace that the form of agreement was virtually stereotyped and, even although the conditions might vary, *portio vicarii* eventually became a recognized style. Early settlements usually arranged for the division of the teinds between vicar and the appropriating body, the most common form being variants of a division by which the garbal or corn teinds were assigned to the 'rector' and the lesser teinds, that is to say those of milk, butter, cheese, wool and the young of animals amongst other things, were set apart for the vicar. Appropriations that occurred after the thirteenth century invariably included both parsonage and vicarage teinds, and this meant that the incumbent only received a fixed wage or pension and was reduced in status to that of a vicar pensioner.[32]

As in the case of perpetual vicarages, there was considerable fluctuation in the value of vicarages pensionary. While most appear to have been above the thirteenth-century minimum of ten merks, later raised to ten pounds sterling, few reached the value of the twenty merks thought necessary in 1549 and still deemed sufficient in the dioceses of Aberdeen, Caithness, Orkney, Moray and Ross, ten years later when the minimum stipend in other sees was increased to twenty-four merks a year. Even a modest increase was difficult to achieve. Thus at Alvah in Aberdeenshire, although the church was the second richest in the deanery of the Boyne, being valued at 51 merks and 10s, and even though the vicar had to meet from his pension the episcopal and archdiaconal procurations together with the ordinary burdens, the incumbent in 1428 was obliged to swear that he would not attempt to have his pension augmented. Evidently this hard bargain was kept, because in 1520, the vicarage was still described as '*vicariam pensionarum perpetuam decem librarum*', and although by then the vicar may have been relieved of certain of his burdens, as he was by 1542, the stipend of the vicar pensioner was far from adequate.[33]

The great majority of vicar's stipends appear to have fallen into this category. Diocesan bishops were not completely insensitive, however, to the plight of the pensionary vicars and attempts to alleviate their plight were made from time to time. In particular, the elevation of the bishopric of St Andrews to archepiscopal status appears to have placed that dignitary in a much stronger negotiating position, especially when legatine powers also came to be granted to a number of the archbishops. Several examples occur in this period of vicars-pensioner having their position improved; an erection of a church into a prebend of St Salvator's college was accompanied by the conversion of the existing vicarage pensionary into a vicarage perpetual. On another occasion a vicar pensioner was, on the petition of the holder of the parsonage and vicarage fruits which were annexed to a prebend of St Mary on the Rock, accorded the status of *vicaria integra et perpetua*. Other isolated cases arise from time to time. Bishop George Browne of Dunkeld (1484–1515) appears to have improved the lot of certain vicars by splitting up large parishes and assigning episcopal revenues to new incumbents. Also within that diocese, the vicar pensioner of Crieff successfully appealed for an increase of stipend on the grounds that his vicarage pensionary was inadequate and not of commensurate value with that of other churches with annexations to the

Chapel Royal at Stirling, which in 1501 had been established at twenty-four merks.[34]

Such processes were no doubt being carried through in other dioceses also, but their comparative rarity indicated that this was only a piecemeal solution to an overwhelming problem. Moreover, even in the cases where a rise in emoluments or status was achieved, it was possible that increased burdens would go far to cancel out the advantage gained. Thus in the case of the vicar pensioner whose status was raised to that of *vicaria integra et perpetua*, the vicar was now to be responsible not only for the archiepiscopal and archdiaconal burdens but also for the cantor's fee – a responsibility normally borne by the prebendary. The vicars pensioner and vicars perpetual had financial problems and both eventually turned to the one source of revenue left open to them, that of mulcting their parishioners. The underpaid vicar could only supplement his meagre income from offerings, oblation and mortuary dues. Of the offerings, that at Easter – when most parishioners made a point of attending their parish church – was undoubtedly the most valuable and priests appear to have been particularly zealous in their efforts to ensure as large a collection as possible. In this respect some vicars clearly failed to stress the voluntary nature of such offerings and some even appear to have made reception of the Eucharist conditional on their payment. An insistence upon heavy mortuary rights is equally evident and the rapacity of vicars in this respect is attested by many contemporary writers.[35]

If greed characterized most vicars and curates, other traits seem at first glance equally reprehensible. In addition to rapacity they are charged with neglect of the fabric of their churches, immorality and a basic lack of education which prevented them from fulfilling their parochial responsibilities. The charge of failing to maintain their churches in good repair is not entirely unjust, as in 1549 the parishioners of Inverchaolin in Argyll 'wad nocht ansuer Schir Robert Maxvell vyker of the fruttis, or to the tyme at he mendit his part of the kyrk'. However, the repair of parish churches was a joint responsibility shared by the 'rectors', who were often the monastic body to which the church had been appropriated, and vicars with their parishioners. The maintenance of the chancel was the responsibility of the parson, whether an individual or a corporate body, and he was equally responsible for the supply of all that was necessary for the service of the altar. Other repairs were a charge on the parish and were to be met by both vicars and parishioners. Appropriating bodies did, however, attempt to place their share of burdens upon the vicars, and the statutes governing the division of responsibilities had to be re-enacted in 1549 and 1559. In many instances internal disputes led to total neglect and individual instances of churches suffering in this way are not hard to find. The ruinous state of twenty-two churches in the deanery of the Merse of 1556 may, however, be taken as exceptional, and may be attributed to the English invasions of the 1540s. Not all appropriations led to neglect and the churches belonging to the bishop of Dunkeld at the beginning of the sixteenth century appear to have been well looked after: glass was regularly replaced in windows; a slater is found roofing the church of St George in Dunkeld and also being paid for his labour in 'winning the slates'; smithy work was carried out on the iron frames of other windows and, most impressive of all, accounts of 1510 relate to the building of the whole choir of Aberlady 'in lime, cut stones and common stones, roofing, pointing, glass windows and iron'.[36]

Charges of immorality were much more individual in their nature, but concern in the sixteenth century about the necessity for clerical celibacy was hardly novel; since the thirteenth century the church had been urging priests to set aside their concubines. Celibacy had been reluctantly accepted by the church in the eleventh and twelfth centuries, but had been seldom practised. If there had been moral outrage it related to the bishops and commendators with their many mistresses rather than to the humble parish priest with his loyal housekeeper who also shared his bed and bore his children. The statutes of the church might be aimed at the parish priest, but satirists attacked the real offenders who would not maintain a 'wife':

> Thinkand it was ane lustie lyfe
> Ilk day to have ane new ane.[37]

In terms of education it is true that most parochial incumbents, in contrast to the higher clergy, were not university trained. Instead they were products of the cathedral schools who, having thereby attained some degree of literacy, obtained their professional qualifications by serving as curates or chaplains in cathedrals or other ecclesiastical institutions. At Dunkeld, boys who intended to enter the priesthood boarded in one instance with one of the canons and in another with one of the vicars choral, and in essence served an apprenticeship rather than a rigorous intellectual training in theology and scripture. In the circumstances it is hardly surprising that many priests emerged with little Latin and only a rudimentary knowledge of their faith. In 1551/2, it was thought to be necessary to advise rectors, vicars and curates to prepare themselves for the task of reading 'lest they expose themselves to the ridicule of their hearers, when through want of preparation, they stammer and stumble in mid-course of reading'. Exceptions, of course, existed and vicars are to be found at church councils and sitting on ecclesiastical commissions; William Wydman, vicar of Keith, was described in a rental that he had transcribed as the 'best wryttar within the bisschopreik of Murray'. Even a low standard of literacy was, however, not a new development; as early as 1216 the papacy had complained of the lack of learning possessed by some parish priests. Lack of education in an illiterate society was not necessarily a serious drawback if the career of the Latinless vicar was socially and economically integrated with the life-style of his parishioners. The vicar who farmed his glebe may have enjoyed a rapport with his flock which was not seriously threatened by his lack of education. Rapacity on the vicar's part might, on the other hand, threaten this relationship and lead to attacks on the church itself. Contemporary satire and the growth of protestant opinions suggest that this process was under way long before the events of 1559/60, yet with the exception of the burning of the parish church of Echt in Aberdeenshire in 1559 evidence of actual hostility towards parochial incumbents is hard to come by. Mobs may have attacked friaries, and on occasions monasteries were also assailed, but their inmates escaped unscathed. In a similar fashion parish churches were purged of symbols of idolatory, but the priests themselves were undisturbed, a fact which is not easy to explain except in terms of lack of popular opposition to the old regime despite its shortcomings. If the church had been able to remove these defects through re-appraisal of its aims and then effect reforms from within its own organization, popular support might well have remained steadfast and the outcome of the events of 1559/60 might have been very different.[38]

4
Reform from Within

Certain sections of both laity and clergy were very much alive to the dangers of a decadent church which had ceased to minister to spiritual needs and had lost almost all semblance of discipline. Criticism took many forms, ranging from serious disputations which not only attacked the church for its malpractices but also offered suggestion for its reformation to those of a satirical nature which by attacking the church for its folly helped to promote self-examination and subsequent amendment.

Some of these, for example the *Gude and Godlie Ballatis*, looked for reformation outside the existing framework of the church; others were merely anti-clerical; some like the works of Sir David Lindsay of the Mount not only offered criticisms but proffered some positive suggestions for reform. Many of Lindsay's works, the *Dreme*, the *Complaynts*, the *Testament* and the *Dialog* or *Monarche* have reforming themes, but the most influential was undoubtedly the *Satyre of the Thrie Estatis*. First performed at Epiphany 1540 at Linlithgow, probably in the banqueting hall, before James v and his queen, Mary of Guise, it was subsequently performed after the king's death at Cupar in 1552 and at the Greenside on the lower slopes of the Calton hill, Edinburgh, in the presence of the regent, Mary, and a large number of the magnates and people on 12 August 1554. The play is a compound of morality play and political satire; the first half concerns the redemption of King Humanitie from Sensualitie and the vices (Flattery, Deceit and Falsehood) which come in her train by the sombre but majestic Divine Correction; in the second half the blemishes of the body politic and particularly ecclesiastic are exposed and 'John the Commonweal', a representative figure of the people is elevated to a place in the government of the kingdom. In this part comprehensive charges – of simony, plurality, oppression of the poor, illiteracy, lack of chastity – are proffered against certain sections of the clergy who are ultimately stripped of their fine vestments and driven off. Lindsay's attack varies in its intensity; the inmates of male monastic houses, with the exception of the monks of Balmerino who are to be asked if 'lecherie be sin', escape general charges of immorality but are condemned insofar as they 'lief richt easelie'. Abbots on the other hand are characterized by one who says of himself:

My paramours is baith as fat and fair
As ony wench into the toun of Air.

Nunneries do not escape so easily, for although the prioress is only accused of repelling Chastity, in admitting the charge she also records:

Howbeit the Nuns sings nicht and days,
Their heart wats nocht what their mouth says,
The sooth I you declare,
Makkand you intimatioun
To Christis congregatioun
Nuns are nocht necesare.

In the *Complaynt of the Papingo*, however, Lindsay modifies this view in respect of the Dominican nuns in the Sciennes. His views on friars are also ambivalent, for at times he may be found praising the various orders of preaching friars for the zeal with which they carried the Christian message to the people; devotion he claims is 'fled unto the freiris'. But in the *Thrie Estaits*, Lindsay suggests that the friars have used their preaching ability to secure advantage to themselves; Flattery in reply to an objection that he cannot disguise himself as a friar because he cannot preach says:

Quhat rak, man, I can richt weill fleich
Perchance I'll cum to that honour
To be the king's confessour.
Pure freiris ar free at ony feist
And marshallit ay amang the best.

The privileges accorded to friars and their failure to castigate other sections of the church for their obvious failings lest they lose their preaching fees are other charges levelled by Lindsay against the friars of whom he seems to have become increasingly critical.[1]

It is, however, the secular clergy who bear the brunt of Lindsay's displeasure. The bishops are decried by the poor man both for their wealth and their immorality:

Our bishops with their lustie rokets quhyte
They flow in riches royally and delyte;
Like Paradice bene their palices and places,
And wants nae pleasure of the fairest faces.
. . . .
But doubt I wad think it ane pleasant lyfe
Aye when I list to part me from my wyfe
Syne tak another of far greiter beutie.
But ever alas, my lords, that may not be,
For I am bound, alace in marriage,
But they like rams rins rudely in their rage!

The greed of the secular clergy as a whole is equally condemned; the lusty parson is accused of being only interested in acquiring teinds, for his preaching his parishioners might wait seventeen years, but the parson would 'nocht want ane boll of beir'. The vicar too would not forsake his financial dues for:

The pure cottar, being lyke to die,
Haifand young infants twa or thrie,
And has twa ky, bot ony ma
The vickar must haif ane of thae,
With the gay frugge that covers the bed,
Howbeit the wyfe be purelie clad,
And gif the wyfe die on the morne,
Thocht all the bairns sould be forlorne

The ower kow he cleekis away
With the pure cot of raploch gray.
Wald God this custome war put down,
Quhilk never was foundit be reasoun.

Identifying the faults was relatively simple, but proposing remedies was more difficult. To some problems, Lindsay presents specific answers; nunneries that fail to fulfil their functions should be closed down:

Thir wantoun Nunnis are now necessair
Till Common weill nor zit to the glorie
of Christis kirk . . .
. . . .
Thair rents usit till ane better tyme,
For Commonweil of all this regioun.

In particular he suggests that their revenues be used to provide salaries for judges. In general terms Lindsay argues that reformation must lie in the hands of the civil power; the crown in particular must use its authority to that end. Temporality decrees that the king:

> Sall write unto the Papeis Haliness
> With his consent by proclamatioun,
> Baith corse-present and cow we sall cry doun.

If, however, the crown fails in its duty, Lindsay would seem to suggest that the estates might take the initiative for when the spiritual lords record their dissent to this mode of procedure, the temporal estates reply

> Wee set nocht by quhidder ye consent or nocht:
> Ye are bot ane estait and we ar twa.

Where appropriate the areas of temporal and spiritual authority might be redefined; and, in seeking the reform of the consistorial courts, Lindsay urged that the example of France be followed so that temporal matters should be reserved for civil courts and only exclusively spiritual cases for the courts of the church. Legislation might also deal with abuses such as simony and plurality:

> That fra henceforth na priests sall pass to Rome
> Because our substance they do still consume
> And als I think it best by my advice
> That ilk priest sall have but ane benefice.[2]

In furtherance of this policy Lindsay had the ear of the king and later of the queen regent; their tacit approval for his suggestions might be inferred from the play's performance for their joint enjoyment at Linlithgow and its later revival at Edinburgh in 1554. No official reprimand followed either performance and no suggestion of heresy appears to have become attached to the play; Lindsay avoided controversial liturgical comment and references to the New Testament in English are muted. When Dame Verity is accused of heresy by Flattery for possessing a New Testamount 'in Englisch toung, and printit in England', her reply may reflect Lindsay's own opinion, but it is one to which little exception could be taken:

> Forsooth my friend, ye have ane wrong judgement
> For in this book there is nae heresy
> But our Christ's word, richt douce and redolent –
> An spring and well of sincere veritie!

Likewise in his attitude towards the papacy: the pope is never disowned or condemned and is associated with some of the reforms advocated by Lindsay. A diminution of papal authority would certainly have followed the implementation of some of the reforms suggested but, as royal power would have grown in proportion to that lost by the papacy, such remedies might have been regarded as representing official royal policy. Some measures, such as the proposed abolition of the right of priests to petition for benefices in Rome, were hardly novel, and had been advocated by the crown since the reign of James I. In this, as in other matters, Lindsay might be regarded as orthodox.[3]

Many of his ideas were in fact acceptable to the church. When Lindsay wrote:

> Ane bishop's office is for to be ane preichour
> And of the Law of God ane publick teachour

he was merely stating a principle on the merits of preaching that had been accepted by the church by the early sixteenth century. The synodal constitutions of Archbishop Forman of St Andrews decreed that monastic houses should send one or two of their members to study theology at university. In this self-same spirit Thomas Crystall, abbot of Kinloss, had sent two of his monks to study theology under John Adamson at the Blackfriars monastery at Aberdeen and several other monks are found at universities in this period. Secular clergy were encouraged in the same manner and in 1544 the new constitution of Kirkwall cathedral stipulated that the chancellor of the diocese was to be at least a bachelor of canon law and to lecture publicly once weekly. Several months before, an enactment in the fifth session of the Council of Trent had likewise decreed that in cathedral churches a theologian should lecture to the canons, and a canonist to the canons and other clergy; Cardinal Beaton had begun the reform of preaching and training of theologians. It was in this tradition, as well as that of Trent, that in July 1548 William Gordon, bishop of Aberdeen, appointed a licentiate in theology, John Watson, to lecture publicly in the cathedral twice a week and to preach there once a month, as well as annually in every church appropriated to the cathedral and its chapter. Watson clearly took his duties seriously and possessed at least three volumes of model sermons. Events at

Trent and decrees emanating from that council were obviously closely followed. Nevertheless, no Scottish bishops attended the Council of Trent, which was convened in 1542 but did not meet until 1545. Cardinal Beaton may have intended to attend and he called a special council at Edinburgh in the year following the council's first meeting in order to raise a tax to send representatives. In the end no delegates were sent, although Scots priests regularly made the journey to Rome during this period. If a Scot, Robert Wauchope, archbishop of Armagh, was present and indeed took a leading part in the council's early sessions, the absence of a distinctively Scottish presence was one that redounded little to the credit of the Scottish episcopate at the time. Yet these selfsame bishops were well aware of the decrees promulgated at Trent and acted with promptitude in drawing them to the attention of the Scottish church.[4]

Strenuous efforts were made to reform from within the existing framework. On the initiative of Archbishop Hamilton, three provincial councils (in 1549, 1552 and 1559) passed a series of reforming statutes. These covered a multitude of problems, some designed to remedy practices that had led to increased alienation between church and laity. Attempts were made to remedy certain defects in the working of the ecclesiastical courts. The statutes of 1549 declared that in future procurators were not to undertake cases that had no legal basis; wherever possible cases were to be expedited lest litigants suffered financial loss through undue delay. Other regulations forbade the pursuit of unjust actions and defined procedure in cases relating to matrimonial suits and the confirmation of wills. Delays were again deplored in 1559, when it was enacted that absolution for excommunication must only be given in cases of genuine repentence and not simply to allow legal actions to proceed. Regulations were laid down for the administration of property from which the clergy drew much of their income. Inflation and increased taxation in the course of the sixteenth century had led to an increase in the practice of long-term leasing of teinds and ecclesiastical property, including even glebes and manses, while the granting of feus or perpetual leases had become increasingly common. The patrimony of the church was being alienated and to check this, it was decreed in 1549 that except for good reasons approved by the bishops such leases should be prohibited. Ten years later the ban was repeated, on this occasion allowing relaxation in favour of the actual tenants and tillers of the lands.[5]

The payment of teind was also to be made more equitable for 'poor tillers or husbandmen' who in future were either to pay their dues direct to churchmen, or if the teinds in question were let by their lawful owners, were to be leased to none but the tillers and cultivators of the lands from which they were derived; the middlemen who had pressurised the poor tenants was apparently to be eliminated, or at least have his economic privileges modified. This too was to be the answer in relation to mortuary dues; in effect a sliding scale was to be established:

> When the dead's part shall have amounted only to ten pounds money Scots, only forty shillings shall be paid to the vicar of that parish as composition for the annal or the mortuary, which was to be paid, and for the uppermost garment; and when the dead's part shall not have amounted to ten pounds, but shall have ranged between that part and twenty shillings, relative payment out of the dead's part shall be made to the vicar in the proportion above related, at the rate of forty shillings to the ten pounds, and when the dead's part shall not have exceeded twenty shillings, nothing shall be paid out of it for the mortuary or the uppermost garment; but if the dead's part shall have exceeded the sum of ten pounds of the said money Scots, then the vicar shall be paid in full . . . as was customary of yore.

Easter offerings were to be similarly monitored for 'the avoidance of popular discontent' for whereas priests at the Easter sacrament had been so solicitous of their teinds and other offerings 'as to seem to sell that most sacred sacrament for the consideration of a garment', they were henceforward advised to come to an agreement with their parishioners shortly before Lent 'so that at the solemn service of Easter the Christian people may have greater leisure for prayer, and may also receive that sacrament with a more ardent spirit of devotion'.[6]

Such concern characterized many of the statutes passed at these three councils. In addition to the measures designed to promote economic and social justice they can be broadly classified into those designed to remedy the moral laxity of the clergy, those intended to rectify abuses in the sphere of spiritual ministrations, and finally those which made a more positive attempt to ensure that the church in combating heresy would not only regain its former vitality, but also prepare itself to meet the changing conditions of the sixteenth century. Statutes designed to combat moral deficiencies in the clergy included edicts against concubinage, the maintenance of the children of such liaisons, non-residence and pluralism. In the case of the latter the 1549 council chose to repeat verbatim the relevant chapter of the seventh session of the Council of Trent which had been promulgated in March 1547. Other statutes forbade the exercise of trade by priests, a prohibition which was repeated in 1549 and 1559, and also banned unseemly dress so that beneficed clergy were to wear only round caps and should not dress:

> in top-boots and doubly-breasted or oddly-cut coats, or coats of forbidden colours, as yellow, green, and such kinds of parti-colour, and shall wear long cassocks reaching down to the ankles in churches, cities, towns and larger villages, but on journeys short cassocks fitted with sleeves, regard, however, being had to the exigencies of time and place; they shall have white shirts with white seams.

Beards too were frowned upon and were forbidden not only 'so that frequent railleries levelled at them for wearing beards might be put an end to, but also as clergymen they might be distinguishable from laymen. Temperance in both eating and drinking was also to be observed 'by the avoiding, in accordance with each one's standing and dignity, delicacy and superfluity in meats and drinks'.

Bishops were to enforce the observation of these decrees, and if they failed in this duty were to be themselves proceeded against in provincial and synodal councils. In 1549 they were reminded that their moral example was of paramount importance 'lest the very persons rashly proceed to the rigorous correction of the morals of others, who are themselves implicated in notorious offences, since from this cause arises the greatest scandal to the laity and the largest proportion of the heresy'. Episcopal authority was also to be used as a means of restoring discipline. Bishops were empowered to visit monastic houses, whether or not they had previously been exempt from episcopal inspection, and were also to assist in the recall of apostate monks and canons. In 1552, every bishop was ordered to make a complete visitation of his diocese at least every two years and to preach in person four times a year; in 1559 this requirement was reaffirmed and they were to preach 'even oftener, as often they can do conveniently'. Archdeacons and deans of Christianity were to reinforce the work of the bishops and all ruinous and dilapidated churches were to be rebuilt and repaired. Great stress was laid upon education in the council of 1549 which repeated word for word chapters on this theme passed at the fifth session of the Council of Trent. In churches where the revenues were slight and the clergy few in number so that no theological lectureship could be maintained, lectures in theology were to be given in the grammar school. Livings originally endowed for teachers of theology must thenceforward be given only to those capable of exercising such a duty; failing which they must appoint a competent substitute. In cathedrals and other churches with numerous clergy, a theologian should lecture to the canons and a canonist to the canons and other clergy. Every monastery was also to have a theologian and emphasis was again placed on sending representatives of the religious to universities to study theology. Practical results again followed these decrees. Andrew Davidson, bachelor in theology was appointed to preach in St Andrews diocese and two other preachers, John McQuhyn and friar James Johnstone, were supplied with pensions from the abbey of Paisley.[7]

Most reforms were directed towards resolving defects among the clergy, but some statutes were aimed at improving the conduct of the parishioners. Attendance at mass was stressed in 1552 when, because it was alleged that 'very few indeed out of the most populous parishes deign to be present at the sacrifice of holy mass on the Sundays and the other double festivals appointed by the church', the names of defaulters were to be noted by the curate and reported to the dean of Christianity for punishment. Disciplinary action was also to be taken against 'those who have fallen into the habit of hearing mass irreverently and impiously, or who jest or behave scurrilously in church at time of sermon' and against those who engaged in trade 'in church porches and churchyards in the time of divine service on the Sundays and on holy days'.

Steps were also taken to ensure that spiritual ministrations were conducted in a more seemly fashion; bishops were to ensure that in their dioceses, parochial incumbents should 'strive with all their might that the word of God be expounded to their flocks, sincerely, and in a Catholic sense; that the true uses of the Church's ceremonies be moderately, soberly and discreetly explained; that false opinions be prohibited, publicly denounced, and confuted'. Injunctions were also made as to the reading of certain prayers and although a statement concerning the Lord's prayer was left blank in the text of the proceedings of the 1549 council, it was enacted that 'at the beginning of all public sermons the ancient and received form of invocation by saying the Lord's Prayer and the Angelical Salutation to the Virgin Mother of God to obtain grace shall be observed; and at the end of the said sermons prayers shall be made for the souls of the departed in the customary form received by the church'. The faults of the clergy were, however, more clearly pinpointed in the regulations of 1552 relating to the reading of Hamilton's catechism which was to be read on all Sundays and holy days for half an hour before high mass 'in a loud and audible voice'. For this task rectors, vicars and curates were to prepare themselves 'by constant, frequent and daily rehearsal of the lesson to be read, lest they expose themselves to the ridicule of their hearers, when, through want or preparation, they stammer and stumble in mid-course of reading.[8]

The issue of this catechism under the authority of Archbishop Hamilton of St Andrews and of the general council of the Scottish church convened at Edinburgh, was intended to ensure that the 'true, Catholic and Apostolic faith may by the exclusion of all kinds of error, be kept intact and uninjured'. To this end it was ordained that:

> a certain book, written in our vulgar Scottish tongue, and, after the most elaborate revision, approved by the opinions and votes of the most prudent prelates in the whole realm, and of the most learned theologians and other churchmen taking part in the present convention, shall be put into the hands of rectors, vicars and curates, as much for the instruction of themselves as of the Christian community committed to their care: which book it orders to be called a catechism, that is to say, a plain and easy statement and explanation of the rudiments of the faith.

No doctrinal condemnation of Lutheranism or Calvinism was necessary: the true faith could speak for itself.[9]

The author of the catechism appears to have been friar Richard Marshall, a Dominican refugee from Newcastle who undertook the task after an invitation to an English secular priest Richard Smith had been turned down on the grounds that he was unwilling to attack all the teachings then employed in the reformed church of England. The catechism itself consists of four sections logically proceeding through various catholic tenets dealing with the twelve articles of the Creed, the ten commandments, the sacraments and finally an exposition of the Our Father and the Hail Mary. It was stated in the preface that its aim was exposition of controversial matters in terms of decisions of the general councils of the church. To what extent this was true has raised questions both about its omissions and its divergence from the teachings then being expounded at the Council of Trent, and attention has centred on its exposition of the role of faith in justification, which does not follow the decree on that doctrine promulgated at Trent some five years previously. More positively, however, the tone of the catechism's instruction on justification might be adjudged to have a protestant ring; in the reception of the sacraments a special trusting faith is stressed, members of the Christian community were 'to believe with certainty' that Christ died for the salvation of mankind. It has been suggested that these interpretations were in deference to a Lutheran request that doctrines previously determined should be reconsidered; Lutheran envoys seeking such modifications were in fact received at Trent in January 1552 and four years previously Charles v had attempted to effect religious compromise by the Interim of Augsburg. However, this appears to savour of special pleading. It is more likely that Richard Marshall, in accepting the modification of teaching on justification, was influenced by his own desire to appeal to moderate opinion in the reformed Church of England.[10]

Other parts of the catechism appear equally unorthodox. There is virtually nothing at all bearing upon the mass as a sacrifice in the chapters dealing with the Blessed Eucharist. This may also be explained by the postponement of the consideration of the doctrine at Trent, but it is odd that so little is said of a topic which figured prominently in protestant attacks upon the church. Even the term mass is avoided in the main body of the text and only appears in the appendix to the final section of the catechism in which some attention appears to have been paid to areas regarded as deficient even in 1552. Other omissions are equally perplexing: the authority of the pope is nowhere referred to and indulgences are also ignored – the issue of indulgences was certainly not considered at Trent until 1563, but the absence of any mention of the papacy is distinctly odd. The survival of the conciliar theory – the doctrine which attributed supremacy in the church to General Councils rather than to the pope – which some churchmen were still anxious to promote in the sixteenth century may explain the fact that papal authority is not stressed, but the total failure to refer to the papacy would appear to go far beyond that point. In these respects the orthodoxy of Hamilton's catechism must remain dubious, but it is doubtful whether an attempt to obtain doctrinal compromise really explains its shortcomings. The purpose of the catechism was to reject heresy and ensure that the catholic faith was kept in all its purity. In many respects this aim was undoubtedly achieved; for example on questions on the authority of the church in interpreting scripture, the sacraments and prayers for the dead, the catechism was totally in line with orthodox Tridentine views. It may be that the decrees of Trent on issues such as justification, made only five years before the issue of the catechism, had not made their full impact on Scotland by 1552. If this were so, it was doubly unfortunate for not only was the use of the catechism seriously impaired but it also meant that on the central doctrinal issues on which the protestants tended to concentrate, the catechism had few positive definitions to which catholics could turn as controversy became more bitter. In this respect the catechism did not measure up to the task set for it.'[11]

Irregularities in saying the canonical hours and celebrating mass may, however, have been more serious challenges to reformers-from-within than that of providing a catechism. This problem was tackled by the 1559 council, which decreed that priests were to celebrate 'oftener than they are wont to do, the sacrifice of holy mass in the presence of the people'; by 1559, parsons as well as bishops were expected not only to preach four times a year, 'but even oftener, at the discretion of the ordinary, under pain of losing the fourth part of the fruits'. Substitutes were allowed for the very young, for the institutions to which churches were appropriated and for elderly churchmen who had 'passed their fiftieth year, and had not hitherto been accustomed to preach'.[12]

The implementation of such suggestions obviously posed problems and therefore a more immediate and practical solution was provided by the preparation of a series of instructions or exhortations on the sacraments of baptism, holy Eucharist, extreme unction and matrimony which 'the several parish or other priests, the lawful ministers of the said sacraments, when about to administer the said sacraments, shall make use of by giving before each sacrament its own appropriate and befitting exhortation, and reciting and reading it publicly and distinctly'. Only one of these exhortations appears to have survived – *A Godlie Exhortation on the Eucharist* – which was a simple practical instruction to be given before a priest administered holy communion. Its purpose was to allow the congregation to understand more easily 'the purpose, efficacy, and use of the sacraments of the church'. Its origin appears to have lain in petitions presented, which not only asked that priests should catechize, but also asked that 'the common prayers, with litanies in our vulgar tongue be said in every parish kirk on Sundays and other holy days after the divine service of the mass and that afternoon prayers be said likewise'. These concessions were not forthcoming but the exhortations went some little way to meeting their demands. The language is simple and direct; the congregation was reminded of Christ's passion upon the cross in remembrance of which communicants ought to receive the sacrament, which is 'the sacrament of lufe and concorde, so that nane of you with dispyte (contempt) in your herte presume to cum to this blyssit sacrament, bot as ye walke be forgevin of your synnis and ressauit in unitie with God, swa aucht ye to forgeve uthir'. The idea behind this series of exhortations was undoubtedly sound, but came much too late. Whether these exhortations are to be equated with the creed of catholic faith dubbed by Knox 'The Twa-penny Fayth' because it was printed and sold for that price must remain doubtful. Other tracts were clearly contemplated and may have been produced; the survival by accident of one of these does not necessarily identify it with the creed described by Knox and it cannot now be ascertained whether the exhortation was ever used for its intended purpose.[13]

Not much is known either of the fate of the first systematic attempt to provide an approach to the nature of and method of dealing with religious controversy from a catholic standpoint. Not until 1558 was this need seemingly met by the appearance of *Ane Compendius Tractive*. The author was Quintin Kennedy, abbot of Crossraguel in Ayrshire, who had studied at St Andrews under John Mair and had completed his education at the university of Paris, probably at the college of the Sorbonne. His career as abbot of Crossraguel to which he was appointed in early 1548 following the death of his uncle William, is obscure; he does not appear to have aspired to a political career, but was present at the provincial council of the church that met in 1549. Whether he spent the succeeding years in theological study or in a life of ease in which conscience eventually triumphed cannot be readily determined; in the preface to his tract he writes that he had been constrained to publish his book for the 'relief of my awin conscience towart sic as I have charge of, conforme to my vocatioun', a statement capable of both interpretations. In any case, and for whatever reason, by 1558 Kennedy had decided to intervene in the religious controversies which were then reaching a critical juncture.[14]

In the *Tractive* Kennedy fully admitted the principal abuses prevailing in the Scottish church; many of these he directly attributed to growing secular influence. It had become a daily occurence 'gyf ane benefice vaick, the gret men of the realme wyll have it for temporale rewarde'. The granting of such benefices to kinsmen was equally scandalous; if any of these appointed, who could frequently neither 'sing or say' and were equally 'norischeit in vyce' were to be mounted on a mule it would be questionable 'quhether he or his mule knawis best to do his office. Perchance Balaames asse knew mair nor thai baith'. Kennedy's remedy for these defects is simple and perhaps unrealistic in view of the fact that the crown had always maintained a voice in the appointment of abbots and bishops for he suggests that 'Geve the Kirk had the auld ancient libertie ... that ane bischop wer frelie chosin be his chapitre, the abbot and prior be the convent of the Kirk; then sulde all hereseis be flemit [cast out], and the peple weill techeit'. If this were the remedy, the crown and the crown alone could ensure that such appointment were offered to suitably qualified candidates. Kennedy's main purpose, however, was not to suggest practical remedies for the reform of the church, but rather to avert precipitate action by the magnates by opposing the protestant claim that scriptural interpretation appertained 'to the Spirit of God' by the which also the scripture was written', that interpretation of Holy Writ could only be effected by members of the true church, by which was meant not any visible church but rather the company, known in its entirety only to God, of the elect through the ages. It was in this belief that the 1560 Scots Confession of Faith stated that if 'the interpretation, determination or sentence of any doctor, kirk or council repugn to the plain word of God written in any other place of the scripture, it is a thing most certain that theirs is not the true understanding and meaning of the Holy Ghost, supposing that councils, realms and nations have approved and received the same'. Two years earlier, Kennedy's tract had set out to refute this view, in a text divided into eighteen chapters. There was, he claimed, only one way to end religious controversies; that is to agree who will act as judge in such matters. That Scripture might be its own judge, as the protestants claimed, was an illusion and a recipe for a multitude of private unorthodox opinions. The church alone, Kennedy claimed, could act as judge of the true meaning of Scripture. In practice, however, this task had been delegated to its appointed leaders. When gathered together in properly convened general councils, they constituted assemblies which were alone capable of interpreting the word of God. The argument was straightforward and direct, but was hardly likely to convince the reformers to whom a summary of the principal line of argument was despatched about April 1559. Kennedy's aim in writing his *Compendius Tractive* had been to demonstrate that there was no theological foundation for rebellion against either temporal or ecclesiastical authority because God had provided all the necessary means for an orderly settlement of doctrinal disputes, but by the time of its publication such disputations were at an end; the claims of Knox in his *Appelation to the Nobility of Scotland*, in which he had appealed to the magnates to further the course of Reformation by force if necessary, were about to be answered. The arguments that might have been used to avert Reformation by revolution were thereafter of only academic importance, and this was to be equally true of Kennedy's post-Reformation tracts – *Ane Litil Brief Tracteit*, *Ane Oratioune* and *Ane Compendius Ressonyng* – in which he discussed the real presence of Christ in the Eucharist and the sacrifice of the mass. By then the opportunity for promoting reform from within was past and by then all that Kennedy could hope to achieve was to persuade some of his fellow Catholics to remain steadfast in their faith.[15]

The outbreak of the Reformation also meant that the statutes of 1559 were to be equally ineffective. But if events had allowed, the willingness to achieve reform was undoubtedly present. Immediately after the 1559 council, Archbishop Beaton of Glasgow held a diocesan synod which adopted the desired reforms, and these were then notified to the archdeacons and deans with specific instructions in certain cases to pursue the appropriate course of action required to effect them. Preaching was to be enforced and penalties invoked against priests guilty of non-residence, pluralism and concubinage; churches were to be repaired and the wearing of clerical dress enforced. The question of church repair was also taken up in the diocese of St Andrews; and Adam Bothwell, commendator of Holyrood, had his revenues sequestrated until windows were repaired in some of the abbey's appropriated churches. In early 1559 in the diocese of Aberdeen the chapter had proposed, at the suggestion of Bishop William Gordon, a whole series of necessary reforms: time did not allow their implementation and this failure has sometimes led to the suggestion that attempts at reform were doomed from the outset.[16]

It is certainly true that little progress had been made in certain directions. The reforms themselves, moreover, were selective and did not deal with certain aspects of ecclesiastical life. Little was said in any of the statutes about collegiate churches or the chapters of cathedrals. Nothing was said about the spiritual requirements or the means of training for the priesthood, one of the areas in which the Scottish church was at its weakest. Above all, however, there was no attempt to measure up to the problem of how the church should proceed if its statutes failed to achieve their desired purpose. The secular arm was appealed to on certain issues, but basically the church hoped to achieve its aims through its own efforts. Leadership was required for reform, but, as the bishops were frequently guilty of more offences than any, reforming policies were vitiated from the outset. Bishops were willing to appoint theologians; they were less willing to reform their lives or to endanger their own livelihoods by placing principles before financial reward.

Yet if political events had not dictated otherwise, all might not have been lost; the proposals of earlier councils were not entirely dead letters and some statutes actually reflected reforms already under way. The need for reform of the church was widely accepted; new attitudes prompted by the rising tide of literacy had made this inevitable. It was universally agreed that the standards of the past would not suffice for the future; explanations of the mysteries of the faith could no longer be left in the hands of ill-educated and inarticulate vicars. Preaching must be an act practised by benefice-holders and not only by a handful of friars and other trained theologians. Other responsibilities must likewise be faced; if the church dictated a certain standard of morality, then it must live up to its own teachings, especially in relation to a celibate priesthood. The poor should equally be the concern of the church which, rather than setting a bad example by contributing to growing poverty through unjust impositions laid equally upon rich and poor alike, must demonstrate its concern for those deserving of its charity. The need for reform was recognized, but the will to reform was less obvious. Bishops, abbots and commendators might pay lip-service to the principle of reformation, but their vested interests lay in the retention of the corrupt system which continued to produce rich dividends. The crown alone could have broken this vicious circle, but it too chose to benefit politically and financially from the existing situation. In time the success of the Tridentine reforms elsewhere in Europe would have modified even these attitudes, but for the time they prevailed. Secular attitudes which had been bred within the church, coupled with even stronger manifestations of secularism outside its ranks, proved too strong for the survival of the existing system. These forces even more than incipient protestantism led to the ultimate failure of the policy of reform of the church from within and to the emergence of a triumphant protestant church.

5
Towards Protestantism: the 1540s and 1550s

As a distinctively popular movement, protestantism had no deep roots in Scotland. Heresy in the fifteenth century was virtually unknown and appears to have been confined to a few individuals who, as followers of the teachings of Hus and Wycliffe, were forced to flee from persecution in England and the continent. Some, like Robert Harding, found uneasy sanctuary in the north, but others – for example his fellow friar James Resby of Perth in 1407, an anonymous heretic in Glasgow in 1422 and the Bohemian Paul Craw at St Andrews in 1433 – were condemned and burnt to death. How far their views gained any acceptance is unknown, although legislation in 1425 demonstrates that the government was concerned lest their doctrines might spread. At St Andrews university, at which an oath to defend the church against lollardy had been demanded from students of the arts from 1417, Lollard sympathizers were still being denounced in 1436, although the fears then expressed appear to have been groundless. Thereafter, 'small question of religion moved within the realm' until after the revolt of Martin Luther in 1517, with the exception of the inexplicable reappearance in Kyle in Ayrshire of so-called Lollards. Their tenets included the rejection of the real presence after the consecration in the mass, of priestly celibacy and of the belief that the mass profited souls in purgatory. Papal authority was disclaimed and it was asserted that true Christians received the body of Jesus Christ every day by faith. Nevertheless when thirty persons, including several prominent lairds from Kyle and Cunningham including John Campbell of Newmills and Andrew Shaw of Polkemmet, were called to account for such opinions before King James IV, it should be noted that he simply admonished them. The advent of Lutheranism posed a more insidious threat, however, and by 1525 Parliament was constrained to legislate against the importation of heretical literature from Europe – and battle was again joined.[1]

In general terms the growth of protestant opinion can probably be measured by the frequency of parliamentary enactments against heretics and by the activity of the privy council. A parliamentary act of 1535 'anent the dampnable opinzeouns of heresy' was followed by a series of enactments in 1540 which ordered the sacraments to be honoured as in the past, permitted only licensed theologians to dispute on the scriptures, forbade those suspected of heresy to discourse on theological subjects and promised rewards for those who accused heretics and revealed their private meetings. These were certainly followed by prosecutions, but their total number was fairly small and they were more often than not followed by abjurations by the accused rather than by legal conviction and sentence. Indeed only four persons – beginning with Patrick Hamilton in 1528 – were burnt as heretics before the seven convicted in 1539 met the same fate, although several more, including Robert Johnson who became a celebrated court composer in England, fled the country rather than face their accusers. It is clear that before 1539 the growth of protestantism was far from a major problem and even Knox, who would surely have dwelt on it in his *History of the Reformation in Scotland*, could find little evidence of it.[2]

An examination of the situation in the various localities bears out this conclusion. In few areas are there signs of active discontent with the church or of more positive attempts to present an alternative. In Ayrshire some of the 'Lollards' accused in 1494, for example Adam Reid of Barskimming, appear themselves as conformists in the early sixteenth century, while relations and dependents of other defendents also signify their loyalty to the existing church; for instance an aunt and sister of James Chalmers of Gadgirth were arraigned before the king in 1494 but Chalmers was still prepared to endow an altar in the parish church of Irvine in 1502. On the other hand, the breaking into the chapel of Dundonald in 1511 and the subsequent ransacking of a chest of its books and ornaments by John Leith, a chaplain taken there by George Campbell of Cessnock (yet another of those accused of Lollardy), at first appears to confirm the continuance of the beliefs expressed in 1494; but closer examination reveals that it was prompted by anti-clericalism or even by secular greed rather than

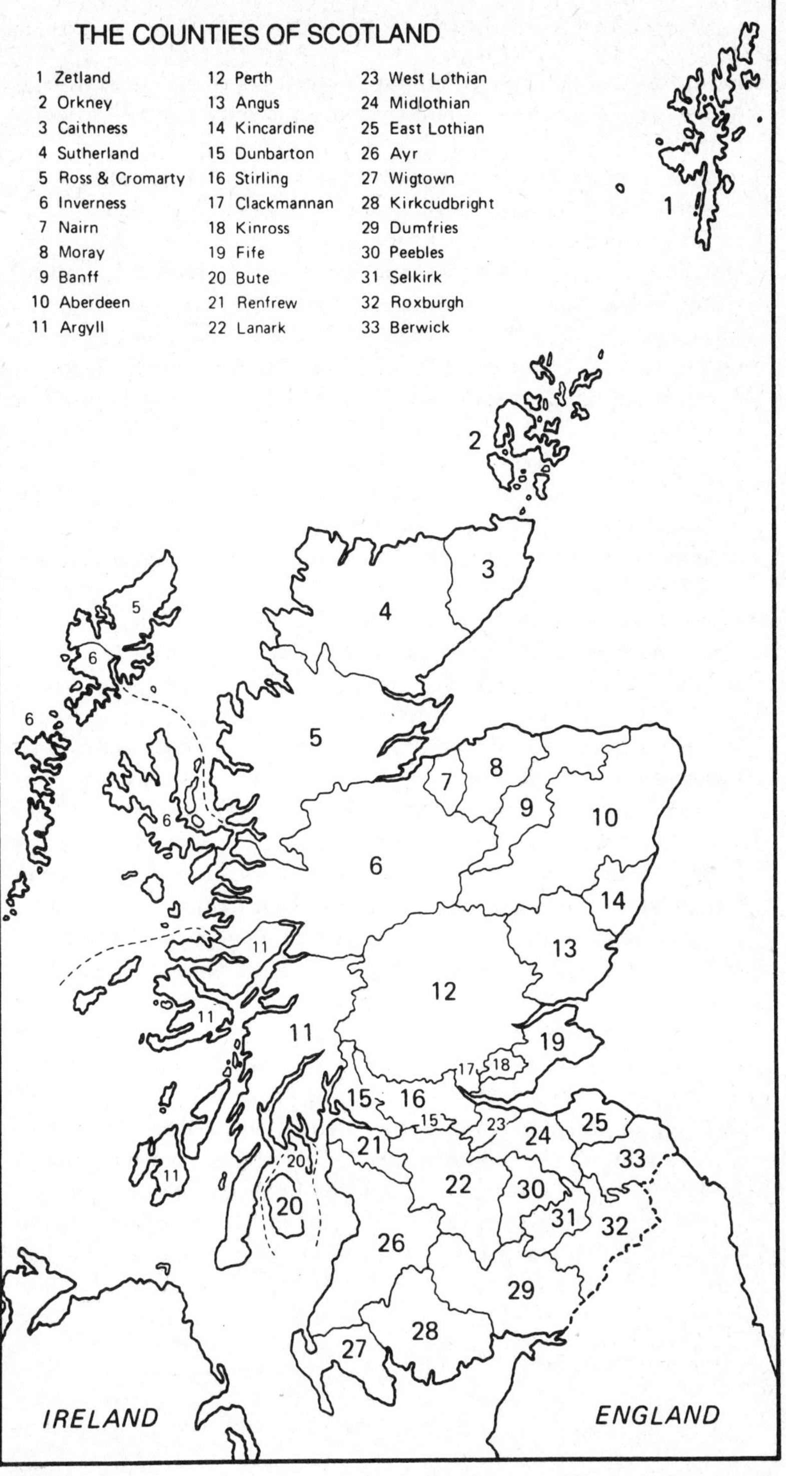
THE COUNTIES OF SCOTLAND
1 Zetland
2 Orkney
3 Caithness
4 Sutherland
5 Ross & Cromarty
6 Inverness
7 Nairn
8 Moray
9 Banff
10 Aberdeen
11 Argyll
12 Perth
13 Angus
14 Kincardine
15 Dunbarton
16 Stirling
17 Clackmannan
18 Kinross
19 Fife
20 Bute
21 Renfrew
22 Lanark
23 West Lothian
24 Midlothian
25 East Lothian
26 Ayr
27 Wigtown
28 Kirkcudbright
29 Dumfries
30 Peebles
31 Selkirk
32 Roxburgh
33 Berwick
IRELAND
ENGLAND

by moves towards church reform. After 1511 there was little sign of further religious discontent for almost twenty years. Donations made to local churches, and in particular to the friaries of Ayr, seem to suggest that for a time religious agitation was unknown; it would not be revived until after the Lutheran upheavals.[3]

The sea-port of Ayr constituted an obvious gateway into western Scotland for Lutheran and later for Calvinist literature, although how far the new religious ideas were actually circulated cannot be assessed. While Ayr provided the focal point for local unrest, its leaders came not from the inhabitants of the burgh but from among the lairds, one of whom, Walter Stewart, brother of Lord Ochiltree, was accused before the archbishop of Glasgow in 1533 of having decapitated a statue of the Virgin Mary in the Observantine friary at Ayr. Others were clearly involved in this incident and the citation demanding their appearance before the archbishop contains the general accusations that certain parishioners of some (unfortunately unnamed) churches had 'sowed Lutheran errors, asserted them both in private and public, and that some of them read the New Testament in English and other writings containing heretical opinions.' The accused laird saved himself by recanting, but four years later in 1537 there are payments for 'serching of the heretiks in the West land' and a summons of the men of Ayr to appear before the lords of council on matters arising from the forfeiture of goods of those who had been 'convict of heresy'. The problem was thus not easily ended. Nevertheless the departure in 1539 from the Observantine friary, within which trouble had evidently arisen, of a friar named John Willock (who was later to become a superintendent in the reformed church) may indicate that traditional support for the church was stronger there at this juncture than the zeal for reform. Information from elsewhere in the west supports this view, although a heresy trial in Glasgow in 1539 which resulted in the burning as heretics of a Franciscan friar and a layman clearly involved a number of people. Among the accused were three monks of Paisley who abjured their beliefs and were deported overseas. A licence was also granted to one of the novices, John Wallace, to visit Rome, the penitentiaries there and the superior and convent of Cluny 'because of great matters moving his conscience'. He had apparently given evidence against his three colleagues, but his own position may have been in some doubt as he was forbidden on his travels to pass to England or other heretical areas. If heresy in the west was more widespread at this juncture than has previously been maintained, there still is little positive evidence of it enjoying any popular appeal, barely twenty years before the revolt of 1559–60.[4]

On the east coast the position seems not to have been markedly different. Nevertheless, as early as 1521 John Marshall, rector of the grammar school of Aberdeen, was summoned before the provost and council for his contempt of the church. In his reply the schoolmaster repudiated the authority of the court of Rome, but whether this view arose from Lutheran teachings or in consequence of a domestic dispute over the school must remain uncertain, for two years later Marshall recanted. Equal doubt surrounds a dispute in 1525 between the chaplains of St Nicholas church in Aberdeen that resulted in a temporary suspension of divine service, but it was certainly reported in Aberdeenshire in that year that 'syndry strangearis and otheris ... has bukis of that heretik Luthyr, and favoris his arrorys and fals opinionys'. The spread of such beliefs may have been assisted by a visit in 1528 to King's college, Aberdeen, of the Danish scholar, Hans Bogbinder, a member of a family that had played an important part in the agitation for reform in Denmark and who was almost certainly influenced by Lutheran doctrine. Evidence of heresy is, however, intermittent. In 1532, Alexander Dick, an Observant friar, laid aside his religious habit, accepted the new doctrines and fled to Dundee for safety and in 1539 'two menne of Abirdene' were imprisoned for helping the convicted heretic Friar Keillor, but there is little indication of general unrest during this period. In Fife, Angus and the Mearns there are also few signs of active protestantism. The execution of Patrick Hamilton at St Andrews in 1528 is indicative only of the place of his trial; and, although the choice of the same town as the execution site of Henry Forrest about 1533 is said to have been made in order that sympathizers in Angus might see the fire, there is no contemporary evidence to support this interpretation. Curiously, there is a similar implication in the account of the deaths in 1534 of two other heretics, Norman Gourlay and David Straton, said to have been burnt somewhere between Edinburgh and Leith 'to the intent that the inhabitants of Fife, seeing the fire might be stricken with terrour and feare'.[5]

If, at first glance, active protestantism seems to have been confined to a few lairds, such as John Erskine of Dun and Andrew Straton of Lauriston, the undoubted spread of protestant literature points to a more positive reception of the new doctrines. In 1527 the English ambassador at Antwerp reported that Tyndale's *New Testament* was being shipped in, some to Edinburgh, but most to St Andrews. Other books which came to Scotland in the same manner included *Patrick's Places* published in Antwerp and John Gau's *Richt Vay to the Kingdom of Hevine* published in Malmo. In 1534 a letter of James v reported that Lutheran books and tracts were being distributed in 'Leith, Edinburgh, Dundee, Sanctandrois, Montros, Abirdene and Kircaldy', and that heresy in consequence was likely to spread.[6]

At St Andrews, indeed, the university and its constituent colleges were certainly deeply involved in a religious ferment which intensified after the death of Patrick Hamilton. Hamilton's teachings in the district may have had a marked effect among the educated classes with whom he associated. Thus the feast of the faculty of arts, intended to symbolize love and friendship, was abandoned from 1534 onwards on the grounds that the sung mass and customary procession offended some members of the university. Of the individual colleges at St Andrews, St Salvator's was orthodox, but St Leonard's was more than suspect; the new doctrines were being taught, sometimes in secret but at other times openly, to those who 'drank of St Leonard's well'. However, while some of the students who favoured heretical opinions chose to leave Scotland, others (notably Gavin Logie and John Winram) remained. Knox in his *History* credits both with the spreading of new opinions but in fact Logie sat on a heresy trial shortly before his death in 1539 and Winram was then also uncommitted, holding to no more than a policy of reform from within the church. Though in 1536 the preaching of Friar Alexander Seton, a Dominican friar from the town's convent, reached a wide audience, there is still no sign of any popular reaction. Indeed, Seton himself was forced to flee to England.[7]

Before his flight the friar had also preached at Dundee where – almost alone in Scotland at this time – protestantism may be said to have possessed some popular appeal. Criticism of the existing order was certainly to the fore among the friars and in 1528 one of them, William Arth, preached there against the licentious lives of the bishops and against the abuse of cursing. In the following decade the weaknesses of the Roman church were most scathingly indicted by the brothers Wedderburn, sons of a Dundee merchant. James Wedderburn, for all that he had received religious instruction from one of the Blackfriars of the town, composed a tragedy (*The beheading of John the Baptist*) and a comedy (*A History of Dionisius the Tyrant*) in both of which 'he nipped the abuses and superstitition of the time'. Both these plays were acted in the burgh, the former at the West Port and the latter in the playfield. In 1540 he was forced to flee to Dieppe. His brother John was a priest in Dundee before becoming a convert to reformed opinions; he too fled, but to Germany where he likewise used his poetic gifts to the full by turning 'manie bawde songs and rymes in gadly rymes', which were to become variously known as the *Wedderburn Psalms*, the *Psalms of Dundee* and the *Gude and Godlie Ballattis*. The book itself falls naturally into two parts, the first being doctrinal and devotional, the second profane but spiritualized. It is profitable, it is explained in a short prologue, for the young and the unlearned to sing the word of God in their mother tongue. Selected passages from scripture were to be set to music and sung as hymns, psalms and ballads. This prologue is followed by the text of the catechism, which includes the ten commandments, the Lord's prayer and passages on the sacrament of baptism and the Lord's supper. Much of the text is simple but effective, as may be seen in a passage entitled 'Of our belief':

> We trow in God allanerlie
> Full of all mycht and Maiestie
> Maker of hevin and eird sa braid
> Quhilk has him self our Father maid:
> And we his sonnis or in deid,
> He will us keip in all our neid,
> Baith Saule and body to defend,
> That na mischance sall us offend;
> He takis cure, baith day and nycht,
> To save us, throw his godly mycht
> Fra Sathanis subtleltie and slycht.

In the metrical catechism that concludes this section, two hymns by Luther are included one of which, on the Lord's supper explicitly recognizes the real presence:

And he, that we suld not forget
Gave us his body for to eit,
In forme of bread, and gave us syne
His blude to drink in forme of wyne

The catechism is followed by spiritual songs and ballads of scripture on the theme of sin and salvation; many are pleasing nativity hymns:

Hay Zule now sing and make myrth
Sen Christ this day to us is born.

A sense of sin is, nevertheless, ever-present, and the twenty-seven psalms of David that follow are also in a sombre vein. The distinctive note in the collection is not to be found in the psalms and hymns, but rather in the ballads 'changed out of profane songs into godly songs'. The religious appeal of verses such as:

Pray God for grace, my lufe maist dear
  Quhilk bocht us with his precius blude,
That we him lufe with hart inteir
  In welth and want be land and flude.

is hard to assess, but it may have been too readily assumed that these ballads served as the marching songs of the Scottish Reformation. As no edition was printed in Scotland before 1560, this would seem unlikely and the ballads would seem to have had a greater influence on the second half of the century. If works like these may have promoted a local spirit of hostility towards at least certain sections of the church, there was still little sign of those active heresies so prevalent in Dundee society. Indeed the only indications of overt unrest were a command to the bailies of Dundee and Perth in 1536 to seek out two men suspected of hanging an image of St Francis, and a letter of rehabilitation granted in 1539 to a burgess named Richard Rollok who had abjured his heresies.[8]

Edinburgh, with its sea-port of Leith, presents a fairly similar picture. If for the first time the evidence points to at least a section of the urban populace embracing protestant doctrine at an early period, few converts were resolute enough to maintain their new beliefs in the face of prosecution. In 1532 'ane greit abjuration of the favouraris of Mertene Lutor' took place at the abbey of Holyrood, but whether those Lutheran supporters were all local persons is unknown. As Scotland's busiest port facing northern continental Europe, Leith was an obvious point of entry for the new religious opinions; and it is significant that amongst those accused in 1534 of professing reforming beliefs were Henry Cairnes, a sea-skipper, and Adam Dayes, a shipwright, both of whom dwelt in Leith, to which town others in the list of accused also belonged. Among the inhabitants of Edinburgh similarly arraigned in 1534 was Henry Hendersoune, the master of the burgh grammar school who, with David Hutchison the provost of the collegiate church of Roslin, was one of the most prominent, and certainly one of those best situated, to propagate reformed opinions. Yet the total number of heretics named in 1534 is only eight, and although a contemporary account declares that 'sindrie utheris baith men and wemen' appeared and recanted, their number was clearly very small; the action taken against them may have effectively curbed their activities for the time being. A similar pattern reappears a little later in 1539, with a handful of burgeses including Martin Balkesky, who was specifically accused of 'having and using of certane Inglis (i.e. heretical) bukis' having their goods restored to them on recantation; only one burgess named as John Braune who apparently remained steadfast in his beliefs, forfeited his property within the burgh. The burning of five convicted heretics in 1539 must have reinforced the message, for Edinburgh remained quiescent in religious matters for at least another decade.[9]

The five heretics executed on the Edinburgh Castle-hill were actually all drawn from central Scotland. Two were Blackfriars, one of whom (John Keillor) had written a morality play on Christ's passion which was performed in Stirling in 1535: another was Thomas Forrest, a canon regular of the abbey of Inchcolm, who had apparently brought some of his younger fellow canons round to his way of thinking 'but the old bottells would not receave the new wine'. As vicar of Dollar in Clackmannanshire, a church appropriated to his abbey, and in close proximity to Stirling, his chief crime had lain in preaching every Sunday from the Old and New Testament in English. The remaining two accused were, respectively, a burgh priest of Stirling and the brother of the laird of Arngibbon in Stirlingshire. No opportunity was apparently provided for the recanting of these five, who were accused as teachers of heresies and as having been present at the wedding of the vicar of another Clackmannanshire parish, Tullibody. Nine others who were arraigned, including two Stirling merchants, were more fortunate, being permitted to abjure; others, including the scholar George Buchanan who had written two poems attacking the Franciscans, fled the country. These trials were apparently occasioned by signs of a rising local dissatisfaction with the church among both the friars of Stirling and the canons of the abbey of Cambuskenneth where in 1538, Robert Logie, master of the novices who had 'embraced the truth', fled to England and was followed by one of his fellow canons and a Greyfriar. However, as at Edinburgh the punishment meted out to those who remained appears to have had a salutary effect and there is little sign of religious unrest in Stirling for many years thereafter.[10]

Over the rest of the country there is little indication that heretical opinions were held. Even where there is some evidence it is notable that the nature of the heresies was limited – the agitation was mainly against images, pretended miracles, the abuse of excommunication, financial rapacity and the immoral life of churchmen. On the more positive side, the use of the scripture in the vernacular was being advocated and the Lutheran doctrine of justification by faith would also seem to have been accepted by those accused of heresy. This doctrine, which is concerned with the means whereby man passes from a state of damnation owing to sin to a state of grace, emerged as one of the major divisions between catholics and protestants. Both agreed that man's justification is brought about by divine grace but, whereas Lutherans argued that man had no truly free will and justification could come about by faith alone, the catholic view emphasized the place of man's free will in allowing him to regain justification by means of penance and the performance of good works. Though the catholic position was not clarified until the sixth session of the council of Trent in 1547, the Lutheran standpoint emerged in Scotland at a much earlier date. Murdoch Nisbet's *The New Testament in Scots* included a translation of Luther's own preface to the New Testament in which the place of faith is stressed while *Patrick's Places*, the work of Patrick Hamilton, was entirely concerned with explaining how man is justified. The charge that he had asserted that 'man hath no free will' and that 'no man is justified by works, but by faith only', figured prominently in his trial and conviction for heresy in 1528. John Gau, a Scot living in

Malmo, also reflected the Lutheran viewpoint in his book *The Richt Vay to the Kingdom of Hevine* (1533), and faith was also stressed in the preaching of the Dominican Alexander Seton in 1535. The circulation of these works was, however, restricted, and in 1539 protestantism remained an ill-defined doctrine to all but a few believers who were unevenly distributed throughout the country; even if in distinct localities they possessed a coherence within their own communities, these groups had little or no contact with one another and were uncertain of the goals for which they were striving.[11]

The executions of 1539 might have proved salutary and decisive if political events in both England and Scotland had not dictated otherwise. In that year, James v demonstrated in no uncertain manner that the willingness to allow criticism of the church either in verse, satire or plain speech, which had characterized the earlier years of his reign, was at an end. Enactments of 1540 strengthened by an act of the following year against heresy and iconoclasm underlined the point and, until James's death in 1542, there is little indication of renewed protestant activity. Only then, with the seizure of political initiative by the governor, the earl of Arran, were circumstances again propitious for those in favour of religious change to demonstrate their strength. Their cause was aided in 1543, as part of Arran's pro-English policies, by an act authorizing the possession of the scriptures in the vernacular. Protestants – to an unknown extent – increased in numbers. It is misleading, however, to accept the attacks on religious houses within certain burghs that occurred later that year, sparked off by Arran's radical tendencies, as attempts to reshape and refurbish the church. As much economic as religious motivation lay behind these riots, and people seem also to have seized upon an opportunity to work off old scores. Once again the national significance of these outbreaks can only be assessed by an examination of the localities in which they took place; this in turn allows for a more accurate estimate of protestant numbers at this juncture in the movement for reformation.[12]

Of the riots that took place in 1543, those in the towns of Dundee and Perth were the most serious. Indeed Perth had hitherto exhibited little interest in the new doctrines and although the bailies of the town, in conjunction with those of Dundee, had been ordered to search for two iconoclasts in 1536, the attack on the Blackfriars monastery seven years later had no apparent antecedents. And the religious motivation behind even this act can be questioned, since the mob's act of defiance in stealing the friars' 'kettle' (containing their dinner) from the fire and parading it through the burgh may point towards a social or economic cause. Nevertheless, a definable group of heretics had now appeared within the burgh and early in the following year several of the inhabitants were accused. As a result four men were hanged and a woman drowned having been accused of acts which included interrupting a friar in the pulpit, 'hanging up the image of St Francis on a card, nailing of a rammes harness to his head, and a cowes rump to his taile, eating of goose on Allhallow even', and 'holding an assemblie and conventioun . . . conferring and disputing there upon holie scripture'. The background of this group, which apparently contained others who only saved themselves by flight, is significant: it included a flesher, a maltman, a merchant and a skinner. It was from this social grouping that further support for the new faith was to stem. Yet, though there was further public activity, the adherents of the new cause, with the exception of Stephen Bell who was accused in 1547 of breaking an image of St Magdalene within the chapel of the town of Leny in Perthshire, remain anonymous until the very eve of the Reformation. It is difficult to escape the conclusion that the repressive measures of 1544 had the desired effect in Perth and its surrounds.[13]

Further north in Aberdeen the position was much the same: in 1543 the magistrates appointed friar John Roger of the Blackfriars of Perth, and friar Walter Thomson for 'preiching and teaching of the trev Vord of God, and their daylie prearis for the estait of the lord governairis grace, the commont weill of this realme, and of this guid towne'. In the next year an attack on the Dominican priory by several burgesses and their colleagues was followed a few months later by the imprisonment at the order of the earl of Huntly of two burgesses, Thomas Branche and Thomas Cusing, for hanging an image of St Francis. Also in 1544 a pardon was issued to a large number of local landowners for holding heretical opinions and reading forbidden books. Those guilty included the earl Marischal, Meldrum of Fyvie, Fraser of Philorth and the provost of Aberdeen. It is clear from the composition of this group that protestantism had spread well beyond the burgh, and in 1547 the bishop of Aberdeen complained that heresy in his diocese was 'thriving greatly'. Nevertheless, this prefaced a period of religious peace in this quarter, apparently undisturbed until the eve of the Reformation. This experience, broken only by the appearance in 1550 of a chaplain in Orkney who abjured unorthodox 'oppynianis' concerning the faith, was to be shared by the entire north of Scotland in which the prevalence of Gaelic in many areas, including the Isles, constituted a further barrier to the advance of protestant doctrine.[14]

It was in Dundee, where the town's two friaries were attacked and sacked by a mob in 1543, that the populace showed themselves to be receptive to the preaching of Friars Guilliame and Rough who taught the use of the scriptures in the vernacular; religious motives may have played a larger part in the riots here than at Perth. The carrying away of chalices , vestments and the Eucharist from the Blackfriars' monastery and the proposal to attack the abbey of Arbroath that was thwarted by Lord Ogilvie point in this direction, and may support the contemporary charge that 'ane greit heresie' raged in Dundee at this time. The lack of stringent action against any of the inhabitants - there was no indictment until ten years later - may also point to a situation in which moderation was felt to be the wisest course of action. The mood within the burgh certainly remained unchanged. In 1554 George Wishart's preaching there appears to have met with general approval; he came to Dundee again in the following year when, with a plague then raging within the town, he received an even greater welcome. If continued sympathy for the reformed cause remained in being thereafter there is little indication of further growth in protestant ideas for another decade after the mid-1540s.[15]

Much the same pattern emerges in the countryside around Dundee, in Angus and also in the Mearns. In 1544 John Roger, the Blackfriar who had earlier taught in Aberdeen and had 'fruitfullie preached Christ Jesus to the comfort of manie' in this area, died, either by accident or by design, trying to escape from the castle of St Andrews where he had been imprisoned, apparently for having ignored a monition against his preaching in the parish church of Glamis. This monition emerged from a general inquisition held throughout the district at this time, which resulted also in the trial of two other priests, David Lyndsay and John Wigtoun: since Wigtoun later attempted to assassinate Wishart, the terms of his release are perhaps questionable. In 1545 Wishart himself returned to his home town of Montrose, 'to salute the church there' with his preaching during his ministrations in Dundee. Montrose, a sea-port, was certainly open to incoming protestant opinions, but undoubtedly the chief influence in the promotion of reformed principles there was John Erskine laird of Dun, who was provost of the town. Through his influence neighbouring landowners, for example the laird of Brigton near Forfar who was denounced with Friar Roger in 1544, may have been won over to the protestant cause. But as in Dundee, support was to be latent rather than active for another ten years.[16]

In the neighbouring county of Fife the religious emergency of 1543/4 had been characterized by the sacking of the abbey of Lindores and the temporary expulsion of the monks, and it was to extend until 1547 owing to the murder of the archbishop of St Andrews, Cardinal Beaton, in 1546. The extent to which even Beaton's death can be viewed as a religious portent is questionable, for although it was justified as an act of retaliation for the conviction and execution of George Wishart as a heretic earlier the same year, the true motivation was possibly political and personal, perhaps largely inspired by Henry VIII of England. However, the seizure and holding of the castle of St Andrews by the murderers for over a year allowed protestants to preach openly in the surrounding area. These protestants included John Knox, who by then had emerged as a follower of Wishart, and who had joined the 'castilians' in April 1547. The episode constitutes a touchstone by which protestant strength can be assessed. Unfortunately, most of the evidence comes from the not unbiased pen of Knox himself. The new doctrine, as he relates it, was 'well liked by the people' and, following his own (Knox's) call to the ministry, 'a great number of the town, openly professed, by participation of the Lord's Table'. Nevertheless, even in Knox's account evidence of opposition is clear. The principal of St Leonard's college, John Annand, was on Knox's admission able to undermine the initial teaching and, if similar success did not attend his encounters with Knox, we only have Knox's word for it; furthermore the counter-attack mounted by John Winram and other representatives of the priory and university in preaching in the parish church each Sunday shows a response that may have checked any move towards protestant ascendency. Any hope of an ecclesiastical revolution came to an end when the castle fell to the French in 1547 and for over a decade there is little further evidence of vigorous protestant activity in the town.[17]

South of the Forth all was quiet, even in 1543. In Edinburgh the burgesses rallied to thwart an attack, which was largely politically inspired, on the Blackfriars monastery; there it was said only a handful including William Forman, one of the canons of Holyrood, 'careyed the name of professioun and knowledge'. Even Knox admits that at this time the burgh was 'for the most part drowned in superstitioun', and when Friar Rough preached therein he was physically threatened by a hostile congregation. In 1545 George Wishart preached in Leith but reaction to him seems to have been slight. Nor was support forthcoming in the surrounding Lothians. When Wishart was apprehended at Ormiston in East Lothian he had been deserted by all but three of the local lairds who had initially befriended him. Although in the period before his arrest Wishart's preaching had been heard in Inveresk and Tranent, his attempt to attract a congregation at Haddington was almost wholly fruitless owing to counter political pressure by the local magnate Patrick Hepburn, earl of Bothwell. Following Wishart's death little further interest appears to have been evinced in protestant teaching, and Knox refers to Haddington with such apparent contempt that it would seem that the inhabitants were not enthusiastic for the new doctrine. Elsewhere in the south-east and in the borders, there is a hint that protestant opinions were gaining favour, although active dissent was noticeably absent. Proximity to England was an obvious factor in this respect and the 'newe appynyonis of England' and the 'ill wynd towartes haly kirk' exhibited in 1544 were thought sufficiently dangerous in the following year to require the rigours of the law. Three years later, however, reforming ideas were still prevalent and the fact that 'part of the legis has tayn new apoynzionis of the scriptur and has don again the law and ordinance of holy kirk' was being advanced as a reason why the cause of 'Inglis men is fawvorit'. Little of this was translated into action, however, and, despite the reports, religious conservatism seems to have remained the norm.[18]

This verdict also holds good for the most of the west coast during this period, with Kyle in Ayrshire proving the exception to the general rule. Even there support was mixed and Ayr itself far from consistent in its attitude to reform. Thus, in 1543, when the use of the English New Testament was authorized by the governor, a Franciscan friar John Routh preached against its introduction and provoked a riot. If this outbreak indicates a popular sympathy for reform in the town, the bailies of the burgh nevertheless supplied the friar with money, a horse and a 'pair of hose and doublet' when he went to face trial for an action that apparently had their support. The parish church of Ayr continued to be maintained by the dean of guild (the titular head of the guild in a royal burgh), and the breaking of images in 1544–45 seems not to have been occasioned by iconoclasm but rather by accident when the town's guns were drawn out of the church where they were stored. The town paid for the removal of the broken figures. Iconoclasm was to the fore, however, in 1545 when George Wishart visited Ayrshire to preach to 'divers gentlemen of Kyle', but the general weakness of support for him is shown by the fact that he had to preach not in church but at the market cross at Ayr. He was also debarred from entry to the church of Mauchline on the authority of Sir Hugh Campbell of Louden, the sheriff of Ayr and by a group of local landowners who feared that 'an ornate tabernacle' might be destroyed. Wishart appears to have restricted his other preaching to the church of Galston and to private houses. Thus, even in Kyle at the time, opinion on religious matters was clearly divided and, although one influential figure, Alexander, fourth earl of Glencairn, seems to have fully embraced the protestant cause, the number of committed lairds may have been few.[19]

This period was a critical one in the battle against heresy, demonstrating the maximum effort by the authorities to curb protestant activities. The execution of Wishart in 1546 was followed by injunctions that names were to be given in of 'heretiks that or relapsis or haldis of apynionis agains the sacrament of the Alter'. Fears that parts of the realm were 'infectit with that pestilencious heresies of Luther, his sect and followaris' grew not unnaturally after the murder of Cardinal Beaton in 1546. In the following month the privy council was apprehensive 'that evill disparit personis will invaid, destroy, cast down, and, withhald abbays, abbay places, kirkis, alswelle paroche kirkis as utheris religious places'. However, with the recapture of St Andrews' castle in July 1547 these fears largely vanished, and events in most parts of the country seemed to justify Beaton's optimistic opinion shortly before his death that 'the heretical opinions which formerly flourished have been almost extinguished'.[20]

Even the greatly strengthened protestantism in England following the accession of Edward VI in 1547 was of doubtful advantage to the cause of reform in Scotland. Areas of the country adjacent to the borders increased their protestant leanings but the impact of reform elsewhere appears to have been limited. Indeed, so long as England proved a safe haven for reformers, no crusade in Scotland was forthcoming. Nevertheless, the arrival in England of John Knox, following his release in February 1549 from the French galleys to which he had been condemned after the fall of the castle of St Andrews, and his appointment as minister at Berwick-upon-Tweed and Newcastle, allowed a number of border Scots to hear him preach at both these centres. The views he expounded were apparently still in the general Lutheran rather than Calvinist tradition. His views on justification were certainly still on Lutheran lines. His approval of Henry Balnaves' treatise on *Justification by Faith* which he received in 1548 confirms his position on this issue and Knox himself was to comment that 'the just live by faith, ever trusting to obtain that which is promised, which is eternal life, promised to us by Jesus Christ'. His sermons certainly appear to have reflected his hatred of the mass and contained denunciations of the catholic claim that the mass was a sacrifice for the living and the dead. Other attitudes expressed by Knox were common enough among protestants; condemnation of the papacy and the rejection of purgatory and a consequent denial of the efficacy of prayers for the dead and to the saints. In one important respect, however, Knox followed in the footsteps of Wishart for in his denial of the real presence in the Blessed Sacrament he deserted the Lutheran compromise, which had denied[21] transubstantiation in the mass but had nevertheless admitted the real presence.

If in such respects Knox's immediate concern appears to have been chiefly to support the Church of England and to counter the disputes that threatened its unity, some relative increase in protestant strength in Scotland may have taken place as a result of his influence in the south in the period before 1553. With the accession of Mary Tudor in that year, and with Knox's flight to the continent, the growth of this influence was jeopardized. The increasing commitment of the border lairds to England was also threatened by this change. While political considerations may not always have been uppermost – as is demonstrated in Roxburghshire in 1553 when the two young lairds of Corsford and Ferniehurst brought an Augustinian canon of St Andrews called Acchisoun to Kelso 'to be the sone raysing in the mornyng ... and maid ane sermond' – they always loomed large. Thus the changes in England may have exerted their own particular influences on political and religious affiliations within Scotland and these were to remain undisturbed until the accession of Elizabeth in 1558. Despite promising beginnings there is, therefore, little indication that either the south-east or the borders were actively protestant during the 1540s and earlier 1550s.[22]

Kyle in Ayrshire, as previously noted, continued its open loyalty to the new opinions almost alone. Support for the cause may even have grown in the 1550s as both political and economic motivations began to dictate a shift from traditional allegiances. An alliance with England rather than with France may have appealed on economic grounds to Ayrshire merchants while many lairds, influenced by events south of the border, may have been moved in the same direction not only by political considerations but also by the opportunity given by opposition to the established church for the secularization of ecclesiastical property. Attacks on religious houses, parish churches and chapels became more frequent in Ayrshire and extended at times into the neighbouring shires of Lanark and Renfrew. This is, at least, the substance of a charge made in 1550 against John Lockhart of Barr who had helped a heretic canon of Glenluce escape from Houston castle. It was in Lockhart's house that Wishart had frequently preached and he with Charles Campbell of Bangour was accused of stealing Eucharistic chalices and ornaments of the mass and breaking choral stalls and glazed windows during the period 1545 and 1548. Such overt action did little to advance the protestant cause. Although Adam Wallace who was seized at Winton in East Lothian and accused of having usurped 'the office of preacher having no lawful calling thereto' came from Fail in Kyle, there is no evidence to suggest that his preaching in the east was part of any missionary endeavour. Nevertheless, although Wallace (who was burnt for his presumption) appears to have been mainly occupied as a tutor to the children of the laird of Ormiston, a laird banished for his support of Wishart, he demonstrated considerable theological knowledge at his trial and his denial of the real presence in the sacrament of the mass may have been reflected in his preaching.[23]

Taking a general view of the 1540s, it is clear that, although a provincial council of the church felt it necessary to pass various statutes in 1549 against heresy and persons who had in their possession 'any books of rhymes or popular songs containing calumies and slanders defamatory of churches and church institutions', and while suitable remedies for the ills of the church were being sought, it was still not unrealistic to maintain that 'complete unity in the ecclesiastical estate' might be preserved. The earl of Glencairn alone amongst the magnates seems to have been firmly committed to protestantism at this point and, if he carried with him those lairds of Kyle who shared protestant feelings with lairds in Angus, Fife and Lothian, they still constituted a tiny minority of sympathizers. If the frequent mention of these lairds in complaints laid before the privy council reveals the existence of an active force against the established church, the fact that these same figures appear time and time again can also be used to demonstrate the limited nature of that support. Moreover, though the movement exhibited strength in the attacks on the existing church structure it also revealed little by way of a more positive attempt to replace it. If some priests followed the example of Campbell of Cessnock's household chaplain, who read scriptures in English to the family and servants, and likewise exhibited their sympathies with the reforming cause, devotion to the mass – as distinct from opposition to the church as an institution whose wealth might be assailed – was still evident. If in this period the church had been able to promote organizational reform, with or without the doctrinal reform envisaged by Archbishop Hamilton, while leaving the church essentially 'catholic', then protestantism might have remained attractive to only a small minority.[24]

The accession of Mary Tudor to the throne of England in 1553, and the assumption of the regency in Scotland by the queen mother, Mary of Guise, from the earl of Arran and the Hamiltons in April 1554, brought the limited attempts at doctrinal and organizational reform to an end until the very eve of the Reformation. This made a protestant solution theoretically more feasible, but the continued weakness of that movement in the localities was still only too evident. Indeed we can only accept as exaggerated the following anonymous account of the immediate pre-Reformation period.

> The greatest fervencie appeared in the Mearns and Angus and Kyle, and Fyffe and Lothian; but chiefly the faithfull in Dundie exceeded all the rest in zeall and boldness, preferring the true religion to all things temporall. But in Edinburgh their meeting was ut in privat houses.

It literally records all the areas of protestant strength; and even within the districts local variations are clearly evident.[25]

Of the areas mentioned by the writer, Edinburgh seems to him the most suspect. However, his interpretation of the position in Lothian may be questioned for although certain lairds such as Sir James Sandilands of Calder were favourably disposed to reform, others were not and it is significant that Knox himself made no effort to extend his preaching beyond the confines of the Edinburgh area. Even there, indeed, his impact is questionable. 'The professors of Edinburgh' who held 'their privat conventiouns ... in the feilds in sommer, in houses in winter' were few in number in 1555. In that year William Harlaw, originally a tailor in the burgh, who had preached as a deacon in the Church of England and is described as 'not verie learned' although 'his doctrine was plaine and sound', returned as a teacher to the Edinburgh protestants. So too did John Willock who had fled his friary in Ayr in 1535. The protestant group, it has been claimed, was 'neither few, nor of meaner sort', but while the latter part of this statement may have been true, the first is undoubtedly open to question since the group originally comprised two separate entities, which even after their union by Erskine of Dun could still meet in a single private house. Other teachers such as John Douglas and Paul Methven of Jedburgh also preached to this Edinburgh congregation, which had its own elders and deacons but, as the visit of John Knox in 1555–56 demonstrated, protestantism clearly lacked popular support. Knox's exhortations had to be carried out secretly, and he quickly discovered that even amongst those professing protestantism some made 'small scruple to go to mass, or to communicate with the abused sacraments in the papistical manner'. When after a month's absence Knox returned to Lothian, he resided not in the capital but at Calder house at Mid-Calder, some miles away, where he stayed for the winter of 1555–56 drawing there 'divers from Edinburgh'. Amongst those who visited him there were Lord James Stewart and Archibald, Lord Lorne, heir to the earldom of Argyll. Both men were to be prominent leaders in the army of the congregation that finally effected the work of reformation, but neither was fully committed at this juncture. Another prominent visitor, John, Lord Erskine, was not to join the reformers until after the death of the Queen Regent whom he had hitherto supported. Those contacts, strengthened by a fleeting visit to Archibald, fourth earl of Argyll who thereafter maintained a protestant preacher, John Douglas, as his private chaplain, were to be perhaps the most significant outcome of Knox's teaching in the area. Although he returned to Edinburgh itself from time to time and on one occasion 'continued in doctrine in the bishop of Dunkeld's great lodging for ten days', the most eminent of his listeners, William Keith, fourth earl Marischal, was less than enthusiastic about reformed principles even after the Reformation had been achieved. There are few indications of a widespread or popular support and, without Glencairn's protection, the opportunity to preach might not have arisen. Nevertheless, the aftermath of his visit can be seen in the complaint of the Queen Regent in September 1556 to the provost of Edinburgh, bailies and council that: 'thair is certane odious balletis and rymes laitlie sett furth be sum ewill inclinit personis of your toun qua has alssua tane doun diveris imagis and contempnandlie brokin the samyn.' A further criticism specifically refers to the breaking of images, but even before this grievance was aired Knox and Willock had returned to the continent. Their departure seems to have had the effect of quietening the situation, and it was not until Willock's return in 1558 that there were again signs in Edinburgh of ecclesiastical unrest.[26]

The most fruitful response to Knox's visits elsewhere during his brief stay in 1555–56 was in Kyle. He received a warm welcome from the lairds there in the first three months of 1556. John Lockhart of Barr, who had already entertained Willock, was Knox's principal host in Kyle although he also stayed with Lord Ochiltree and several other lairds. For instance, Knox celebrated communion for the earl of Glencairn at Finlayston in Renfrewshire. Most of his contacts were still among established reformers, yet the major purpose of his visit must have been to extend the cause of reform. How far he could claim to have had any success in this cannot be easily assessed. Knox, nevertheless, had been accepted as the doctrinal leader of the Scottish protestants. Since taking up residence in Geneva in 1554 his faith had become Calvinist in tone. Calvinism permeated his religious thought. Only two sacraments, that of baptism and of the Lord's Table, were regarded as valid and the doctrine of predestination, which accepted that God has pre-selected some men for heaven and others for eternal damnation, figured more prominently in his writings as the years proceded. The doctrine is explicitly stated in a letter written 'to his brothers in Scotland' in 1557 and is exhaustively analysed in his *Answer to the Cavillations of an Adversary respecting the Doctrine of Predestination*. This extension of Calvinism may have been Knox's greatest achievement during his visit to Scotland, for although Knox in other respects claimed great triumphs, communion was celebrated only in private houses and he made no attempt to preach in churches as Wishart had done, nor indeed did he preach to the masses. While this may have been prudent, in view of the authorities' concern about his preaching even though they were at first uncertain that the culprit was Knox, it only demonstrates again that the movement in Kyle even at this late date was not a popular one, but was very much restricted to a few influential magnates, the principal among these being Glencairn. It was these men, with their following among the local lairds who, as they became increasingly involved in the struggle against French political intrusion into Scotland, decided to couple secular and political aims with religious beliefs.[27]

A similar picture to this is to be found in Angus and the Mearns when, on two occasions, Knox visited John Erskine of Dun. To Dun, which lay midway between two burghs with protestant leanings, Brechin and Montrose, 'resorted the principal men of that country to hear him preach', although Knox himself apparently (and perhaps surprisingly) made no attempt to visit Dundee which had so enthisiastically received earlier preachers. Early in the following year (1556) he revisited Dun and 'ministered the communion at the request of the gentlemen of the countrie about, speciallie of the Mernes'. Thereafter the lairds appear to have been active in converting others to their views and in doing so went outside the confines of their own district. Nevertheless, neither in Kyle nor in the Mearns was their pressure consistently maintained. Indeed Knox's seemingly premature return to the continent in July 1556 may have been occasioned by despondency at his lack of success. If he was despondent, then he was not unjustified. In October 1557, when he was at Dieppe and prepared to return to Scotland to initiate further religious reform at the invitation of the earl of Glencairn, Lord Lorne, Lord James Stewart and Erskine of Dun, he received a letter from a friend who had spoken with 'all those that had seemed most frank and fervent in the mater; and that in none did he find such boldness and constancie as was requisite for such an interprise, but that some did ... repent that ever anie such thing was moved.' Despite the fact that the initial signatories to Knox's invitation had included a landowner from the Mearns and one from Ayrshire, opinion had apparently shifted in both districts. The same situation may also have obtained in neighbouring Fife, a county which seems to have been relatively unaffected and had remained unvisited by Knox. Not until the appearance of a fresh wave of preachers in the following year, when 'manie in Angus and Fife beganne openlie to renounce their idolatrie', did protestant expectations in these and other parts of the country again rise. But why did matters change in 1558? The answer seems to lie in politics.[28]

The impending marriage of Mary, queen of Scots to the Dauphin Francis, eldest son of the French King Henry II, increased fears that Scotland would be even more effectively dominated by the Queen Regent and her French advisors and would become an appendage of France. Thus many nobles and lairds were prompted to align themselves with the pro-English reforming party, who, in December 1557, had drawn up the 'First Band', a pledge to work for the recognition of a reformed church. This had initially attracted few new supporters, the earl of Morton being the only influential figure to join the signatories who had invited Knox to return earlier in the year. By early 1558, however, there was increasing support from the lairds and barons who proceeded to draw up proposals for reformed worship. The marriage of Mary on 24 April 1558 was accompanied by a well-known 'secret' assignation of her kingdom to the king of France if she died without heirs, and this added to the political support for the party which had also embraced church reform.[29]

The volatile political situation created by these events continued throughout 1558. Encouraged by these developments and by the accession of Elizabeth in England, protestant preachers again took up their cause in the Scottish localities. In several towns protestant sympathizers began to form themselves into more highly organized groups, appointing elders and deacons from their own number to ensure that a proper order among the new protestant congregations might be maintained. According to one commentator 'God also blessed this weake beginning, that within few moneths the face of a church was erected in sundrie places'. Of these Dundee was undoubtedly the most committed. There it was reported that 'the faithfull ... exceeded all the rest in zeall and boldness', a revival brought about after the arrival in the burgh in 1558 of John Willock and Paul Methven. Largely through Methven's efforts, it is said, 'the town of Dundie beganne to erect the face of a reformed church publiclie, in which the word was preached openlie, and the sacraments truelie ministered'. Nevertheless, burgesses shuttled him 'from ane nighbour to another' and he was forced to leave the town for a while in May 1559 after being denounced by the Regent for preaching at Easter and administering the sacraments to several of the 'leiges of the burgh'. By this date, however, the committment of the inhabitants was assured, and Dundonians were to play a prominent part in the final outcome of the Reformation movement.[30]

When not occupied in Dundee, Methven moved around the surrounding countryside and in the summer of 1558 preached 'in sindrie gentlemens places in Angus and also in Fyfe'. Thus he administered the sacrament in the parish church of Lundie eight miles distant from Dundee, and also at Cupar in Fife, ten miles away. His activities in Fife undoubtedly met with some popular response and may have occasioned the burning for heresy of Walter Myln, an aged priest who, refusing to say mass, had left his parish of Lunan in Angus in the early 1540s. Myln's execution at St Andrews in 1558 may indeed have fostered sympathy for the protestants and aided growth of reforming opinion in the town; yet according to Knox as late as June 1559, the protestant lords could not look to St Andrews for friendly support since 'the town at that time had not given profession of Christ'.[31]

On the west coast Ayr followed the example of Dundee and there too overt protestantism can be attributed to the support of the lairds in the surrounding hinterland. And in Kyle even more than in Angus the process of spreading protestant beliefs may have been maintained up to Knox's departure in 1556, either by itinerant preachers drawn from the household chaplains of families with reforming tendencies or by beneficed priests with sufficient protestant sympathies to adopt the new beliefs. In Ayr itself the council began to identify more and more closely with the reform movement, and in May 1558 accepted into their jurisdiction Sir Robert Leggat, curate of the neighbouring burgh of Prestwick, who had marked protestant sympathies and who assumed thereafter the duties of vicar and curate of Ayr. For a period, co-existence appears to have been possible: in an account of 1558 payments to the town's friaries appear side by side with a payment for the minister's chamber rent, which also, incidentally, indicates that the curate was already acting as minister. Nevertheless, although Knox may have been justified in describing Kyle as 'a receptacle of God's servants of old', it is clear that many Ayrshire inhabitants in the county as a whole remained true to their old faith.[32]

Such an attachment to the old church is equally evident in Edinburgh which, although exhibiting discontent with the existing church in 1558, was far from being committed to the protestant cause. Incidents such as the theft of a statue of the patron saint of the burgh, St Giles, which was afterwards burnt, followed by a similar incident on St. Giles's day when another statue of the saint, borrowed from the Greyfriars by the burgh authorities for a religious procession through the town, was torn down and eventually thrown into a sewer, doubtless demonstrate that at least the brethren were growing more bold and probably increasing in strength. But they were still numerically weak; and although John Willock, from his sick bed, is reported to have taught some of the nobility, barons and gentlemen of the district, it is also noted that several of these 'fell backe after'. Such hostility to the course of reform was certainly not restricted to Edinburgh. At Aberdeen in 1559 the cathedral chapter thought it necessary to proceed against heretics in the diocese and in particular against those involved in the burning of the parish church of Echt and in the casting down of the images; otherwise there was little or no sign of reforming zeal, the presence of the powerful earl of Huntley – nephew of the bishop of the diocese – ensuring that reformed principles had few active adherents. In other burghs the religious sympathies of the inhabitants were equally clearly with the existing order. At Peebles on the very eve of the Reformation in March 1559 the bailies and burgesses demonstrated where their loyalties lay when they intervened to prevent a preacher from using 'any new novationes of common prayeris or preching' and declared that they would not 'assist to him nor none of his sect nor opinioun'.[33]

The course of affairs at Peebles was repeated throughout southern Scotland. Although the recommitment of the church of England to protestantism in 1558 presented a fresh opportunity to revive sympathy in the border districts, the reformers claimed little support in these areas. Not until September 1559 could Knox report that 'Christ Jesus is begunne to be preached upon the south borders ... in Jedburgh and Kelso'. If in the period of the Reformation more support was to be forthcoming from this quarter, political considerations were again as important as any commitment to the protestant ideal. This is amply demonstrated by the careers of the two young lairds Ferniehurst and Cessford, who had brought a preacher to Kelso in 1553: Ferniehurst emerged as a staunch supporter of the Queen Regent and her daughter, Mary, queen of Scots, and continued to embrace catholicism; Cessford, now diametrically opposed in political attitudes to his one-time friend, supported the protestant cause. Such considerations were to be vital for the outcome of the Reformation movement. On religious issues alone it is clear that the greatest strength of protestant support, with the exception of Kyle, was confined to a closely demarcated area on the east coast. Beyond these areas the reformers were clearly numerically weak. Yet political considerations were to favour this militant minority and enable them to achieve their religious goal.[34]

6
The Triumph of Protestantism

The catholic church had failed to promote effective reform; the protestant party in Scotland found it equally difficult to promote its case in the face of hostility from the civil authorities. Had it not been for the fears aroused by the marriage of Mary, queen of Scots, which prompted many of the magnates and lairds to associate themselves with the pro-English reforming party in the First Band of 1557, the support necessary to achieve Reformation might have been withheld. The revival of protestant preaching in 1558 and the continuing political resistance to the Francophile policies of Mary of Guise were encouraged by the accession of Elizabeth in England and led to further support which in the following year grew more rapidly still. In the course of 1559, commencing with the 'Beggars' Summons' which appeared on 1 January and threatened appropriation of the friaries in favour of the poor before Whitsunday, 12 May, the movement also became more noticeably militant. The arrival of Knox from the continent on 2 May coincided with a determined effort by the Queen Regent to deal with the new situation. Dundee and Perth had already made their profession of faith and other burghs subsequently joined them. Stirling, which had not exhibited any overt protestant activity since 1538, accepted the order of Common Prayers in June 1559, a step already taken in May by Perth which had been quiescent since 1543. Both towns demonstrated their zeal more practically by destroying their friaries. The earlier policy of conciliation towards protestants by the Queen Regent may partially explain the absence of visible protestantism in either of these towns for more than a decade before this date. At all events neither seems to have been greatly favoured by protestant preachers until Knox delivered his famous inflammatory sermon in St John's kirk at Perth in May 1559, and he himself was to describe the inhabitants of that burgh as 'young and rude in Christ', confirming that the burgh was not actively protestant before that date. The burgh of Montrose, no doubt subject to pressure from the neighbouring laird of Dun and his associates, conformed during May: yet, while Montrose and its neighbour Brechin may have been open to the persuasion of the preachers who were active in Angus and Mearns from 1558 onwards, contemporary accounts are curiously silent about both towns. In Brechin the cathedral clergy at least – of whom only one conformed and served in the reformed church – must have provided an active opposition to the reformers, and this may explain why Brechin is not included with Montrose among those who 'received the Evangel' in May 1559. At St Andrews too the burgh had still not 'given profession of Christ' in late June 1559. Only after the arrival of the Lords in the burgh and after a sermon by Knox did the provost and bailies, as did the commonality for the most part, 'agree to remove all the monuments of idolatry'. The phraseology used by Knox here suggests a far from unanimous decision in the matter by the populace and, although the reformed church at St Andrews was quickly established thereafter, this burgh follows the pattern established at Perth and Stirling rather than that at Dundee and at Ayr.[1]

At Dundee the attempted apprehension of Paul Methven in May 1559 led to widespread support for him; Knox, newly arrived in Scotland, hurried from Edinburgh to Dundee and 'craved earnestly that he might be suffered to assist his brethren and to give confession of his faith with them which was granted'. James Halyburton, provost of the burgh who had been charged to arrest Methven and convey him to Stirling, instead not only warned the preacher to quit the town for his own safety, but after the riot occasioned by Knox's sermon in Perth raised a large contingent of townsmen who, with others from neighbouring burghs joined with the magnates, lairds and their supporters to form the so-called 'army of the congregation'. The very title they chose revealed their commitment to the protestant cause. In Ayr too the final step in this direction was also taken in May 1559 when the burgh accounts reveal that 'ane prechour' had been brought from Edinburgh – John Willock, who was unavailingly denounced by the regent on 10 May for his actions. On the day following his denunciation the organ loft of the church was closed, and some days later the bailies and dean of guild of the burgh 'dischargit the schaplandis [chaplains] of said kirk and their service'. Before the year was out Knox's colleague at Geneva, Christopher Goodman, had been appointed minister at Ayr while in November 1559 an assistant minister and schoolmaster was appointed to 'say and reid the commoun prayeris and minister the sacrament in the minister's absence'. The intervention of the nobles and lairds had thus been decisive in Ayr. Apparently this was also true at Dalmellington in the same county where a minister, Leonard Clark, seems to have been acting by November 1559. Both in respect of the events which followed, and in the support given to the 'congregations of the West country', the Ayrshire lairds played a dominant role – and an all-important part in deciding the final outcome of the Scottish Reformation. There were similar events at Peebles where the town council reversed their earlier policy of banning protestant preachers when the local lairds joined the lords of the congregation, a change clearly dictated by political rather than religious considerations.[2]

In Edinburgh, Knox preached in St Giles church on 29 June 1559 and was subsequently elected minister to the burgh. Yet he decided to leave when military support for the reformers dwindled in the face of the Queen Regent's superior forces; it was left to John Willock to celebrate public communion in the church after the departure of the protestant forces from the town on 26 July. Even after a brief re-occupation of the town, the lords of the congregation were again forced to retire. On this occasion, indeed, the true feeling of many of the inhabitants was revealed since the protestant army was berated by the Edinburgh citizens, much to Knox's despair. Indeed he wrote: 'The sword of dolour passed through our hearts, so were the cogitations and determinations of many hearts then revealed. For we would never have believed that our natural country men and women could have wished our destruction so unmercifully, and have so rejoiced in our adversity.' The mass was restored in St Giles at a service held by the archbishop of St Andrews, and Knox's claim that in September 1559 eight burghs – Edinburgh, St Andrews, Dundee, Perth, Brechin, Montrose, Stirling and Ayr – were all committed to his cause must be amended in at least this respect. It was not until 1 April 1560 that the gospel (in the eyes of the reformers) was truly preached again in Edinburgh, in what undoubtedly remained an hostile atmosphere. Elsewhere this hostility was even more marked. In the burgh of Old Aberdeen, in which both university and the cathedral chapter remained committed to the old faith, little support for reformed principles was forthcoming; when the destruction of the houses of the Black and White friars in New Aberdeen, for which the burgesses had little affection, was reported in early 1560 it was also said to have been achieved by 'certain strangers' who may be identified with the congregation of Angus and the Mearns. If 'some neighbours and indwellers of the burgh' assisted in this process, their motives appear to have been economic rather than religious. The burgesses successfully repelled an attack on the parish church of St Nicholas of New Aberdeen and St Machar's cathedral in Old Aberdeen suffered only minor damage. Alexander Anderson, principal of King's College, effectively protected the church there although the domestic quarters appear to have suffered considerable damage. External considerations led to the acceptance of a reformed minister, Adam Heriot, a former canon of St Andrews before 19 July 1560, but his task in an area where protestantism had many implacable opponents could not have been an easy one.[3]

Elsewhere in Scotland the determining factor in any area in promoting the reformed faith was the attitude of the local lairds. Indeed even in burghs that showed some readiness to accept reform, pressure from outside the town was necessary before most, if not all, of the councils finally decided in favour of protestantism. Where a neighbouring laird who favoured the protestant cause was also provost, as at Montrose and St Andrews, this may have been decisive; it was clearly decisive at Perth where Lord Ruthven was provost of the burgh and committed both himself and the citizens to advance the Reformation. Nevertheless, it is clear that the immediate interest of the magistrates and lairds who led 'the army of the congregation' was political and, in the marching and counter-marching that characterized the ensuing skirmishes between them and the forces of the Queen Regent, the principal stress was always laid on the struggle against French domination. For a time in August 1559 when 'fower ensignes of Frenchmen' arrived at Leith the final outcome remained uncertain, but it is notable that the fear of continued French supremacy induced even pro-Catholic magnates to join the congregation and also led to an appeal for effective military intervention by the English. Elizabeth was finally to respond to this request in March 1560; this was fortuitously followed by the death of Mary of Guise, in June.

These two factors proved to be decisive. A campaign which the congregation and their protestant supporters in Scotland could never have won by their own efforts was successful. The treaty of Edinburgh between France and England in July 1560 guaranteed the end of French influence in Scotland and, in the parliament that followed, the victorious lairds honoured their commitment to their protestant allies by accepting on 17 August a reformed Confession of Faith. To what extent political reasons engineered the acceptance of the new protestant faith must remain debatable. What is certain is that, even in those burghs that supported the congregation, there must have been only small bands of protestant sympathizers before the achievement of military and political success. The view so often stressed by historians that the success of the Scottish Reformation depended upon popular urban support must therefore be questioned. In most burghs support for protestantism stemmed initially from a small minority of the populace who were only permitted to seize the initiative and win over their fellow citizens through the intervention of the local lairds.[4]

If this interpretation is correct, the distribution of the reforming lairds throughout the country might determine the likely support in the various localities for the protestant cause. A ready-made guide exists in the list of about one hundred lairds who attended the Reformation parliament of 1560, although it should be stressed that the list is defective and not all of those present were supporters of the new ecclesiastical regime. Nevertheless, the pattern produced by plotting the holdings of these lairds reveals that the great majority came from a few well-defined areas in which protestantism had already been clearly evident - Kyle in Ayrshire, Lothian, Perthshire, Fife, Kinross, Angus and the Mearns provide almost half the number. The southern counties of Berwick, Roxburgh, Dumfries and Kirkcudbright, which may of course have been greatly affected by the new relationship with England, constituted about a fifth of the group. Of the other Lowland counties, Renfrew, Stirling and Peebles were poorly represented despite the ultimate support for change in the burgh of Peebles. Lanarkshire, on the other hand, where protestant sympathies had not been very evident before 1560, supplied at least five members although this was not many in relation to the size of the county. The rest of the country provided only a handful. Aberdeenshire, Banffshire, Inverness-shire, Moray and Ross-shire together produced fewer reforming lairds than Kyle. The evidence therefore confirms the earlier conclusion that the greatest strength of protestant support, with the exception of Kyle, was confined to a closely demarcated area on the east coast. Beyond these areas the reformers were clearly numerically weak. Yet political considerations favoured this militant minority and enabled them to achieve their religious goal.[5]

The objects of the reformers in this respect were determined by Calvinist doctrine. Little or nothing of the original Lutheran tenets can be detected in either the Scots Confession of Faith which outlined the reformers doctrinal viewpoint or in the first Book of Discipline in which the organizational structure of the new church was advanced. The Confession which was accepted by parliament on 17 August 1560 was followed a week later by enactments abrogating papal authority and forbidding the saying of the mass. Nevertheless, as early as 29 April of that year the great council of Scotland had commissioned certain ministers to draw up a book containing their 'judgments touching the reformation of religion'. Such a work had been completed by 20 May; it was not, however, debated in the August parliament, but was revised and expanded in the months that followed and was not ready for consideration by a convention of nobility and barons until January 1561. The programme for reform, now termed a 'Booke of Dyscipline' was then presented by its authors and six whole days were spent examining and discussing its proposals before it received a somewhat lukewarm approval. On certain issues its recommendations, if controversial, were clear cut; the compilers laid claim to all the spiritual revenues of the old church but only sought possession of part of the temporality, tacitly relinquishing the monastic temporality to the commendators. Otherwise the benefice structure of the old church was to be dismantled and a new system to meet the needs of the parishes, schools, universities and the poor was to take its place.[6]

In practice the wholesale transfer of patrimony could not be implemented and a series of administrative and financial expedients, which involved the use of ministers, exhorters and readers, arose to take its place. In January 1561 the lords had decided that benefice holders who acknowledged the reformed faith should continue to receive their revenues provided that they contributed to the upkeep of the ministry. Some may have done so, while others who refused to conform may have had their stipends confiscated, although there is no evidence to show that such revenues in any way alleviated the lot of the reformed clergy, many of whom were dependent upon the charitable support of friendly lairds. It was clearly in the interest of both parties to achieve an amicable settlement and this became all the more pressing after the return of Mary, queen of Scots, from France in August 1561. On 22 December, four of the bishops offered one quarter of their revenues to the queen to be deployed as she thought fit, but this was considered inadequate by the council who deemed one third to be a more appropriate amount. On 15 February 1562, this requirement became statutory; the old possessors of benefices were to be allowed to retain two-thirds of their revenues for life while the reformed church was maintained from whatever portion of the remaining third the crown chose to allow.

The solution may have been statesmanlike but was obviously unsatisfactory to the reformed church and one of the most striking features of the immediate post-Reformation era is the apparent poverty of the ministry. Knox, who as minister of the High kirk of Edinburgh himself enjoyed a more than adequate salary, complained bitterly of court expenses; the guard and the affairs of the kitchen, he claimed, were more important than the ministers' stipends. Yet there was some justification in the crown's claim that it too required adequate finance and, in appropriating ecclesiastical revenues it was doing no more than its predecessors who had increasingly relied upon ecclesiastical taxation. The continued appropriation of two-thirds of the revenues to the old possessors was less defensible and the assembly with some justification could claim that 'neyther by the law of God neyther yet by any just law of man, is any thing dew into thame, quho now most cruelly do exact of the pure and riche, the twa pairts of thair benefices as they call thame'. Only in 1567, when Mary's power in Scotland was tottering, was something done to meet the situation, when in a last desperate attempt to uphold her failing political position, she granted succession to the lesser benefices to the reformed church at last. Even then no attempt was made to evict incumbents from benefices and, although collection of the thirds was now placed in the hands of church collectors, rather than those of the crown, the new arrangement proved to be singularly unsuccessful as the collectors lacked the means of enforcing payment. No machinery, moreover, existed for dealing with succession to the larger benefices, and this question was to remain in abeyance as civil war raged between king's men and queen's men. Any resolution of the problem might have been expected to await the ending of that conflict had it not been for the execution for treason of John Hamilton, archbishop of St Andrews, in April 1571. The government without recourse to the church appointed John Douglas, rector of St Andrews university, to the vacant archbishopric on 6 August 1571 and at the same time proceeded to nominate and provide John Porterfield to the see of Glasgow, vacant through the forfeiture in September 1570 of the absentee James Beaton. Strenuous protests by the kirk at this mode of proceeding led to a commission on 8 September 1571 empowering the church to examine the two archbishops but no machinery, other than that of notifying the king and regent of their findings, was made for ecclesiastical admission to their benefices. The appointment of James Paton as bishop of Dunkeld on the same day as the announcement of the commission and again without reference to the church, underlined the unsuitability of makeshift arrangements and on 16 November Erskine of Dun wrote to the Regent Mar stressing that the admission of all spiritual office-bearers must be controlled by the kirk. As a result of his insistence on this particular point a convention of the kirk eventually met with a committee of the privy council to settle these issues. Their meeting at Leith ended in a compromise between two opposing views; the wish of the kirk to dissolve the benefices, including the bishoprics, and that of the regent representing the interests of the crown who wished to initiate an Anglican-type episcopacy in which bishops would have been subject to the authority of the crown. In the event the kirk, for the time being, accepted episcopacy but the crown conceded that while nomination would rest with the crown, bishops-elect were to be examined by chapters of ministers and that after consecration they would be subject in spiritual matters to the authority of the General Assembly.[7]

These arrangements, which were ratified by the assembly in August 1572 and reinforced by an Act of Conformity in 1573, have been seen as a statesmanlike solution to the problem of settling the organization of the church and also as providing welcome financial relief for the reformed cause; its terms have been regarded as a binding arrangement on both parties which received general approval. Even Knox, who had bitterly opposed the initial appointments of Douglas and Porterfield, in his last injunction to the General Assembly before his death that 'all bishopricks vacand may be presented, and qualified persons nominat thereunto, within a year after the vaiking thereof, according to the order taken in Leith' seemed to approve. However, this view appears to overlook the fact that the assembly in giving its approval in 1572 was insistent that the agreement should be regarded as 'ane interim' measure and that some members of that body were most unhappy about the adoption of titles such as archbishop. If there was unease about the situation, it was not unjustified. The Regent Morton chose to encourage bishops to ignore the authority of the assembly, while as a counter-measure that body in its turn decreed in 1576 that bishops should accept a congregational ministry, an edict which some bishops accepted but which others, including Patrick Adamson, the newly appointed archbishop of St Andrews, refused to obey, firmly declining the assembly's jurisdiction.[8]

In such circumstances that Leith agreement, of which many ministers had been suspicious from the outset could not be expected to endure. In its search for a solution to its dilemma the church found it necessary to re-define its position; and this definition came in the promulgation of the second Book of Discipline in 1578. Leadership for the adoption of this course of action was found in Andrew Melville, but he should be no more credited with the compilation of the second Book of Discipline than Knox with the drawing up of the first. It was a composite work and as such enjoyed the support of most of the survivors of the first generation of reformers. The redefinition of the principles that governed the polity of the Scottish church may have led to some departures from the organizational plans of 1560, but such 'innovations' were generally speaking merely a statement of existing practice. Eighteen years experience had led to certain changes of procedure but their appearance in the second Book of Discipline can be seen rather as approbation than as innovation. The views of the church on certain issues had changed over the years; they would continue to change after the acceptance of the second Book of Discipline. In such years of uncertainty no agreement would be viewed as permanent whether it was the first Book of Discipline, the Convention of Leith or the second Book of Discipline. Nevertheless, with the exception of the claim for the restoration of the church's patrimony in full, the two books diverged very little on basic issues. The one constant, which governed all else, lay in their unanimous belief that church and state were separate and distinct entities.[9]

The problem of church-state relations had faced the reformers from the outset but, although their views were quite clearly stated in certain of their pronouncements, they were less clear as to how the power of the church should be exercised in practice. Thus although Erskine of Dun affirmed: 'there is a spirituall jurisdictioun and power which God hath given into his Kirk, and to those who beare office therein; and there is a temporall power givin of God to Kings and civill magistrats', no such explicit statement appears in the first Book of Discipline, although a clear distinction is drawn between civil and ecclesiastical jurisdiction. The organization of the church is explicitly defined at congregational level, but little is said of any body comparable to the General Assembly although reference to 'the whole councell of the kirk' and even to the 'Assemblie of the Universale Kirk gathered within the realme', must surely refer to such a gathering. The views of Knox, it has been argued, are less ambiguous and he certainly made statements to the effect that 'the Reformation of religion in all points, together with the punishment of false teachers doth appertane to the power of the Civil Magistrate' and he also affirmed that 'na power on earth is above the power of the Civill reulor; that everie saule, be he Pope or Cardinall, aught to be subject to the higher Poweris'. In similar vein the Confession of Faith of 1560 states that 'to kings, princes, rulers and magistrates we affirm that chiefly and most principally the conservation and purgation of religion appertains; so that not only they are appointed for civil policy, but also for maintenance of the true religion and for suppressing of idolatry and superstition'. Nothing in these statements, it has been claimed, suggests 'that a church should be independent of the civil magistrate, and nothing at all is inconsistent with the ecclesiastical supremacy of a "godly prince".' But for the impracticability of having a catholic queen as head of the church, Scotland would have followed the example of England and accepted the 'godly prince' as head of the church.[10]

Against this view may be placed the theory that such statements about the role of the civil magistrate suggest nothing more than an active partnership between church and state in the promotion of the true faith. The magistracy, in the form of the 'great council of the realm', was at times expected to take the initiative, even in the matter of the nomination of superintendents but this, it is clear, was only to be a temporary expedient until the affairs of the church were more settled when control over this and other matters could be assumed by the kirk itself. The 'council of the church, with ecclesiastical magistrates and the council of the realm' with civil magistrates, were expected to function quite separately, although in the perfect Christian commonwealth their efforts would be complementary. The General Assembly which came into being before December 1560 was clearly distinguished from the great council of the realm and, although its composition of ministers, nobles and burgesses mirrored that of the three estates, its intended image was that of the whole Christian community. It was not created with the sole intention of holding the power of the crown in commission until the advent of a godly prince. Indeed when that occasion did arise the assembly maintained its stance as supreme arbiter on ecclesiastical affairs. The appeal of Erskine of Dun to the regent on 16 November 1571 re-asserts the kirk's position on the matter, that spiritual and temporal jurisdiction were quite separate and exercised in a distinct manner by different bodies.[11]

This distinction is equally evident in terms of the assembly's composition; it was in essence an ecclesiastical gathering. The primary element in its membership were the ministers and the commissioned members who represented kirks, provinces or shires, burghs and sometimes universities. The nobles and barons who attended came as individuals and not as commissioners, nevertheless their presence wielded a powerful influence. Their practical assistance was certainly welcomed from time to time; in 1563 the earl of Glencairn was asked to accompany the superintendent of the west on a visit to enquire into the financial state of the hospital at Glasgow and in 1569 yet another assembly delegation was led by Andrew, Lord Ochiltree. The commitment of some of these lords is unquestionable and may be seen in the formalization of their position after the deposition of Mary in 1567; thereafter magnates were individually invited to attend by letters missive, and even when that practice ceased many continued to do so. In 1590, for example, a number of magnates were present and Lord John Hamilton and Ludovic, duke of Lennox, each offered 'all kinds of assistance according to his power'. The position of barons or lairds was very similar. Their presence and influence in the early assemblies is hardly surprising for as a social class they had figured prominently in the early years of the Reformation movement. They were among the first to profess the reformed faith in Scotland and their attendance at the Reformation parliament had been one of the notable features of that assembly. Thereafter, as the records show, they were equally prominent in the General Assemblies of the kirk. Thus, three lairds were appointed to a body to petition the privy council in 1561, and four of a group of five appointed to approach the queen in 1565 were lairds. In the same year, the three lairds of Cornell, Sornbeg and Dreghorn undertook to provide stipends at Riccarton and Dundonald, and other examples illustrating the commitment of men of this class to the reformed church are readily available. Their position in the assembly was, nevertheless, open to doubt. At first they appear to have attended because they were committed to the cause of Reformation, but while on occasions they may have represented, under a variety of nomenclatures such as 'commissioners of shyres', reformed congregations or certain areas, more often than not they represented no one but themselves. While this was feasible in the assembly, a similar attitude to attending parliament highlighted the need to regularize and regulate their attendance in both bodies. Abortive moves towards parliamentary representation in 1567 appear to have led in the following year to the assembly act, which established that 'Commissioners of Shyres sall be chosen at the synodall conventioun of the diocese, be consent of the rest of the ministers and gentill men that sall convene at the said synodall conventioun'. The projected appointment of such commissioners initially made little difference to the position of the barons who continued with the magnates to attend as individuals. By the early 1580s this practice had, however, ceased and only those who were appointed commissioners were able to take their places in the assembly. The barons had at last become an identifiably representative group but, as few elected commissioners seem to have appeared as a result of the cumbersome machinery of 1568, the representation and influence of these lairds in the supreme court of the church was severely curtailed and may have been further weakened by an assembly decree of 1598 which gave presbyteries, in which ministers alone were to be found, the nominal right of sending one baron each, as synodal representation declined thereafter.[12]

Burgh representation was also regulated by this act which allowed two commissioners from Edinburgh and one each from other royal burghs. Limitation had not existed previously, probably because so few burghs sent representatives, and the 1568 act had merely stated that commissioners were to be appointed jointly by the town and 'kirk of their awin tounes'. In this respect, practice appears to have varied; Edinburgh town council regularly appointed commissioners from 1562 onwards but at St Andrews, which also appears to have been frequently represented, the kirk session and not the council acted as the appointing body. Universities too appear to have been intermittent in their representation, but the renewed emphasis placed upon the doctor or theology professor in the second Book of Discipline may have stimulated attendance. Every university had its own procedure for commissioning its personnel and at St Andrews from 1597 this involved the ministers nominating three of their number to the council of the university, which in turn would commission one of them to the assembly on the understanding that the successful nominee would not be eligible for service for another three years.[13]

Commissioners drawn from the shires, burghs and universities were not prominent in sixteenth-century assemblies; the most important element in its membership were the bishops, superintendents and commissioners of the assembly who attended by virtue of their office and the commissioned ministers who represented the kirks. At first ministerial members were only present by permission of the superintendent; other ministers were only allowed to attend if they were parties in a case to be heard before the assembly. Not everyone obeyed this order and the assembly of 1568 which admitted 'the pluralite of voyces' decided to adopt new procedures for selecting commissioners. Representation was felt to be the only answer to the problem and it was enacted that ministers should be chosen at the synodal convention in a similar fashion to the shire commissioners. Even then representation was uneven and in the sixteenth century ministers, other than bishops and commissioners, from the six northern synods of Orkney, Caithness, Ross, Moray, Argyll and the Isles were represented only by John Ross, minister of Tain, who attended the assembly of April 1581 and by a few representatives from Moray who attended the assemblies of April 1581 and August 1590. Elsewhere the procedure laid down in the 1568 act were followed until they came into conflict with commissioners appearing from presbyteries – these courts had received legal recognition in 1592. For some years two sets of commissioners appear to have attended assemblies and this problem was not tackled until 1598, when not only the right of synods to send commissioners was re-stated, but also a new ordinance established which allowed presbyteries to send 'thrie of the wysest and the gravest of the brethren' to assemblies. In practice synods ceased to commission members shortly after this date and ministerial representation came thenceforward from the presbyteries.[14]

The character of the assembly was thus well established shortly after 1568; if magnates and barons appeared occasionally as individuals, the primary element in its membership was ministerial together with a handful of lay commissioners drawn from the shires, burghs and universities. Such lay commissioners were, however, almost inevitably elders. From 1561 university teachers had acted as elders of the St Andrew's kirk session and the involvement of the synod and kirk session in the appointment of shire and burgh commissioners is likely to have resulted in the selection of elders. Nevertheless, some doubt must remain as to whether the few commissioners who attended sixteenth-century assemblies did so as elders or as commissioners who might fortuitously hold office within the kirk. Whatever their exact status, an assembly consisting of only ministers and elders was not an unknown quantity during the 1570s. In this respect the proposal of the second Book of Discipline that: 'nane or subject to repaire to this assemblie to vote but ecclesiasticall persons to sic a number as shall be thocht gude be the same assemblie, not excluding uther persons that will repaire to the said assemblie to propose, heir and reason. ...' was not making a violent break with the past, but rather reflecting what might already for some years have been considered accepted practice.

This was also the case with the explicit restatement of the two kingdom theory, which far from being innovatory merely reinforced, in the face of Morton's attempts at state intervention, the reformers' original concept of the division between church and state. The concept that 'as the ministers and uthers of the ecclesiastically estait be subject to the magistrat civill, so ought the person of the magistrat be subject to the Kirk spiritually, and in ecclesiasticall government' would have been perfectly familiar to the compilers of the first Book of Discipline and was certainly not an invention of Andrew Melville's.[15]

The rejection of the distinct office of bishop does, however, appear at first glance to have been a more radical break with previous practice. The second Book of Discipline only accepts four offices in the kirk: 'the office of pastor, minister or bishop; the doctor; the presbyter or elder; and the deacon'. As to bishops, it declares 'they ar all ane with the ministers, as befoir declairit. For it is not a name of superioritie and lordship, bot of office and watching'. The first Book of Discipline, on the other hand, had proposed a form of superintendence in the church, based on the chief town of a neighbourhood. Ten or twelve such centres had been thought expedient and charge was to be given to the superintendents of such districts 'to plante and erect Kirkes, to set, order and appoint ministers ... to the countries that shall be appointed to their care where none are now'. In fact, because of financial constraints and political uncertainty only five superintendents were ever appointed although the greater part of the country was supervised by using ministers commissioned by the assembly for that purpose and by the utilization in a similar fashion of three conforming bishops whose duties, nevertheless, arose from powers conferred upon them by the assembly and not from their episcopal status. The exact status of the superintendent might, however, be questioned. It has been argued that the superintendent was in effect a godly bishop, that aversion to the title of bishop only arose because unreformed bishops still held office. Their personal status and prestige was certainly considerable, and contemporaries may have viewed them with the same awe that they would have accorded to a bishop. Some of the superintendents may have even thought of themselves in such a light and the remark at John Winram's election as superintendent of Fife in April 1561 that 'of Christ Jesus and of his apostolis we have command and exempill to appoynt men to sic chergis' is paralleled by the inscription on his tombstone which describes him as 'bishop of the people of Fife'. This equation of bishop with superintendent was also to be made by Erskine of Dun (superintendent of Angus) in November 1571, when at the height of the controversy over the nomination of bishops by the state, he declared that he understood 'a bishop and a superintendent to be but one office'.[16]

Within the terms of the agreement reached at Leith in early 1572, Erskine's statement was accurate; the superintendent, in common with the new-founded bishops, possessed administrative and disciplinary functions which in an episcopal system would have pertained to the bishop and were later in Scotland accorded to the presbytery. Initially the superintendent had exercised judicial functions in matters of divorce which if maintained would have paralleled the consistorial jurisdiction of episcopal courts; but these rights had been lost by 1563 and actions for adherence that superintendents continued to hear within their courts (which merely consisted of the kirk session of the chief town in their province) were of a disciplinary rather than of a judicial nature. Even the superintendent's administrative and disciplinary actions were, however, subject to the restraints of the conciliar system through which the reformers sought to organize the church. They were subject to correction by their fellow ministers and elders and the assembly regularly surveyed their attempts to carry out the policies it laid upon them and rebuked them if their success had been less than expected. It is hard to find any parallel between this mode of proceeding and similar proceedings in an episcopal church; hence the attempt to correlate superintendence with episcopacy, in any meaningful sense of the word, breaks down entirely in terms of spiritual authority. The superintendent had no sacramental powers in ordination or confirmation for the apostolic succession had been specifically renounced; spiritually the minister and superintendent were one. The agreement reached at Leith did not alter this situation; bishop and minister were still one. Here too the second Book of Discipline only restated accepted theory in more positive terms.[17]

In purely practical terms the device of exercising discipline and administrative functions through individuals who were themselves responsible to the courts of the church had not worked. Had the benefice structure been dissolved and a full complement of superintendents appointed, the office might well have persisted. As conceived the office was not a purely temporary measure to ensure that kirks were established and reformed ministers appointed, nor should it be regarded as an expedient pending succession to the bishoprics. On the other hand, the agreement reached at Leith was an expedient that allowed the church to retain the essential features of the office of superintendent and, by compromising their original plans for dissolving the benefices, obtaining instead succession to the existing bishoprics. Such a solution clearly left many problems outstanding and many people within the church still obviously hoped that they would eventually attain their original goal, but as an expedient the Leith settlement had much to commend it. There was equally an element of risk; the adoption of the title of bishop and the acceptance of the old diocesan boundaries was calculated to invest holders of the office with an even greater sense of importance than that enjoyed by the superintendents. In essence the system broke down, not on questions of principle, but for the very practical reason that the bishops by asserting their personal authority and defying that of the assembly created a situation in which the concilar nature of the church was in danger of being undermined. In consequence because the name 'has been abusit, and yit is likely to be', the distinct office of bishop, even within the strict limitations understood by the reformers, had to be abolished. The fears expressed by some in the kirk as early as 1572 had become a reality, and a new solution to the problem of exercising administrative and disciplinary functions had to be found.[18]

This was the one new problem that faced the compilers of the second Book of Discipline and significantly it was the one to which no immediate answer appeared to be forthcoming. With the benefit of hindsight the genesis of the presbytery, the court of the church that was eventually to fulfil the administrative and disciplinary duties previously upheld by superintendents and bishops, can be discerned in the concept of a common eldership between kirks. This device already operated in larger burghs in which ministers, elders and deacons from different districts met, and in terms of the second Book of Discipline, was to be paralleled in the country at large, so that 'thrie or four, ma or fewar, particular kirkis may have ane commoun eldarschip' to hear ecclesiastical cases. Had the idea been developed to its logical conclusion (which appears to have been the intention), individual kirk sessions might well have disappeared and so too might many of the parishes; in devising the scheme, the compilers of the second Book of Discipline may have had plans for a comprehensive reorganization of parochial boundaries. The creation of a common eldership was, however, the first priority and here a ready-made solution was often at hand with the common meetings known as the 'exercise', which were already held between ministers and elders of different districts for the interpretation of scripture. Their possible use was quickly spotted and by July 1579 the General Assembly had decided that 'the exercise may be judgit a presbyterie'. From there it was but a short step for the assembly to devise a scheme in October 1580 for establishing and constituting some fifty presbyteries from about 600 parishes. This resulted in the following year in a scheme for thirteen model presbyteries in the lowlands. The incompleteness of the scheme and the considerable number of parishes that they each contained did, however, mean an end to any plans for the abolition of individual kirk sessions and the conciliar structure of the church was thenceforth to embrace four courts ranging from the General Assembly through the synod to the presbytery and ultimately to the kirk session. The emergence of the presbytery was to possess great significance for the church, but the institutionalization of the rather loosely framed proposals of the second Book of Discipline owes as much, if not more, to ideas developing within the church after its compilation than to the contents of the book itself. Not for the first time the kirk was adopting new stratagems to meet changing circumstances; practical responses to the challenge from the former regent Morton, who had refused to ratify the second Book of Discipline, clarified their thinking and his final fall from power in 1581, and the seizure of the young king by the Ruthven raiders allowed the kirk to translate thoughts into action.[19]

Edinburgh presbytery was functioning by May 1581 and at Stirling a presbytery was formally constituted on 8 August; the others quickly followed. Elders appointed for life according to the second Book of Discipline, attended some of these early presbyteries, although a marked reluctance to do so appears to have materialized at a fairly early stage. These developments were checked, however, by the king's escape in June 1583 and under the direction of James Stewart, earl of Arran, the administration in 1584 passed the Black Acts reaffirming episcopal authority and subjecting the church to crown and parliament. With the exception of kirk sessions, convocations of ministers were not to be allowed to meet without the king's consent and it was stressed that this provision was especially directed at 'that form lately invented in this land, called the presbytery'. Melville and other prominent presbyterians found it provident to leave for England, and this had for the time being the effect of allaying opposition. Nevertheless, the king's situation was politically unstable and within two years compromise had again to be reached with the church. In 1586, the Black Acts were modified to allow the continuance of presbyteries with, however, the retention of the office of titular bishop but also with an affirmation of the rights of synods and General Assemblies to deal with ecclesiastical causes. Gradually the position envisaged by the presbyterians came nearer to realization; by 1593 some forty-seven presbyteries existed at least on paper and were formally recognized by the assembly. As they became established, they gradually usurped the duties technically pertaining to the bishops and presentations to benefices were increasingly directed in their direction. This increase in business may have discouraged elders from resuming their seats in these courts and although some presbyteries such as that of Edinburgh continued to encourage elders to join in their deliberations, these attempts appear to have been unsuccessful. The dominance of the presbytery was, nevertheless, assured and final victory seemed to have been secured by the crown's acceptance of the new ecclesiastical organization in the so-called 'Golden' Act of 1592. If hidden threats to the future were contained in the reaffirmation of the crown's rights in calling assemblies of the church, this was not apparent at the time; the wishes of the crown on ecclesiastical polity had been thwarted and even if the total division of church and state envisaged in the second Book of Discipline had not been achieved, the future of the presbyterian church must have seemed assured.[20]

Although, after three decades of doubt, the polity of the church seemed at last secured, it is interesting to note that no such conflict or ambiguity had surrounded the ordering of the congregational courts. Even before the Reformation was effected, the reformed privy kirks possessed a rudimentary organization at a congregational level. Elders and deacons had been appointed to conduct their affairs in association with the minister and this example was followed elsewhere as further reformed congregations were established in the months following the victory of the reformers. In some areas, however, kirk sessions were not to be established until the seventeenth century and one of the expected advantages of the scheme of common eldership advocated by the second Book of Discipline would have been to take care of a situation in which kirk sessions either did not exist because there was no minister or where established sessions failed to operate and discipline was unexercised in consequence. With an eye to these changes, the character of the office of elder, and deacon, was also redefined. The first Book of Discipline had ruled that 'the electioun of elderis and deaconis aught to be used everie yeare once ... least that by long continuance of such officiaris, men presume upoun the libertie of the Churche'. By 1578, however, the second Book of Discipline could declare that the office was perpetual: 'elderis anis lawfully callit to the office and having gifts of God meit to exercise the name may not leive it again'. This proposal, it has been argued, differed only in detail and not in principle from that enunciated in 1560, for in practice elders had been continued for many years, and then after the second Book of Discipline, annual elections or more frequently elections at irregular intervals remained a feature of the system. Elders, according to the first Book of Discipline were indisputably laymen, but from the second book it is possible to assert that the elder's office was an order in the ministry, because it was defined as 'a spirituall function, as is the ministrie'. Outwardly, however, the eldership remained a lay office, though it is not easy to resolve actuality with the statement of the second book. Perhaps it is not necessary to do so; it was in essence a device, which many learned arguments on the nature of the eldership have tended to obscure, to bridge the gap between the desirability of having elders present in the General Assembly and the requirement that 'nane or subject to repaire to this assemble to vot bot ecclesiastical persons'. The underlying concept of the elder's office remained basically the same. Deacons, on the other hand, were to be more restricted in their functions; whereas the first Book of Discipline had allowed that deacons whose duties were essentially financial might 'also assist in judgement with the Ministers and Elders', the second Book of Discipline maintained that the duty was purely financial. In this instance, however, practice in some churches decreed otherwise; in a few, such as St Andrews, disciplinary cases were heard by a session that included deacons, and in many instances deacons continued to assist at communion. Once again theory and practice were frequently poles apart.[21]

This was equally true of the qualifications expected of those who exercised the duties of the eldership, for the requirement of the second Book of Discipline that elders should be 'men of judgement and habilitie' tended to be equated with the selection of 'men of best social standing' while goodness and judgment became synonymous with rank and wealth. A comparison between those who were elders and those who were deacons of the St Andrews kirk session between 1559 and 1600 shows that whereas lairds, merchants and master craftsmen were prominent among the elders, the diaconate was drawn almost exclusively from guildsmen and tenants. This social distinction between elders and deacons is also exemplified in the holding of civil appointments within the burgh, as a considerable number of the elders were bailies but only a handful of deacons aspired to this office. Thus, although deacons and elders were initially equal in status as members of the session, and deacons could at first fulfil the same duties as elders and even officiate at communion, their office was certainly regarded as socially inferior to that of the eldership; this was to be further accentuated when the duties of the deacons were gradually restricted to those of administration.[22]

Even among the elders, however, social distinctions can be observed. Tenants and guildsmen appear to have been fairly equally represented on the kirk session of St Andrews and a considerable proportion also came from the university. This representation apart, however, St Andrews appears to have been fairly typical of other burghs in which the actual power was invariably divided between lairds and guildsmen. The influence of the lairds was not so obviously apparent in rural parishes in which tenants and small proprietors constituted the eldership, but it is difficult to believe that the wishes of the local lairds carried no weight in decisions of the session. As in the burghs the ability of the lairds to influence the nominal elections to the eldership may have been decisive. If election in theory lay with the parishioners, selection rather than election appears to have been more common practice, the right of the congregation being restricted to a right to object to nominees. Thus at Elgin in 1593 'the minister maid nominatioun of the names of all the eldaris that ar to be chosin publictlie upoun Sondaye nixt in presens of the hail auditoris for this yeir . . . quho desyrit to undirstand gif thair wes ony occasioun lauchful to be schawin quhy thei nocht beir that office and nothing being proponit or opponit in the contrar the minister proceidit to the nominatioun of the deacones'. The clearest indication of the closed nature of the session and its almost unchanging composition comes, however, from St Andrews in 1595 when the election proceeded in the following manner:

> Maister Androw Melvill, Rectour of the Universite, and remanent membris thairof, quha wer elderis this last yeir removit, the haill remanent sessioun remaning be voting electit elderis of thame that was removit, quhilk being done, thai enterit agane in sessioun; and eftir four or fyve brethering elderis and deaconis being removit, the remanent sessioun remaining electit and chusit elderis and deaconis, quhill the haill number of the brethering passit throche. And thaireftir the haill bretherng of sessioun being togidder at ane tyme, the personis nominat of new to stand in electioun being red in presens of the haill sessioun, the sessioun be voting electit elderis and deaconis to be adjonit with the rest now electit, to stand for this yeir in to cum.

In some respects, this closely parallels the election of town councils at which, by rather similar methods, continuity of personnel was assured. Aberdeen provides another example of this practice in 1605. There the elders and deacons of the session were 'nominat and chosin be the sessioun of the yeir prceeding' and having undergone public censure they accepted office and gave their oaths 'for faithfull administratioun of thir officies for the yeir to cum'.[23]

Privilege and position may have been required to obtain a seat in the session, but that in itself was not always sufficient to defend an offending elder from receiving the same punishment as he may have meted out to others. In 1598, for example, an elder accused of adultery was found unworthy 'to bruik the office of eldership' and ordered 'to stand in the porch dur bare hedit and bair futtit with seck clothe, betuix the secund and thrid bell, and then on the penitent stule, and to continew during the will of the session'. However, on occasion, influence and status does seem to have swayed the issue and the ordained punishment have been tempered in consequence. Thus, in December 1585, James Douglas, provost of Elgin and an elder, having been found guilty of fornication declared himself willing to accept the censures and commands of his fellow elders, but at the same time reminded them that repentance 'consistit not in the externall gestour of the bodie or publict place appoynit for the samyn but in the hart, of the quhilk he had God and his own conscience giving him witness'. He therefore asked that he might remain in 'his awn place the tyme of preaching and the sermon' and to appear simply before the minister to declare confession of his sin and his penitent state of mind. The elders after hearing this good advice accepted his argument and, 'hoping alwayis for a bettir example of him in tymes to come grantit the samin and to declair his uprycht mening ordanit him to repair the North Windok foryain the pulpit sufficientlie with glass quhilk the same James acceptit'. If punishment of a kind had been imposed, and in this respect justice had been done, it was nevertheless clear that the status of the offender had probably carried more weight than his arguments.[24]

Moral lapses were punished as they arose, but elders and deacons were also subject to the censure of their fellows at the privy-censuring. In the early days of the Reformation this censuring took place at congregational meetings held for that purpose. In 1566 the communicants of the Canongate parish were given such an opportunity, the minister, elders and deacons submitting themselves to 'the judgments of their brethren and the censorse of the kirk'. Criticisms on this occasion were few but an elder and a deacon were admonished 'to wait bettir upon thair vocation'. Such inquisitions before the congregation were still in vogue at Aberdeen in in 1574 when the session ordered the minister to charge 'all and sundrie within this toun to compeir on the nixt Assembly day to try and examin the lyffes of the minister, elders and dyaconis and to lay to thair charge sik thingis as thai know to be sklanderis to the kirk'. Somewhat later, however, such occasions seem to have been restricted to those who were actually members of the session. The minister and the more prominent members of the session were removed individually, others in groups, when complaints were invited. Among the faults found against the elders of St Andrews in May 1596, it is recorded that one 'payis na thing to the contributione of the puir'; another was accused that 'he, being an elder, suld be in company with thame that brak upe the tolbuth dur and electit the counsell' in time of sermon, while yet another was urged to 'mend his rasche speking in the sessioun'. Admonition was usually deemed to be sufficient, but later that year one of the deacons was removed from the session because he was 'inobedient to the magistrates and an evill payer of his dettis'.[25]

In the hands of this body, which contained its own share of human frailty, lay the task of assisting the minister in all public affairs of the kirk. Included in this was the punishment of moral lapses, especially those not normally punishable by civil courts. If the reformers would have welcomed the support of the secular authorities in this respect, they did themselves assume the right of fining and excommunicating offenders against their authority. Moreover, if the civil courts never obtained the statutory powers that they had sought, the support of magistrates in towns, in which many of the bailies tended to be elders, could be counted upon in cases of exceptional difficulties. Thus at St Andrews in 1569 in the case of two relapsed fornicators, the session 'referrit the punition of them to the magistratis' while on another occasion the course of justice was made even speedier by committing an offender into the hands of the bailies present in session 'to be civilie correckit and punist'. Punishment was not always restricted to imprisonment. In 1601 at Elgin, Eduard Alcorne and his two sons were committed to the steiple 'quhil they be beltit for thair gryt enormiteis and play at prophane pastymes on the Sabbath the tyme of preaching'. The exercise of discipline in this manner brought an involvement between church and society that has never been surpassed. The indifference of the pre-Reformation church had been replaced by an intense interest in the lives of each individual member of society. The moral transgressor may have resented the interference of the session, but even the most intractable and stubborn was made to accept its authority and on occasions even amity could result. Thus at St Andrews in 1596 after James Smyth and John Welved had declared that 'thei had na hetred maleis nor invy againis nane of the memberis of this sessioun nor counsell', those who were present rose up 'and with thair hartis foirgave all men and tuik every persoun in the session be the hand in feir of God and luif'. This incident, more than all the institutional changes envisaged in either of the Books of Discipline, characterized the spirit in which worship in the reformed church was conducted.[26]

7
Worship

If the reformers' complaints about the 'distancing' of church from people in pre-Reformation times were to be met and overturned then it was by drawing the populace into church affiliation, into regular church attendance, into a sympathetic and supportive attachment to their ministers that this could be achieved. For these reasons emphasis was placed upon the parish, and it is only by an examination and analysis of progress made in this respect in all parts of the country that the success or failure of the new church in gaining the attachment of the people at large can be judged.

The reformers expected that Divine Service in principal burghs at least would be conducted on week-days as well as on Sundays, although not unnaturally the principal services were held on the latter. In many towns, a daily service was held by a reader and usually took the form of 'common prayers with some exercise of reading the scriptures'. The appointment of Thomas Duncanson as reader at Stirling in October 1560 was on condition that he read the common prayers once a day and twice on Sabbath. In Glasgow in 1595 the session ordered prayers to be read at seven in the morning in the High Kirk and at five in the evening in the New Kirk. The hours of daily service probably altered with the season and in Edinburgh the town council instructed the keepers of the church of St Giles to open the doors of the kirk at seven in the morning in winter and five in summer and to shut them again at four in winter and six in summer. This service consisted also of the singing of psalms and the reading of chapters of Holy Scripture; these were taken systematically. It is possible that the psalms too were sung according to a set consequence. The exact form that such services took is not entirely clear, but in 1597 the kirk session of St Andrews ordered their reader, Robert Zuill, 'to reid every day, morn and evin, except the dayis of publict teacheing, ane chaptour of the New Testament and ane uther of the auld befoir none, begynand at Genesis and Mathow with ane prayer befoir and eftir, and evining sum psalmes with ane prayer befoir and eftir'. Attendance at daily service was not obligatory and if work was not suspended during the hours of common prayers, no-one was to be hindered from coming. At Elgin in 1599 it was enacted that: 'Na persone or personis (except fishar sellaris and cadegaris [fish dealers]) remain in the fishe mercatt the tyme of prayeris, nor yitt that na man or woman be vagand on the streittis, idlie sittand under stairis, nor at pastyme on the calsaye [causeway] under the paynis of 6s 8d.' Attendances would, however, be inflated in other ways and in St Andrews in 1583 the poor bedesmen were instructed to 'keep the prayaris ilk day'.[1]

In addition to the daily reading of the common prayers, the Reformers advocated that there should be 'one day beside the Sunday appointed to the Sermon and Prayers'. In many places it was customary to have two days, usually Wednesday and Friday, assigned as preaching days. These services were taken by the minister for readers were strictly forbidden to preach, although even at these services the reader may have been associated with the reading of prayers and scripture. It was originally intended, however, that common prayers should not be said in conjunction with the sermon on such occasions, but while this may have been followed for a time, it soon became the custom to read prayers on the preaching day as well as on others. The first Edinburgh edition of the Book of Common Order published in 1562, which officially displaced the English Book of Common Prayer, contained a prayer of intercession which was to be said after the sermon on a Wednesday; in the following year an order of the privy council relating to the repair of parish churches associated their use with 'the preaching of the Word of God, ministration of the Sacraments and reading of the common prayers'. At St Andrews in 1597 it was concluded by the session that the sermon should begin at eight hours on Wednesday and Friday and should be 'endit by nyne houris, prayeris and all, or thairabout'. More strenuous efforts were made to ensure that attendance was maintained on these preaching days. The bedesmen at St Andrews were also expected to attend the sermon, likewise at Perth where citizens in receipt of alms from the session were evidently excused daily prayers but were required to be present on Sundays and on the preaching day. Abstention from work was required, although this was not always easily achieved. At Perth the session, when it discovered that merchants were remaining in their booths and tradesmen continuing in their employment and thereby absenting themselves from the Thursday sermon invoked the aid of the dean of guild and the deacons of the incorporated trades to charge their members 'that every Thursday, which is the ordinary day of preaching, they should leave the exercise of their own calling for that time of preaching and frequent the kirk'.[2]

Whatever the success of such endeavours, even more strenuous efforts were made to ensure attendance on Sundays. The service itself was an amalgamation of the weekday services offered by the reader and minister. After the ringing of a warning bell some half-hour before the commencement of worship, a second bell marked the beginning of the reader's service. Thereafter the reader read the scriptures, certain of the prayers, and led the congregation in the singing of metrical psalms. The close of this part of the service, which lasted about an hour, was marked by the ringing of a third bell, during which the minister entered the pulpit and began by offering a prayer. A psalm was sung, followed by another prayer and thereafter he preached the sermon. This was followed by another prayer, the Creed, another prayer and the Benediction. This part of the service followed the Book of Geneva, which was the form of worship drawn up for the use of the English congregation at Frankfurt in 1555. Nothing is said about the reading of scripture in this part of the service although this almost certainly preceded the sermon in which the minister, as advocated by the first Book of Discipline, interpreted the chosen passage. Ministers were not always free, however, to select their own subject matter. If the elders at Perth in 1586 only asked the minister to leave his 'ordinary text' and choose some part of the scripture likely to move the hearts of the people, the kirk session of St Andrews, in a much more positive fashion enacted that the minister should proceed in preaching of the second book of Samuel and book of Kings following.[3]

The second service on the Lord's Day was usually held in the afternoon and part of this at least was usually reserved for catechizing. This was in accordance with the first Book of Discipline which stated that:

> After noon must the young children be publictlie examined in their Catechisme in audience of the pepill, in doing whairof the Minister

> must tak gret deligence, alsweill to cause the Pepill to understand the questiones proposed as the ansueris, and the doctrine that may be collected thairof

The catechism referred to was Calvin's, which was bound into editions of the Book of Common Order. Other catechisms that came into use thereafter included that of Heidelberg and *the Little Catechism or the manner to examine children before they be admitted to the Supper of the Lord and the Form of Examination before the communion* drawn up by John Craig. Catechizing became so much a part of the Sunday afternoon services, that this second diet was sometimes called 'the catechisms'. So much importance was indeed placed upon it that in 1580 the General Assembly ordered that such a diet was to be held in every church. In this manner the Scottish people became familiar with the doctrine and beliefs of the reformed church.[4]

This was also achieved in other ways. For example parliament enacted in 1579 that:

> All gentilmen houshaldaris and utheris worth thrie hundreth merkis of yeirlie rent or abone and all substantious yemen or burgesses likewise houshauldaris estemit worth fyve hundreth punds in landis or guidis be haldin to have a bible and psalme buke in vulgare language in thair houssis ffor the better instructioun of themselffis and thair fameliis in the knowledge of god within yeir and day after the dait heirof ilk persone undir the pane of ten pundis.

This enactment was not a dead letter as, following upon its provisions, the town council of Edinburgh ordered all citizens to obtain the books, while in 1591 the kirk session of Elgin ordered persons covered by the act to produce their psalm books and have them noted by the clerk of their assembly. In order to facilitate the printing of the Bible, subscriptions were taken in advance through money obtained from parochial collections. Even then printing was slow and in 1576 a further nine months was eventually allowed to the printer who promised at the end of it to deliver the books 'bund in blak and claspit' to every parish that had subscribed. Demand was such that private enterprise was sometimes encouraged to meet the need. The offence of an Edinburgh printer, Thomas Bassendine, was not only that he had printed psalters without licence of the magistrate or revising of the Kirk, but also that at the end of the psalm book was to be found 'ane baudie song callit Welcum Fortoun' – a secular love song on which a hymn was based in *Gude and Godlie Ballads*, of which the wrong version may have been printed. Religious censorship and control was to be steadily exercised in the future and it was in this manner that the church was not only to protect its official viewpoint, but also to promote it throughout the kingdom.[5]

The great emphasis laid upon attendance at both Sunday services meant that every effort was made to ensure that no possible diversions existed that might detain the congregation from their parochial duties. At Aberdeen the town council insisted on church attendance by the burgesses, their wives and families, and in 1598 drew up a tariff of fines to be levied on defaulters, the husband being responsible for his wife and the master for his servant. In the burgh of the Canongate the prevalence of drinking resulted in brewers and tapsters of ale being forbidden to permit 'any maner of person ... to drink keip companye at table in commoun tavennarris or houssis upon Sondaye the tyme of preiching' under the penalty of a forty shilling fine. Similar enactments appear at St Andrews where in 1595 the elders and deacons of each quarter of the town were instructed to note all who were absent from the sermon in 'taveronis, aill-houssis, caichpellis and utheris partis' and report the transgressers to the session. As at Aberdeen, masters were held responsible for their servants and punished for their offences. Fines payable to the 'box of the puir' were frequently levied, but at Glasgow a piper, Mungo Craig, was threatened with excommunication if he should 'playe on his pypes on the Sondaye fra the sunne rysing quhill the sunn goinge to'. Banishment might also be threatened and at St Andrews in 1600 Bessie Miln, after confessing to 'hir braking the Sabath day', agreed to her own banishment if she committed the offence again. Recalcitrants were often dealt with by the civil authorities. At Elgin James Roy, who was accused of 'playing this last Sunday upon his gryit pyip at aftirnone in tyme of preaching', was not only to stand in haircloth and make public repentence, but also to 'remane in the stepill till he find caution to do so'. At St Andrews five men who were imprisoned by the magistrates for three hours for 'vagand in tyme of sermone on the Sabath day' were warned that sterner punishment would follow if the offence was repeated. The offences committed by inhabitants of the burgh on this score were numerous and the various charges included playing in the golf-fields, 'playing at the golf eftir nune', 'playing and casting the hammer', 'laying out skynnis to dry', selling flesh, threshing corn and, most frequent of all, absence from church. Many who attended services may have done so for fear of the session and the stool of repentance and some of the more reluctant worshippers were obviously anxious to leave church as soon as the opportunity arose. The problem of preventing members of the congregation rushing out of church before the Benediction was pronounced attracted the attention of several kirk sessions. At Glasgow in 1587, such offenders were to be censured while at Perth the session instructed that the bailies and elders were to guard the kirk doors and prevent all but those who were sick or 'evil at ease' from leaving before the blessing. A fine of 6s. 8d. was imposed at Elgin in 1596 on those who were guilty of this offence. At St Andrews too offenders were to be reported to the session and among the many crimes of which Alexander Wilsoun was accused in 1593 were 'playing on the Sabbath, extraordinar drinking and dinging of his wyffe' and 'passing furth of the kirk befuir the blessing be gevin aftir sermone'. Nevertheless, a new enthusiasm for church-going can be detected as the century progressed and in St Andrews in 1600 it could be recorded that upon the 'Saboth day aftir nune, in this sumer seasoun, the peopill convenis sud frequentlie to the preaching that the kirk may nocht conventientlie contene thame'. In consequence other arrangements had to be made for additional services.[6]

The new-found involvement with the church can also be seen in the central act of the reformed faith – the communion service. In the pre-Reformation period the partaking of this sacrament had been increasingly restricted to Easter and as a reaction against this the early reformers had advocated more frequent communion. Practical considerations militated against this and the General Assembly decreed in 1562 that communion was to be administered four times a year in burghs and twice a year in rural parishes. These guidelines were seldom observed; in the sixteenth century the chronic shortage of ministers made it impossible in some areas while in others ministers neglected this sacrament altogether. In Edinburgh in 1574 it was alleged that the 'Table of the Lord has not this long time past been ministered'. The kirk session of Perth in 1583 decided to have only two celebrations each year. The fixing of the dates for the celebration of communion was equally erratic, but economic and sometimes personal considerations clearly influenced the choice. At Elgin in 1591 the session decreed that the service was to be held when leisure may be had at the issue of the barley seed; two years later they sounded the opinion of 'the greatest number of honest men ... in respect of the busy time of the year'. At Anstruther in 1592 it was to be 'before the people go the fishing'.[7]

In their insistence that the Sacrament of the Lord's Supper was a feast rather than a sacrifice – a belief which departed not only from catholic practice but also from the viewpoint of many of their protestant associates in Germany – the reformers laid stress upon the corporate action of the participants and to this end communion was administered by ministers and elders to the communicants sitting around a table covered with a white cloth in the manner of the Last Supper. In this respect their critic Ninian Winzet argued that the reformers were not following the scriptural guidelines that they had adopted as their standard. Objections were not only raised to the historicity of the cloth but also to the role of elders in distributing the elements, the argument being that the minister in the manner of their Saviour was alone to be entrusted with that action. The pre-Reformation practice of morning communion was – inconsistently, argues Winzet – retained and celebrations began at a very early hour. At Glasgow the service started at four in the morning; at Stirling it was half-an-hour earlier and at Elgin the first bell rang an hour earlier than that. In Edinburgh servants and 'sic utheris that plessis to cum' were expected to attend a service which began at four a.m., with ministration of communion one hour later, reaching its conclusion at seven a.m. A second service began at nine a.m., with ministration again one hour later, in order to finish before noon.[8]

The service itself followed 'the manner of the administration of the Lord's Supper' contained in the Book of Common Order and began with a reading of the warrant, followed by an exhortation which was an invitation to the Lord's Supper and excluded from the table all unworthy persons who lived contrary to the word of God. The exhortation finished with the doxology and thereafter, with the communicants already seated, the minister left the pulpit to consecrate the bread and wine; the prayer of consecration was followed by a prayer of thanksgiving and the doxology. The bread was then distributed by the minister and elders to the communicants who divided and distributed it among themselves. The cup was then passed from hand to hand. As the people were communicating, passages of the scriptures 'which may bring in mind the death of Christ Jesus and the benefit of the same' were read by the minister. As each company retired from the table, they were dismissed with a blessing, and another group took their place; it was customary for a psalm to be sung by the congregation. After the last table had been served, the closing prayers were offered by the minister. The service ended with the singing of a psalm and the benediction.[9]

The elders, although not mentioned in this respect in the Book of Common Order, played an important part in assisting the minister at the administration of the sacrament. If this practice was not a part of the elder's duties by right, it quickly became accepted usage. In the Canongate church in 1564, four men were appointed by the minister to serve at the communion, 'thai berand office'. At St Andrews in 1596 nine men were chosen 'to servie the taball with bred and wyne', only one of whom was an elder while eight were deacons. In 1598/99, half of the elders and deacons were selected to serve 'the tabill the first Saboth and the remanent the next Saboth'. This assistance was much needed, for the congregation of St Andrews had over three thousand communicants. This and the necessity of finishing before noon also explains the need for ministrations on two successive Sundays. At Edinburgh as early as 1574 the inhabitants resident in different quarters of the town communicated on different days. At Anstruther in 1592, when all present could not be served 'befoir twell hours' they were told to be patient till 'ye next day that sall be fund meitest'. By the seventeenth century, celebration over three Sundays was not unknown, but when the minister of Campsie applied to the presbytery of Glasgow in 1594 for such an extension he was ordered to content himself with 'the said twa Sondayes . . . and to lippen [ask] for na mae Sondayes togidder but onlie the said twa'.[10]

The elements used at the Lord's Supper were bread and wine. Communion was administered in both kinds and, in returning the cup to the people, the use of a common cup or cups – to which Winzet also objected 'sen our Saviour useit ane breid and ane coupe' – was a visible sign of equality between all communicants. The medieval custom of using unleavened bread was continued in some areas, but in others ordinary bread was used. Unleavened bread usually took the form of shortbread and was particularly popular in the south-west of Scotland. Elsewhere leavened wheaten bread was used, but early accounts relate only to the quantity purchased and to the price rather than to its quality or nature. At Edinburgh in 1561 'twa duzzon of breid price ye pece 14d were purchased for the first communion', and for the second and third communion at each '8 dozen of breid'. The wine used appears to have been chiefly claret and the considerable quantity used may have been to demonstrate visibly the restoration of the cup to the people. At Knox's three communions in Edinburgh in 1560 no less than twenty-three gallons were consumed at a cost of £11. 14s and in 1578 for one sacrament Sunday alone, no less than twenty-three gallons costing £41.[11]

There is, however, apparently no connection between the quantity of wine consumed and the riotous behaviour of the communicants at some celebrations of the Lord's Supper, because parishioners in the medieval church appear to have exhibited the same tendencies. At Stirling in 1597 the session took the congregation to task for the 'great misordur amongis the pepill of this congregatione at the last ministratione of the Lord's Supper, in rash and suddan cuming to the tabill, in spilling of the wyne, and in thrusting and shouting in thair passage out at the Kirk dur aftir the ministratione'. In future the people were to be 'admonishit to use thame selfis mair reverentlie'. This is curiously reminiscent of the plea made in 1559 in the Godlie Exhortation:

> Thole nocht your parochianaris to cum to this blyssit sacrament misorderlie. But put them in order be your ministeris before the altare, and require tham to heir yaw reid the afore wrytten exhortation, without noysse or din, and to sit styll swa in devotioun with devote hert and mynde, quhill they be ordourlie servit of the said blyssit sacrament.[12]

In many places the 'mixed chalice' or the mixing of the wine with water was a practice carried over from the pre-Reformation church. As far as can be ascertained the actual mixing took place before the service began. In Edinburgh churches the cost of the elements was borne by the burgh treasurer, but in other places the pre-Reformation practice, which placed the onus on the 'parson' of the parish, continued and was in fact reaffirmed by an act of parliament in 1572. Henry Sinclair, the unreformed bishop of

Ross who was also 'parson' of Glasgow, had in the latter capacity no scruples about providing bread and wine 'to the halie communion' of the reformed church. His successor as parson, Alexander Lawder, had other thoughts, however, and 'being lauchfullie requirit to furneis and ministrat breid and wyne at the ministratioun of the communioun' refused to do so. Difficulties were also encountered in obtaining suitable communion vessels for most such objects had been seized at the Reformation. Individuals frequently appropriated them to their own use and town councils sold them for a variety of purposes. At Stirling in 1561 two silver chalices were sold and the money spent in repairing the streets; at Edinburgh part of the return from selling the silver work of St Giles was used for the 'reparation and decoring of the kirk'. Elsewhere the returns were appropriated to more general purposes. The upshot was the same as far as the reformed church was concerned. Denied the use of their predecessors' communion plate they were forced to fall back on wooden or pewter platers and mazers or loving cups. Winzet's gibe that the reformers were forced to use 'basins and cups furth of any prophane taveroun' has no doubt its origin in this dilemma.[13]

Those who wished to communicate had to obtain a ticket or token from the session before they were allowed to do so. Tokens were distributed by elders and deacons in the various districts for which they were responsible, but where examinations and preparatory services were held, the tokens were handed out after these meetings. Tickets might be refused for a variety of reasons. At St Andrews in 1598/99 it was decreed that 'na tiquotis be gevin to sic as hes nocht payit thair pairt of the contribution to the puir'. Debarment through refusal of tokens might also result from lack of knowledge of basic reformed tenets and in 1595 the St Andrews session enacted:

> It is statut that na persoun be admittit to the communioun, but sic as confessis the treuth with us, and subtractis nocht thame selfis from precheing and catichising; and that can say the Lord his Prayer and Ten Commandimentis, and that can ansour to the questiouns of the Litill Catechisme.

Such examinations usually took place a week or so before the communion. The examination in Edinburgh in 1573 was on the Tuesday afternoon preceding communion: any who failed to present themselves and their household as requested were debarred from the communion or fined. Those who failed their test might on occasion be granted a special trial and in some cases those who failed were admitted to communion if they could find a surety who would guarantee that the defaulter would make the grade by the next communion. The most common cause of exclusion from the table was, however, moral turpitude. In 1573 the General Assembly ruled that any guilty of drunkenness who disregarded the church's warning should be excluded. Six years later it decided to debar such people who 'after admonitioun will pass to May playes'. Butchers and others in St Andrews who broke the Sabbath by trading were threatened with exclusion from communion. Such misdemeanours warranted the lesser excommunication and in this respect were regarded in a somewhat different category from those who were refused a token for the offence of failing to pay ecclesiastical dues or through ignorance of basic Christian doctrine.[14]

Those excluded from communion may have been unaware of the nicety of this distinction and failure to receive a token or ticket was dreaded by most. Counterfeit or 'fengyeit tikatis' were not unknown and at St Andrews in 1583 a young tailor, Andrew Brown, was accused of presenting himself to the Lord's Table, 'he nocht being at examinatioun, nocht resavand ane tikket, bot he his maisteris tikket'. On occasions the kirk had to be searched for intruders who had hidden in the church after morning prayers and hoped thereby to participate in the communion service. In most cases lack of a token meant exclusion from the church, but in Dunfermline and possibly a few other churches it was the space around the communion table that was not to be entered by the tokenless parishioner. Every effort was made by the ministers and kirk sessions to keep sinners from the communion table. In the final resort recourse lay in the 'fencing of the tables' by the minister. This was a final challenge to the conscience of the communicant who was warned in no uncertain terms of the dire consequences of communicating while unfit to do so. Those who took communion must also have attended the whole service and the reformers would not allow anyone to communicate who had not heard the immediately preceding service. In such ways the reformed kirk and the ministers defended the purity of the sacrament of the Lord's Table.[15]

In the last resort persistent offenders might be threatened with the greater excommunication, which not only declared the offender to be 'separated and cuttit of from the congregacion and misticall body of Christ Jesus, and all benefitis of his trew Kirk (the hearying of Goddis Word only except); delivering hymn oneto sathan, for the distruccion of the flesche, that the spirit may be saved in the daye of the Lord', but also enacted 'that none of the faythful fearyng God, fra this hour furth, accumpany with hymn in commonyng, talkyn, bying, selling, eating drynkyn or other way quhatsoever, except that be appoynted of the Kyrk for his amendment'. Punishment invariably followed non-compliance with these injunctions, and an Elgin elder was made to confess his fault, which, he rather ingeniously claimed, had arisen through accompanying the corpse of an excommunicate person 'not altogidder villinglie but rather accidentlie'. Even close relations were debarred from the company of an excommunicate and in 1604 Arthur Settoun was admonished by the session of Aberdeen that he should not 'intercommon with Maister Alexander Settoun, his brother's sone, an excommunicant papist nor resave him in his house, kep companie, eating or drinking with him in tymes cumming'.[16]

Withdrawal of the right to communicate in such circumstances was readily defensible, but doubts were at times expressed about the failure of the reformed church to make provision for communion for the sick and dying. Winzet with his usual perceptiveness enquired how it was that:

> Ane faithful man haveard na uthir impediment, bot wantand cumpanie to communicat with him sacramentalie, may nocht resave that sacrament him allane, without errour or idolatrie. Quhou can he be him allane, sa lang as he is a membre of Christis Kirk?

To constitute a true sacrament the reformers believed that its administration must be celebrated in a parish church and not in private. In the pre-Reformation period Knox and other reformers had celebrated communion in private houses, but this was forbidden after 1560 and reconfirmed by an act of the General Assembly in 1581. Similar objections were raised to private baptism which, as the only other sacrament recognized by the reformed church, had also to be administered in the parish church at the time of the public preaching. To allow exceptions seemed to admit some justification for the catholic doctrine that baptism was a necessary preliminary to human salvation. Whereas the pre-Reformation church had admitted the validity of lay baptism in exceptional circumstances, no such latitude was allowed by the reformers. Several ministers who baptized in private were severely disciplined; in 1580 the General Assembly ordered the 'brethren of the Exercise of Edinburgh' to deal with Thomas Cranstoun, minister of Ashkirk, who had baptized bairns and preached in private houses; in the following year Alexander Forrester, minister of Tranent, who had baptized an infant in a private house for which offence he had been suspended, was only restored to office on condition that he made public repentance in his parish church.[17]

Parents desiring baptism for their children had to be able to repeat the Lord's Prayer and the Apostles' Creed, and in some instances a knowledge of the Ten Commandments was also required. According to the Book of Discipline every church was to have a basin for baptisms and it appears that these took the place of fonts, which had been previously used. Insistence on the ceremony taking place on a preaching day was only relaxed in very special circumstances, but exceptions were made from time to time along the lines laid down at Perth in 1584 where it was decreed that another day might be possible if 'the midwyff deponit on hir conscience the bairne war waik'. The normal insistence upon preaching days did cause problems, however, as feasting and celebrating after the baptism was inappropriate on Sundays. In 1581 parliament enacted that banquets after the baptising of bairns were prohibited, but the alternative policy of ensuring baptisms took place during the weekday-preaching service was probably wiser. In Edinburgh in 1592 baptisms were to take place only on Thursdays at half-past eight, while at St Andrews in 1597 the sacrament was to be 'ministered in tymes cuming upon Weddinsday and Friday', although at both some latitude was to be allowed at the minister's discretion.[18]

The ceremony, which followed the order of baptism as expressed in the book of Common Order, was relatively simple as the reformers had rejected 'spattil, salt, candill, cuide [the chrisom used in baptism] (except it be to keape the barne from cald), hardis, oyle and the rest of the Papisticall inventions'. After his sermon, the minister remained where he had preached and the father, or some other godly man if the father was unavoidably absent, presented the child to be baptized. A short prayer was followed by a short exhortation on the nature of the sacrament and the duties in which it involved the parents or godfathers. Whoever presented the child had then to make his own confession of faith and promise to bring up the child accordingly; the child was then baptized by sprinkling with water and the minister ended public worship with various prayers and dismissed the congregation with the blessing.[19]

One striking feature of the baptismal service is that godfathers (who were later to be discouraged) were very much in evidence. Indeed it seems that godmothers too had not been entirely unknown in the earliest days of the Reformation for Winzet enquired of the reformers 'Quhy hald ye godmotheris in the beginning and now repellis the samin?' No answer to this question was forthcoming, but godfathers continued and indeed multiplied as the years went by. Nevertheless, it is quite clear that in normal circumstances it was the duty of the father not only to present his child for baptism but also to hold it in his arms before the pulpit. The role of the godfather was that of a witness and they are frequently referred to as such. At St Andrews in 1584 it was decreed that:

> in all tymes cuming, witnes, that salbe advertisit and warnit be the parentis to the baptisme of the barnis, sall sitt still in their awin places, quhairin thai salbe in for the tyme in the kirk; and none to stand up tyme of baptisme bot the parent and father of the barne haldand up his awin barne him selfe onlie, except tua or thre witnes at the maist.

The problem was not theological but rather one of space. At Aberdeen in 1622 where it was claimed that the number of godfathers had risen to twelve or sixteen whereas in former times it had been the custom to invite 'only tua godfatheris at the most', it was conceded that 'thair can not be places gottin to the godfatheris to sitt upon' and unedifying wrangles had taken place in consequence.[20]

Unseemly behaviour might also characterize wedding ceremonies, and here too problems faced the reformed church. Some measure of continuity between existing practice and the new helped to ease the transition to the reformed usage. Banns continued to be published three times in the parish churches of both parties and, although certain relaxations were allowed on the question of marriage within the forbidden degrees, the more immediate relationships remained prohibited. Prohibitions of other kinds were, however, introduced; marriage was not allowed to anyone who was deficient in Christian instruction. An ability to repeat the Lord's Prayer, the Ten Commandments and the Apostles' Creed was usually required. Those who desired to be married had to be diligent in attendance at church and the St Andrews session threatened in 1572 and again in 1579 to refuse marriage to any couples who profaned the Sabbath. At Perth in 1578 the session was concerned that the contracting parties should be instructed in the true knowledge of the cause of marriage and to this end were to visit the reader before arranging for the proclamation of their banns. Somewhat later at Elgin in 1637 the session introduced new and somewhat different criteria when it ordained that:

> None heirafter sall have the benefits of mariage specially they of the purer sort except that first they set caution that they be diligent and carfull in that vocation God has called them to quhereby they nor ther posterity be burdensome to the toun through ther sleuth and negligence but that they indevore be all means lawfull to acquire ther owne liveing except that poverty came through long seiknes or through sum sensible visitation otherwayis, and this is first execute on the persone of David Gray a man past forescore and ten yeiris being contracted to a young woman, its ordeant that their bands be stopit and no mariage granted them.

If no impediments existed, the banns were called and the marriage arrangements set in motion. Marriage was no longer regarded as a sacrament and the ceremony in the Book of Common Order was simple and straightforward. After an exhortation the minister enquired of the couple and then of the congregation as to the existence of any impediment to marriage. Each partner in turn was then asked as to whether they could take each other as husband and wife and after the reading of Christ's words on marriage from the nineteenth chapter of Mathew, the minister assured the couple that if they believed these words they were now joined in wedlock. He commended them to God and the ceremony ended with the singing of a suitable psalm. No prayers were required as this order was always used at a normal preaching service; nor was there any pronunciation of the couple as man and wife, as in accordance with the law and practice of the medieval church and the law of Scotland, the public announcement of consent to marriage was all that was required.[21]

Marriage was always in church and stern measures were taken against any who attempted to perform the ceremony privately. On the whole few seem to have broken the General Assembly statute of 1571 which ordered all marriages be solemnized in the face of the congregation, although Peter Watson, commissioner for Nithsdale, was censured in 1577 for conducting a ceremony in Drumlanrig castle. The prohibition was renewed in 1582 and six years later a reader was deposed for marrying in a private house. If opinion on this issue seems to have been fairly unanimous, many more doubts were to be raised about the day on which marriages might take place. According to the first Book of Discipline marriages should be solemnized on Sundays in the forenoon, but marriages did take place on other preaching days. A ruling of the General Assembly in 1579 would seem to suggest that even this rule might be breached, but in practice marriages continued to be solemnized only when there was a sermon. Sunday had long remained the favourite day for marriages, but the subsequent festivities greatly troubled kirk sessions.[22]

In 1570 the session at St Andrews complained vigorously about newly weds who on the day of their marriage failed to attend church in the afternoon 'and at evin eftir supper insolentlie, in evil example of utheris, perturbis the town wytht rynning thair throw in menstralye and harlatrys'. At Edinburgh even delaying the celebrations to the following day could bring disapproval and Thomas Acmoutie and his spouse were reprimanded for 'superflowis bankatting with conventioun of freindis maid upon the Monenday at ewin nixt aftir the solempnization of thair mariage'.[23]

In order to curb this problem at least as far as the Sunday was concerned, some kirk sessions tried to prohibit marriage on that day. The session of St Cuthberts, Edinburgh, in 1592 decreed that marriages should take place on Thursday at half-past eight before the preaching; all Sunday nuptials were forbidden at Stirling and at Perth, where the session in 1586 had tried to limit Sunday marriages to the afternoon service, it was decided six years later that marriages should be restricted to Thursdays. Whether the wedding took place on a Sunday or on a weekday, the newly-married couple were expected to hear the sermon and it was enacted at Glasgow in 1600 that those who failed to stay for the sermon after their marriage should be accounted totally absent.[24]

Such problems were not associated with the burial of the dead, as funerals had to be carried out without any of the ceremonies formerly in use. There was to be neither singing nor reading lest anyone present should think that such works profited the dead. However, the Book of Common Order suggested that the minister might repair to the church if it be not far off and make an exhortation to the people on the significance of death and resurrection. The injunctions of the first Book of Discipline also left room for a burial service and it may be that where the church was at a distance, such a service did take place. It was certainly accepted that ministers might preach at the funerals and Knox himself preached at the funeral of the Regent Moray, who in being buried in the church of St Giles, Edinburgh, also breached the reformers' stipulation that burials within churches be forbidden. The burial of the poor was, however, a very different affair, but every effort was made to ensure that they were seemly. To this end the General Assembly decreed in 1563 that: 'a beere be made in every paroch to carrie the dead corpes to buriall, and that village or house wher the dead lyes, with the nixt house adjacent thereto, or a certane number of every house, sull convey the dead to the buriall, and eird it saxe foote under the eird'.[25]

In their prescription for the administration of the sacraments of Holy Communion and Baptism and in their attitudes towards the ceremonies connected with marriage and burial the reformers were guided by scriptural authority. This likewise dictated their attitude towards the observance of festivals and saints' days. Though the latter were invariably condemned by opponents of the catholic church, the greater Christian festivals such as Christmas and Easter were recognized. This seems to have been initially the attitude in Scotland too and even in 1559 the leading protestant ministers were charged to hold communion at Easter. Nevertheless, the first Book of Discipline adopted a somewhat different attitude, suggesting that:

> keping of holy dayis of certane Sanctis commandit by man suche as be all those that the Papists have invented, as the Feistis (as thai terme thame) of Appostillis, Martyres, Virgenis, of Christmess, Circumcisioun, Epiphany, Purification, and uther found festis of our lady: Quhilk thingis, becaus in Goddis Scripturis thai nather have

commandiment nor assurance, we juge thame utterlie to be abolischet from this realme.

No mention is made of Easter, Ascension or Whitsunday, but even observance of these days had come to worry the reformers and in dealing with the measures for the celebration of the Lord's Supper the first Book of Discipline clearly intended to break with the Easter communion, which has been accorded special significance by the pre-Reformation church. How far this intention was carried out in the first few years after 1560 cannot be clearly ascertained, but attitudes certainly hardened and by 1566 the General Assembly in approving the Helvetic Confession of the church of Zurich 'would not allow the days dedicat to Christ, the circumcisioun, nativite, passion, resurrection, ascension and pentecost days, but took exception against that part of the Confession'. Nevertheless, the General Assembly decided in 1570 that communion might be administered on Easter day where superstition was removed. This was the crux of the question and in 1575 an assembly that had petitioned the Regent Morton that Yule day and saints days should be abolished, also re-affirmed that communion should not be administered at Easter if that day was kept superstitiously.[26]

Such prohibitions may have been desirable in the eyes of the church, but popular sentiment frequently militated against such an approach. Yule in particular proved obdurate despite the activities of kirk sessions in punishing those who continued to observe it either as holiday or a holy day. In 1573 ten persons were brought before the session of St Andrews for observing Yule and an unrepentant Walter Younger spiritedly told the elders that 'he is ane yowng man and saw Ywil-day keipit halyday, and that the tyme may cum that he may see the like yit; and thairfor would nocht becum oblist nor astrictit in tyme cuming to work or abstein fra work that day, bot at his awn plesure.'

Amongst many others called to account for celebrating Christmas were a number of Glasgow merchants who in 1583 had closed their booths on Christmas day; a group of Aberdonians in 1574 who were charged with 'plaing, dansin, and singin of fylthe carroles on Yeull Day at evin', and the parishioners of Rutherglen. In 1599 twenty-two girls were charged with having sung carols in the ruined cathedral of Elgin at Christmas. Transgressions at other major festivals appear to have been less common, but general condemnations of such days indicate that they were no less frowned upon. At Aberdeen in 1574 the deacons of various crafts were warned to desist from observing any holy day or festival which was used of 'auld tyme befor; bot to keip only the sabet day, callit the Sounday'. Memories and tradition died hard and in 1577 a number of the citizens of Perth were disciplined for taking part in a 'Corpus Christi' procession. Other local festivals which were equally difficult to suppress may have had little religious significance, but were nevertheless unacceptable to the reformed kirk. At Aberdeen it was forbidden for the burgesses and other inhabitants to convene to choose 'Robin Huid, Litill Johnne, Abbot of Ressoune, Queyne of Maii or sicklyk' while at Perth the session condemned resorting in May to the Draggon Hole, as well by young men as women, with their piping and drums striking before them. In the latter instances issues of morality were perhaps as important as religious issues. Economic considerations could also play their part and explain the privy council proclamation of 1561/2 ordering all lieges to abstain from eating flesh 'in the spring of the year called Lentryne'. Such prohibitions were repeated at regular intervals but at least one commentator was at pains to explain that such enactments were not 'for cause of relligioun, but to save the yong foulis and beasts'.[27]

The kirk's emphasis in its teaching was not, however, on prohibition but rather in the positive teaching of the Word. Its success in this respect can be measured in the increasing familiarity of the people with its scriptural precepts. The success of the reformed church in recapturing the enthusiasm of the people can, however, best be seen in a part of worship on which the reformers did not initially lay any particular stress – the singing of psalms. The first Book of Discipline merely commented that in some churches the psalms might be conveniently sung, in others perchance they could not. Nevertheless, the people undoubtedly came to know their psalters and its harmonies. Burgh councils in particular were conscientious in this respect. At Perth two bailies were deputed in 1592 by the kirk session to speak to the council that 'ane musician be had for uptaking of the psalmes in the kirk'. Earlier in the same burgh the master of the song school, who had previously been granted rents formerly belonging to the Greyfriars in recompense for his labours in instructing the youth of the town in music and in taking up the psalms, declared himself content to receive in lieu whatever the council wanted to bestow upon him during his work and good service. Much was obviously achieved as a contemporary statement attests that:

> Both pastors and people be long custome, or so acquainted with the psalms and tunes thereof; that as the pastors or able to direct a psalm to be sung agrieable to the doctrine to be delyvered, so he that taketh up the psalm is able to sing anie tune, and the people for the most part to follow him.

In this respect the best evidence for the success of the reformed church and the new enthusiasm for worship that it had engendered is seen in the reception given to John Durie, minister of Edinburgh on his return to that burgh in 1582 after his sentence of banishment had been lifted by the king. At the Gallowgreen Durie was met by a crowd of two hundred,

> but ere he came to the Netherbow their number increased to 400, but they were no sooner entered but they increased to 600 or 700, and within short space the whole street was replenished even to St. Geiles Kirk; the number was esteemed to 2,000. At the Netherbow they took up the 124 Psalm, '*Now Israel may say*', and sing in such a pleasant tune in four parts, known to the most part of the people, that coming up the street all bareheaded till they entered in the kirk, with such a great sound and majestie, that it moved both themselves and all the huge multitude of the beholders . . . with admiration and astonishment.

This was one incident, but the enthusiasm and the sincerity behind such a demonstration cannot be doubted, and is a far cry from the apathy and lassitude of the pre-Reformation church.[28]

8
Consolidation and Recusancy

In time protestantism was to be effectively embraced by the vast majority of the Scottish people. Nevertheless, for over a decade, religious issues hung in the balance and recusancy remained a problem until the end of the century. There is considerable evidence in support of a Jesuit claim in 1562 that 'a large number of the ordinary common people are still Catholics'. Thus acts of parliament in 1560 indicated that notwithstanding the 'reformation already maid ... yit notheless thair is sum of the Papis Kirk that stubburnlie preserveris in their wickit idolatrie' and as late as 1573 the General Assembly, reminiscent of pre-Reformation enactments to the same end, enjoined that 'The multitude of hereticall books bought in this countrey shall be burnt; and that proclamation be sett out in strait manner, that none bring home hereticall books, nor press to sell them.'[1]

The extent to which such general comments truly reflect support for the catholic church can, however, be best determined by a close look at the localities. The information at hand is, however, imperfect; that relating to conversion to protestantism is almost nonexistent and in these circumstances an analysis of data relating to the settlement of a reformed ministry in the regions is the only index available for judging the reformer's success after 1560. Evidence of continuing loyalty to catholicism is, however, more readily at hand. Turning first to those areas in which protestantism was at its strongest during the pre-Reformation period, even Ayrshire continued to demonstrate a remarkable degree of loyalty to the old faith. The parishioners of four Ayrshire parishes – Maybole, Girvan, Kirkoswald and Dailly – were all accused of continued loyalty to the old church in 1560. At Dailly, it was said 'the masse is openly said and maintained'. The earl of Glencairn may have promoted the advance of reformed principles but two other prominent Ayrshire magnates, the earls of Cassilis and

Eglinton did their best to maintain the mass. The abbot of Crossraguel, Quintin Kennedy, and many of his family likewise protected catholics in Ayrshire, especially in the southern part of the county known as Carrick; in the northern part, Cunningham, the Montgomery family with Eglinton at its head acted in a similar fashion. An instance of a more general attempt to revive catholic fortunes on the west coast was provided in 1563, when several Kennedy lairds helped to organize a public celebration of the Easter mass at Maybole and Kirkoswald, with two monks of Crossraguel taking part. Nevertheless, the rapid establishment of a reformed ministry at Ayr, Ochiltree and Mauchline in Kyle was paralleled in Cunningham with early appointments at Irvine, Stevenston and Kilmarnock. Other protestant appointments quickly followed and were sometimes facilitated by the conversion of the sitting incumbent. Elsewhere a ready supply of converts, many of whom were drawn from the ranks of unbeneficed chaplains and former students of St Andrews university, was at hand. In consequence few charges in Kyle and Cunningham were still vacant in 1567. Evidence for service at many of these churches does not, however, much precede this date and a petition on the 26 June 1565 by the lairds of Carnell, Sornby and Dreghorn for a minister to be placed at Dreghorn indicates that the task of providing a reformed ministry was still an active problem. Readers at Beith and Craigie only appear in 1574 and the difficulty may not have been fully solved until the early 1570s. Progress was certainly much slower in Carrick. In 1562 Robert Hamilton, minister of Mauchline and Ochiltree was appointed by the General Assembly to preach in the unplanted kirks of Carrick in which, with the apparent exception of Straiton where the vicar was obliged in 1562 to pay twenty marks annually to an unnamed minister placed in the church by the reformers, evidence of service only regularly appears in 1567. Even then four of the ten churches in the district remained unmanned. Although two of these were provided with incumbents by 1568, evidence for service at Kirkcudbright-Innertig and Maybole does not appear until 1571 and 1572 respectively. Nevertheless, Ayrshire, with one or two possible exceptions, appears to have been provided with a reformed ministry in advance of the Act of Conformity, which in consequence made little impact upon the county. Mass, however, was still being celebrated at Eglinton in 1571 and Gilbert Kennedy of Crossraguel was maintaining catholic sacraments and baptizing children in that area as late as 1588, attesting even at that date to an Ayrshire that was not entirely and fervidly protestant.[2]

In Fife and Kinross the provision of a reformed ministry was rapidly achieved. At St Andrews the reformed ministry of Adam Heriot predated that of the reformed cause, but other appointments were being actively confirmed shortly after that event. At Aberdour a minister was in office on 24 October 1560 and at Ceres a former student of St Andrews university was adjudged fit for the ministry by the General Assembly on 20 December 1560. Nearly every parish in the two counties had an active reformed ministry before 1563, even if on some occasions compromise arrangements such as that at Largo (where the incumbent 'ministered every other Sunday') might prevail. Of the eight parishes in which a reformed clergy cannot be identified by that date, early service may still have occurred in four charges and was certainly established in all parishes before 1567 and was therefore uniform throughout these counties.[3]

In both counties catholicism lacked champions with the status of the recusant families in Ayrshire and this may explain the apparent ease with which conformity was achieved. Yet there were individuals who would not be browbeaten into an easy acceptance of religious change – the kirk session register of St Andrews contains many spirited encounters between resolute catholics and their protestant opponents. Thus William Myretoun of Cambo gave this warning to the minister of Crail in 1561: 'My brother is and salbe vicar of Crayll quhen thow sal thyg [beg] thy mayt [meat] . . . I sal pul ye owt of the pulpot be the luggis [ears] and chais ye owt of this town.' Others were no less forthright in their comments. Declarations by citizens such as 'God give Knox be hanget' and 'The Divill burn up the Kirk or [before] I come into it' are only a few of the many recorded signs of resistance to the Reformation in this area. Such was the problem that the kirk session of St Andrews carried out an interrogation in 1572 of persons habitually absent from communion. In March 1572/3, the session made further enquiries about all known papists and a list of priests who had held altarages in the town's churches was to be compiled. Such priests were required two months later to appear and make confession of their faith within fifteen days. Absence from communion tended to be taken as an admission of recusancy;

Lady Ardre and Lady Culuthye and their servant John Lundy were 'suspectit of papistry' on such grounds, and Besse Brown, servant of Sir George Brown, was described as 'ane papist and never came to communioun'. Punishment was severe and Robert Brand 'ane papist and maintainer of papistry' was warned that a fine of ten pounds for the poor's box would follow a second offence. It may be doubted whether all non-attendance at communion could be equated with recusancy and the glib remark of Walter Adie that he would 'by ane poynt of wyne and ane laif' and would 'haif als gude a sacrament as the best of them all sall haif' may be questioned in this respect. Nevertheless, the problem was evidently a real one, and in 1595 the session in conjunction with the magistrates decreed that those who were persistently absent from communion 'salbe esteemit papists'.[4]

In Angus and the Mearns there was a similar situation; Dundee possessed a reformed ministry from 1558, Brechin was served by a minister in 1561 and the majority of parishes had obtained a reformed ministry before 1563. A few parishes were deemed not to require service, but only a handful of bona-fide parishes apparently remained unfilled until 1567. In this respect the Mearns appears to have fared better than Angus as every parish (with one exception, which did not possess a reader until 1574 but was supervised before that date by a neighbouring minister) appears to have obtained a parochial incumbent by 1563. In Angus this was true of the majority of parishes, but a few appear to have remained unsupervised even after that date; eight other parishes, which were under the supervision of neighbouring ministers in 1563, had to await the late 1560s or early 1570s before obtaining incumbents of their own. Both supervision and service were deferred until the 1570s at four others, including Lintrathen where the vicar was reported as early as 1560 to be 'content to abyde sik reformatioun as the lordis of our secreit counsale pleais mak'. If a completely reformed ministry was delayed until a decade after the Reformation, the influence of the lairds in favour of protestantism appears to have been fairly conclusive, although the absence of early kirk session registers in the area makes it impossible to assess the incidence of recusancy in the same way as for Fife. Few of the pre-Reformation beneficed clergy are reported as conforming and serving in the reformed church, but if this was so it is in marked contrast to the pattern in some other areas of Scotland.

The schoolmaster at Arbroath was accused in 1563 of 'infecting the youth committed to his charge with idolatry' and in the following year an aspirant to the ministry incurred disfavour by claiming 'there was a mid-way betwixt papistrie and religion'. Religious questioning was no more encouraged by the reformed church than by its predecessor, and the magistrates of Dundee, indeed, threatened those who indulged in public debate on such issues with the permanent loss of burgess rights.[5]

Towns, more effectively than rural parishes, could curb dissidents among their ranks but even in 'protestant burghs' the support given to the new church – even by magistrates – was sometimes in question. At Perth, which obtained a protestant minister in the person of John Row on 20 December 1560, the session alleged in 1585 that 'threw negligence of the bailies sundry were not punished who condemned the kirk and ordinances'. 'Papistical magistrates' were still giving cause for concern in the General Assembly of 1591. Of the inhabitants of the burgh, one had been hanged at Edinburgh in April 1566 'under one colour of tresoun for the religious caus'. Another, accused in 1578 of remaining at home at time of the service 'without any exercise of religioun', had previously subscribed to the articles of faith and may have been a former priest. Jesuits were thought to be at work in Perth in 1587 and the continued allegiance of at least some of its inhabitants throws further suspicion on the extent of the burgh's conversion to protestantism in 1559. A baker who was charged in 1596 with 'baking and selling great loaves at Yule' may have placed commercial profit before religious convictions but his real crime in the eyes of the session was of 'cherishing ane superstitioun in the hearts of the ignorant'.[6]

In rural areas of Perthshire the reformed church faced a much more difficult task. The county contained three medieval dioceses; most of Dunkeld lay within its bounds as, with the exception of one parish, did the entire diocese of Dunblane. Eastern Perthshire mainly belonged to the diocese of St Andrews, and contained over twenty parishes. Although Perth, which stood at the heart of these parishes, was almost immediately reformed, those surrounding it seem to have been slower to follow its example. Only about one third of the parishes appear to have had protestant incumbents by 1563. Four years later, however, all the remaining parishes with the exception of two (which did not receive readers until 1574 and

1568 respectively) appear to have received a reformed ministry. The movement for reform appears in this respect to have moved from east to west and this trend is also discernable in the diocese of Dunkeld, where Bishop Robert Crichton had refused to accept the Confession of Faith and was the only Scots bishop to receive the papal nuncio da Gouda in 1562. He clearly exercised a strong influence over both his cathedral and parochial clergy, few of whom chose to conform and serve in the reformed church. With the exception of William Drummond, pre-Reformation vicar of Cargill who served as reader there in 1561/2 and Andrew Simpson, the pre-Reformation schoolmaster of Perth who became minister there in 1564, there is little sign of a reformed ministry before 1566 when William Ramsay appears as minister of Inchaiden and reader at Moneydie. The majority of the reformed ministry in this diocese, even at Dunkeld itself, does not appear before 1567, but a build-up occurred thereafter and this resulted in an almost full complement of incumbents by 1574. This situation is paralleled in Dunblane in which two successive bishops, both named William Chisholm, followed a conservative course. The rate of conformity was at first slow and although Dunblane itself had a reformed minister by 2 July 1562, only Comrie, Dunning and Monzievaird, all of which lay in the eastern part of the diocese, appear to have possessed a reformed ministry before 1567. Only at that stage does evidence for a reformed ministry become more plentiful and thereafter its growth continued until 1569 by which time only Kippen, at which a reader does not appear until 1574, appears to have lacked a reformed incumbent.[7]

In Perthshire the concessions made to the reformed church in 1566 by Mary, queen of Scots and her subsequent fall from power were clearly the decisive factors in finally determining the progress of the reformed faith. In such circumstances it is hardly surprising that the preservation of catholic belief is strongly attested. In 1564, a priest was accused of 'drawing of the pepill to the chapel of Tuleborne (Tullibardine) fra ther parroch kyrk'. Five years later four priests of the diocese of Dunblane were condemned to death but were subsequently reprieved and 'bund to the mercat crose with their vestments and chalices in derisioun'. The county contained a large number of recalcitrants; indeed, early monitions against priests who said mass at the chapel of Foss near Dull and also at Logyrait clearly were ineffectual and were destined to remain so until after 1573 when stricter measures came into force once parliament had passed the Act of Conformity. Nevertheless, in March 1573/4 it was alleged that the bishop of Dunkeld had admitted as reader at Logyrait, who had recently used 'popish rites' at a funeral. As late as 1580 it could be reported that many papists were dwelling in Dunblane.[8]

If recusancy presented a problem even in areas in which protestant ascendancy had been fairly quickly established after the Reformation, it might be expected to have presented an even greater problem in those localities where support for the reformers had been initially weaker. This was indeed the case in the Lothians and south-eastern Scotland, with Edinburgh in particular continuing to show favour to the old faith. In Berwickshire the growth of a reformed ministry was slow. Although an exhorter had been appointed at Greenlaw by 1561, only eight or nine parishes had a settled ministry before 1563, and although thirteen other charges had been filled by 1567, vacancies still existed in at least fifteen parishes. With the exception of the vacancy at Simprin, these had been filled by 1574, but not before a stern warning from the privy council had persuaded a few former priests to desert 'mass-mongering' and to concentrate on their duties as reformed clergy. In some churches the mass still flourished for at least a decade after parliament had abolished it in 1560. At Fishwick, for instance, in 1563 a priest said mass every Sunday; and the same was true at Nenthorn and also of Greenlaw which had a catholic patron. As late as 1569, in fact, the mass was still being celebrated in a large number of Berwickshire parish churches; and the incumbent priests, some of whom had at length paid lip-service to conformity and service in the reformed church, were summoned in that year to appear before the privy council. Eighteen years later the General Assembly was still accusing Lord Home of allowing kirks in his patronage to lie waste while encouraging the activities of a priest, Andrew Clerk. In East Lothian also, the reformed ministry made slow headway. Only at Oldhamstocks where the parson conformed and served, at Bolton where the vicar did likewise, at Tyninghame where the curate became reader, and at Haddington and Tranent which had a reformed ministry before 1562, was early service assured. Elsewhere protestant incumbents were not evident until 1567/68 and even then the minister of Dunbar was instructed to minister the sacraments to kirks thereabouts. No reader was evident at Athelstanford until 1574 and at Garvald, where the parish chaplain was cited as a priest before the privy council on 17 October 1569, he later appears a conformist and exhorter in 1571/72. Supervision over four churches was still in the hands of the minister of North Berwick in 1571; three years later, two of these had obtained readers of their own but another two were thought not to require them. In such circumstances recusancy flourished. In 1569 it was alleged that the parishioners of Whitekirk had 'never heard the word twice preached, nor received the sacraments, since the Reformation'. The influence of a local catholic, Lord Seton, who maintained a catholic chaplain in his house, may have encouraged recusancy in this area - and as late as 1593 a schoolmaster at Haddington enacted a play for his scholars, one of whom baptized a cat in the name of the Trinity 'in derisioun of the Kirk'.[9]

If the reformed ministry was slow to take root in East Lothian, this was not the case in Midlothian and West Lothian. The churches of Edinburgh and those of its immediate neighbourhood were quickly provided with a reformed ministry which included John Knox at St Giles and William Harlaw at St Cuthberts in Edinburgh. At least six other parishes possessed incumbents before 1562 and most others were similarly provided by 1567. Several parishes even at that date posed problems, the priest of Temple being called before the privy council in 1569. Most of the outstanding vacancies had been filled by 1574, but in a few parishes supervision from a neighbouring parish was all that had been achieved. Recusancy though uncommon was not unknown and Currie was one of the parishes in which the General Assembly urged punishment in December 1564 of 'sick as has steiked the doores of the paroch kirks, and will not opin the samein to preachers that presentit themselves to have preachit the word'. Edinburgh and its neighbouring burgh of the Canongate (in which catholic allegiance was encouraged and strengthened by the presence of Mary queen of Scots) were, however, the recusant centres in this area. Attempts to remove catholics from the burgh such as a proclamation of 2 October 1561 'Commanding and charging all and syndry monks, friaris, priests and all utheris papistis and prophane personis, to pass furth of Edinburgh within xxiiii hours next after following, under the payne of burnying disobeyaris upoun the cheik and harling of thame throw the toun in ane cart' were countermanded by the queen, as was a proclamation of 1562 restricting the holding of public office to professed protestants; this had to be withdrawn 'for eschewing of the queen's anger'. The queen's chapel at Holyrood became the centre for catholic activity within the burgh and could be described indeed as 'nothing less than a Catholic parish church'. In 1563 twenty-two men and women were 'delatit for arte and parte of the cuming to the chapell of our soueran ladeis Palice of Holyrudehouse . . . and swa becumyng manifest transgressouris, violatouris and breakaris of our souerane ladeis Proclamatiouns . . . aucht to be adiugit and punesit to the deid'. Within it children were baptized, sometimes from conviction of the parents, as in the case of an Edinburgh merchant, John Graham, who openly defended the doctrine of the mass, but on other occasions to escape the censures of the kirk when the children in question were illegitimate. Marriages were frequently celebrated there, but while the queen's influence in her political ascendancy could secure the release of David Hoppringill of Edinburgh whom the magistrates had imprisoned for a catholic marriage, the plight of Paul Wallis, accused of fornication in September 1566 (because his marriage in the queen's chapel was not recognized by the Canongate kirk session), was much more perilous as the queen's political influence declined. The queen's presence encouraged many who would have agreed with the parishioner who claimed 'my hart gevis me to the mess and thairfor I can nocht come to the commonion'. The catholic schoolteachers of the burgh and neighbouring Leith also remained active; one, William Robertson, defied all the efforts of the magistrates to dislodge him and another, the priest John Scott, claimed exemption from the authority of the Canongate kirk session 'because he was of the Queen's religion' and because he had royal permission to teach in the burgh. The protection of the queen was an important element in all this, for a Leith schoolmaster was less fortunate in 1572 when he was 'accusit for saying of masse . . . was condemnit be an assyse and thairoftir hangit'. Before the deposition of the queen in 1567 active catholicism was very evident among the Edinburgh populace: and in March 1565 as many inhabitants of that burgh were reported to have been present at a mass as those who attended the protestant service. The apprehension of the priest Sir James Carvet, who had officiated at the mass and was thereafter tied to the market cross in his vestments and subjected to egg-throwing, occasioned a riot when catholic supporters took it upon themselves to intervene on his behalf. Faced with such intransigence, the General Assembly could only appeal on 25 June 1565 'that the word of God might be established, approved and ratified, throughout the whole realme, alsweill in the Queen's Majesties awin person as in the subjects'.[10]

With recusancy so prevalent in areas which had had clear protestant sympathies (of however limited a kind) before the Reformation, the situation elsewhere could hardly be other than inimical to religious change. Nevertheless, in at least two areas - Galloway and Orkney - in which hostility had been evident at first, the bishops conformed and remained to serve their dioceses in the reformed church; their conversion induced a substantial percentage of the clergy to follow their example and this in turn may have led to a more general conformity. In Galloway some difficulty was experienced in 1560 with the prior of Whithorn and his servants in Cruggleton; Whithorn, with its catholic patron, was to be a trouble spot for many years to follow. Despite that, however, the example of Bishop Alexander Gordon promoted a reformed ministry that was already some thirty strong by 1561. In Galloway, at least the reformed church quickly took root.[11]

Similarly, in Orkney and Shetland, Bishop Adam Bothwell became a protestant and remained to supervise the establishment of a reformed ministry in the diocese. Initial resistance was clearly evident, and was expressed at a demonstration at Birsay in Orkney led by one of the local lairds who was accompanied by 'a great nowmer of commonis'. The demonstrators proceeded to a chapel near which the bishop himself was lying sick, and obliged a priest to say 'masse and marye certaine pairis in the auld maner'. However, once restored to health and assisted by some reformed clergy from outside the diocese, Bothwell entered into the task of reformation so vigorously that by 1567 nearly every church in the diocese had a protestant incumbent.[12]

The provision of a reformed ministry in these distant dioceses was not paralleled in other outlying areas. Much of the Western Highlands and Islands was to lack ministers for more than half a century after the Reformation; this in no small measure was due to the resistance of local chiefs who saw the new faith as a threat to their accustomed way of life. Only in Argyllshire, an area largely controlled by Archibald, fifth earl of Argyll, who had followed his father in supporting pre-Reformation protestantism and where the ascendancy of the reformers had actively destroyed 'places and monumentis of ydolatrie,' were signs of an active ministry to emerge. This was due not only to the support of the earl, but also to the administration of John Carswell, superintendent of Argyll, whose stated aim in undertaking a translation into Gaelic of the Book of Common Order in 1567 was to help his Christian brethren who needed teaching and comfort and lacked books. The supposition must be that his concern was for the well-being of a small literate group of Gaelic ministers, but their number must have been very small and their activity extremely restricted. In most parish churches the pre-Reformation clergy simply continued to hold their benefices as before and it was left to Carswell to further the work of a reformed ministry as best he could. Appointments to Glenorchy before 1562 and Ardchattan, Dunoon and Lochgoilhead by dates in the early 1570s attest to the success of his efforts, but the majority of parishes even within the bounds of Argyll were outside the influence of either earl or superintendent and remained devoid of protestant service.[13]

This situation was similar in the Islands, the first appointments to Hebridean parishes not coming until 1609; even then language difficulties meant that reformed ministers were few in number and catholicism lingered on after the death of priests (who could not be replaced) in the form of half-remembered beliefs and practices. Pilgrimages by sea to Ireland may have maintained the faith more fully in a few islands and in 1615 it was reported of Islay (where the Macdonalds had very close connections with Northern Ireland) 'that the religioun that the cuntrie pepill has heir amongst them is Popishe'. But memories could not endure for ever, and religious belief was left to wither away. Thereafter, with a few possible exceptions, the ecclesiastical affiliation of the inhabitants of these areas was to be determined by intermittent missionary activity, by both catholics and protestants, during the course of the seventeenth and early eighteenth centuries.[14]

Over much of the rest of Scotland, where protestantism had been little evident in the pre-Reformation period, the success of the reformed church was to rest on determined missionary activity. In 1562 it was reported to the General Assembly that 'the north countrie for the most part was destitute of ministers'. In the same year a commissioner was sent to Moray to preach and 'if it sall chance that he sall find anie qualified persons', he was to take steps to have them appointed to the ministry; nevertheless, a year later, the need to form a reformed church in 'Murray, Banf and the cuntreis adjacent' was still being debated before the Assembly. The problem was not uniform. In some parts of the diocese of Moray, which lay in Aberdeenshire and Banff, reformed service had been achieved with reasonable speed. Keith had a minister in 1560; four others had reformed incumbents before 1563, one with supervision over the parish of Drumdelgie, and six others were served by 1567. In the most distant parts of these counties equal success had not been achieved, and seven parishes do not appear to have possessed incumbents until shortly before 1574. Some parishes in Moray and Nairn were just as late in conforming. In the deanery of Elgin, however, a reader served Forres in 1563; evidence for reformed incumbents at Alves and Elgin appears in 1565 and 1566 respectively and by the following year fourteen other parishes in the deanery had obtained reformed service leaving only four others to obtain incumbents before 1574. In Strathspey, reformed incumbents were less forthcoming; Alvie had a reader by 1563, but only six other parishes possessed readers by 1567/68; the special commissioner appointed for the task of planting churches asked to be relieved of his duties in 1572; and seven parishes are not recorded as possessing a reformed ministry until 1574. A similar pattern emerges in the deanery of Inverness, comprising mainland Inverness-shire. The town of Inverness possessed a minister in 1561 and the parish of Moy an exhorter in 1564, but service in ten others was delayed until 1567/68. The following year seems to have been an active one in the establishment of a reformed ministry: at Farnua a presentee to the parsonage was to be examined to assess his qualifications to serve as minister and in the same year two readers appear. Nevertheless reformed incumbents only appear at four other parishes in 1574, and the task of establishing the reformed church in this area was a slow uphill task. The kirk session records of Elgin not only reveal cases of catholic baptism (carried out on one occasion by one of the ex-monks of Pluscardine), but also a persistent devotional respect for a former shrine in the Garioch to which inhabitants of the burgh still repaired. If a measure of conformity was achieved after 1574, Jesuit activity and popular sentiment contrived to act as barriers to total success. In 1593 two men from the parish of Elgin were accused of accompanying Jesuit priests to the house of Lady Sutherland and assisting them at mass; the minister on this occasion offered to counsel the offenders 'if they are in doubt of their religioun'. Less compassion was shown in May 1597 in the cases of Janet Wardane accused of private prayer in the disused Chanonry Kirk and Isobel Umphray prevented in 1601 from praying at the grave of her child.[15]

The problems faced by the General Assembly in Moray and Inverness were also present in Ross and Caithness. In Caithness, despite the fact that the earl was an acknowledged catholic, reformed service was achieved at Bower and Thurso by 1561. Thereafter, the presence of a third reformed bishop, Robert Stewart, who was granted a commission to plant churches in his diocese in June 1563, speeded up the process of establishing protestant worship and resulted in a further nine reformed clergy being established by 1567. Five others were in office by 1570, but the task was far from easy. At Farr a prospective minister was to be examined in 1572 and three other parishes were provided with incumbents by 1574. Nevertheless, the parish church of Assynt was still vacant in 1574 and a minister did not finally appear until two years later. Recusancy in this area may have been encouraged by the earl of Sutherland who with his wife and friends were condemned by the General Assembly in 1587/88 as 'contemners of the word and sacramants' and 'suspectit laitlie to have had mess'.[16]

In Ross the task of establishing the reformed church and extirpating catholicism had been made all the more difficult by the appointment of a devout catholic, John Lesley, as bishop in 1566/67. Even before this, however, the response to the reformed faith had been slow and only a few protestant clergy appeared in the early 1560s. Logie Wester and Urquhart possessed ministers in 1562 and Alness was served by an exhorter in the same year but thirteen other parishes had to wait until 1567–9 for a reformed ministry, when the forfeiture of the bishop following the deposition of Mary, queen of Scots, allowed some leeway to the reformed church. Most parishes were apparently not held by protestant incumbents until the early 1570s and clergy only appear in another fourteen parishes in 1574 and even then two charges were without individual service. The rehabilitation of Bishop Lesley on 13 March 1587 reversed this trend and in the following year the General Assembly protested that he had given the parsonage of

Kinken in Ross to Alexander Lesley 'a professed papist'. Jesuits, encouraged by the earl of Huntly, were also active. Time, nevertheless, was on the side of the reformers, and the long delays in filling benefices with protestant incumbents may have done much to allay opposition; a more decisive and early protestant attack on long cherished beliefs would otherwise have stimulated a sharper reaction in defence of older practices.[17]

In areas somewhat less distant from protestant strongpoints in central Scotland, where the reformed church was more active in the years following the Reformation, resistance was certainly more spirited. In Aberdeenshire the presence of the earls of Erroll and Huntly and various other influential members of the Hay and Gordon clans including the bishop William Gordon, actively encouraged catholics to maintain their beliefs. For a decade after the Reformation the 'trew religioun' made little headway in this area and in 1570 the church's commissioner in Aberdeen asked to be relieved of his duties since 'there was no obedience in these parts and the ministers were not answered'. Nevertheless, despite its apparent conservatism in religious matters, the diocese of Aberdeen, which included most of Aberdeenshire, parts of Banff and a few Kincardineshire parishes, possessed a reformed ministry within a remarkably short time. The church of St Nicholas of Aberdeen had an appointed minister before 19 July 1560 and although a reader does not appear in the cathedral of St Machar until 1567, the tiny old Aberdeen parish of Snow possessed a reader by 1563. The other seven parishes in the deanery of Aberdeen were similarly served by this date, even though two neighbouring parishes were forced to share a reader. Service of similar proportions is found in the other deaneries of the diocese at this time. By May 1563 twenty-four parishes had reformed incumbents and another eight had readers before 1567. Of these remaining parishes, a presentee to the parsonage of Fetterneir in 1571 was to be examined to ascertain whether he was qualified to serve as minister; he apparently failed to meet the grade as the minister of Tough had been assigned supervision of the parish by 1574 when it was also declared that the church 'neides na reidare'. Readers were, however, installed by this date at the two hitherto unfilled charges. In the deanery of the Boyne the same pattern prevailed and a minister was installed to serve the adjoining parishes of Aberdour and Tyrie by December 1560; the latter, with nine other parishes, had individual incumbents by 1563. Deskford was filled by 1567 and although Ordiquhill was served from Fordyce and Farscan from Rathven, this merely maintained the medieval pattern of service. Only at Forglen, over which the minister of Turriff nominally exercised supervision but at which there was no reader, were difficulties apparent. In Buchan, events followed much the same course, twelve parishes having reformed incumbents by 1563. Of the remainder five were provided with service from 1567; so too at Fetterangus supervised from Deer. Only at Lonmey, which was apparently still vacant in 1574 despite the joint presentation of the minister of Deer in that year, is there any indication of an extended problem in providing a reformed ministry. Only two such problems existed in the Garioch in which twenty parishes had incumbents in 1563 with two other parishes filled by 1567. At Oyne and Furvie, however, ministers do not appear until 1570 and 1574 respectively. Nevertheless, out of a total of some 102 parishes in the diocese of Aberdeen, three-quarters had an established parochial ministry by 1563 and all but seven parishes had reformed incumbents by 1567. Despite the difficulties posed by an active recusant force in this area, the reformed church clearly established an early bridgehead from which it could establish its own position.

An increase in catholic support brought about by increased Jesuit activity in Aberdeenshire in the 1580s and 1590s was, however, to test its strength. Seven churches were said to be destitute of pastors in 1587/88 and it was also asserted that ministers in various other Aberdeenshire parishes had been deprived. Physical violence against protestant incumbents, such as an attack in 1599 on the minister of Slains while on his way to his kirk, was certainly not unknown. Catholic patrons like the earl of Erroll were also accused of withholding stipends and in 1597 the minister of Cruden declined his charge for this reason. Jesuit activity was widespread in the area and in March 1592/3 no fewer than twenty-seven influential persons in the north-east, most of whom bore the names Gordon, Lesley, Hay or Cheyne were obliged by the privy council to give surety not to aid the Jesuits. Such assurances were fairly pointless and the records of the presbytery of Ellon provide evidence not only for non-attendance at protestant services by prominent local families like the Woods of Boniton, the Cheynes of Essilmont and the Gordons of Gight, but also of active catholic ministrations. Such actions helped to sustain a catholicism that was never to be entirely eradicated. In the burgh of Aberdeen dissidents could be more effectively countered. Even this took time for, although the acting principal of King's College and several of the regents refused to subscribe to the reformed Confessions of Faith in 1560, they were allowed to remain in office until finally purged in 1569. Nevertheless, a report of the General Assembly's commissioners in 1587/8 reported that Jesuits came and went freely in the two burghs, in which they celebrated mass and distributed literature. In consequence the reaction of many of the inhabitants to the enforced religious changes continued to be echoed in the words of a local stalwart, Marjorie Urquhart, who in 1575 informed the kirk session that so sharp was the 'prick on her conscience' that she 'culd nocht be fulle of the present religioune now in Scotland'.[18]

This sentiment would appear to have much support in Renfrewshire where, although an early reformed ministry appeared at Renfrew and Erskine in 1561, at Eaglesham in 1562 and at six other parishes by 1563, in the same year six beneficed clergy took part in plans for the public celebration of mass and at least one, at Neilston, took place. The celebrant Stephen Wilson continued as a thorn in the flesh of the reformed church for many years thereafter. In 1571 the reader at Neilston (who first appeared in office in 1570) was mobbed by a crowd which swore that 'he suld have thair hert blude gif thai brocht not again thair messe priest Sir Stevin Wilsoun'. Not until 4 March 1580 did retribution finally catch up with Wilson who, then described as 'mass priest of Neilston many years and rebel put to the horn for continual disobedience in abusing the sacraments, saying mass, and dissolving marriage at pleasure', was to remain in prison until his trial. The area around Paisley, where a minister did not appear until 1572 and then had to be released from his duties in 1578 because of his parishioners' 'contempt of discipline', was a region in which hostility to the reformed church was particularly violent – on one occasion a recusant there declared that his minister and all other heretics should be 'hangit'. In 1597 the minister of Lochwinnoch, which only obtained a reader in 1574, rode into Paisley to be confronted by a group of catholic sympathizers who came with ale and other provisions and 'powrit drink in the maris mouth and thereafter dansit and sange Saule Masse for the minister's deid meir'. Elsewhere in the county, Eaglesham and Erskine were parishes with a history of recusancy, resistance to the discipline of the kirk in the latter being attributed to Lady Mar and her chaplains, one of whom had his service books and vestments confiscated; his case was brought before the General Assembly in February 1587/8.[19]

No such problem appears to have arisen in neighbouring Lanarkshire, as a reformed ministry was established at Cambusnethan in 1561 and in twenty other parishes before 1563. Twelve others, including a shared ministry and readership, were similarly served by 1567/68. Evidence for reformed service is missing at Lanark until 1569, but apart from two churches, which did not possess readers until 1569 and 1571 respectively, the county was fully served at an early date. Problems appear to have been of a secular rather than a recusant nature; as late as 1587/88 the minister of Lanark could not reside in the town because the vicarage had been usurped by a servitor of the Lord Chancellor.[20]

Further down the Clyde, in the Lennox, which included Dumbartonshire and parts of Stirlingshire within its bounds, the evidence is more disparate. In several parishes that apparently shared a minister, there is evidence for reformed service in 1560/61. In most others a reformed ministry had been established by 1563 and by 1567, with the exception of Baldernock which did not obtain a reader until 1568, the whole area was apparently adequately served. Difficulties did exist, however, and at Fintry in 1568 it required an order of the privy council before the exhorter there could take possession of the glebe, manse and yard which had been withheld since 1560. In 1587/88 the laird of Fintry was accused of stealing away 'the hearts of the commons by banqueting at Yuile', in ceremonies which it was said had lasted three days during which time 'all Papistical ceremonies wer used'. The General Assembly reported at the same time that there were 'great bruits of suspicion of messes in many places of the countrey, which have genered in the hearts of the people contempt of the Word and Ministers'. There are other similar complaints, but it would appear that the Assembly statement that there were scarcely four ministers to twenty-four parishes in the Lennox in 1588 may literally relate to the office of minister and exclude the readers who were already placed in the majority of charges.[21]

In the borders, the situation was equally mixed. In Peebleshire, a minister had been established at Linton in 1560 and almost the whole county was served by a reformed ministry before 1563. The only exceptions were at Skirling, which shared an exhorter with Dolphinton in 1567 but was again vacant in 1574, and Traquair which did not possess a reader until 1567. Other parts of the borders were not so well served. John Guild was reader and teacher of the youth at Selkirk in 1563 but outlying parts of that county were not so well treated. Yarrow was served by an exhorter from Selkirk in 1568, but by 1574 the minister of Ashkirk had assumed responsibility for this church and that of Ettrick. The establishment of a reformed ministry in Teviotdale was a slow process in all but a few key parishes. Incumbents had been found for Jedburgh and Melrose in 1562; three others were similarly provided by 1563; Bedrule possessed a minister by 1564 and Lindean a reader in the following year. If seven parishes had been provided for by 1567/68 not all placements were reliable: the exhorter in Ancrum in 1563 was one of the priests called before the privy council in 1569 and one of his parishioners was accused at the same time of keeping a religious statue in his house. The accusations may have been salutary for at least fourteen parishes obtained incumbents shortly after that date, but another eight parishes were still vacant in 1574. At Maxton a vicar cited in 1569 conformed and served as a reader by 1574; Abbotrule obtained a reader in 1576 and at Mow a presentee to the vicarage was to be assessed as to his ability to serve as a reader. Vacancies and recusant readers continued to cause problems in 1587/88 and Teviotdale was then singled out as an area in which there was a serious lack of ministers. Lord Home, the laird of Edmestoun and other principal landowners were accused of corruptness in religious matters, and Home in particular of maintaining Mr Andro Clerk 'a malicious enemie to the Gospell and Ministers thereof'. Other professed catholics were named but, more seriously, it was alleged that the sacraments were profaned by deposed readers and some that 'never bare office in the kirk'. Among the named recusants were Thomas Ker in Old Roxburgh, Thomas Hall in east Teviotdale, James Scot called vicar of Ashkirk and Thomas Neulatt, vicar at Bassendean. Some of these charges, including the keeping of holy days and superstitious pilgrimages, were repeated in 1590 when two readers were accused of profaning the sacraments.[22]

Scarcity of qualified ministers contributed greatly to this state of affairs. This too was the problem in Dumfriesshire, parts of which were destitute of a reformed ministry for many years after the Reformation. It was here and in adjacent Kirkcudbrightshire that catholicism was to make one of its determined stands. In Eskdale all five parishes remained devoid of protestant ministers until the seventeenth century. Adjacent parishes in Annandale were also left vacant or only intermittently filled after 1574. Of the parishes lying east of Annan only three possessed readers in 1567 and may have been again vacant by 1574. With the exception of Trailtrow, appropriated to the hospital of that name, all these Annandale parishes were independent parsonages in the patronage of the recusant and absentee archbishop of Glasgow or of the local lairds who appear to have been indifferent to Reformation principles. Efforts, if any, to provide protestant incumbents were evidently unsuccessful, and as late as 1602, reference was made by the General Assembly to kirks within the borders of Annandale 'quilk has bein desolat continuallie, sen the reformatioun of the religioun within this countre'.[23]

West of Annan, the remaining Annandale parishes present a more complex picture. Two parishes lacked readers until the mid-1580s, but the remainder all possessed ministers or readers by 1567/8. By 1574, however, most of these charges were again apparently vacant. Old age and lack of commitment to religious change revealed by the Act of Conformity in 1573 may explain these vacancies, many of which (despite being filled in the late 1570s and early 1580s) were again apparently vacant before the end of the century. In 1608 some twenty-eight charges in Annandale were still said to be vacant. If the evidence does not positively indicate that the old church retained its former influence a further reference in 1608 to 'the great necessitie of the Kirks of Annerdaill, Ewisdaill and Eskdaill and the rest of the Kirks of the Daills quhilk are altogether unplantit ... in the quhilks it is regraitit that in many of them the holie communioun was never celebrate' illustrates the nature of the problem.[24]

Although Annandale was inimicable to change, neighbouring Nithsdale was much more amenable to protestantism. On the Dumfriesshire side of the Nith no fewer than eight pre-Reformation clergy conformed and served in the reformed church. Elsewhere, though conformity is not attested, protestantism was quickly achieved. Only in two parishes was there apparently no reformed service as late as 1574. At Kirkmichael, the task could not have been an easy one as the laird was hostile to change. On 27 December 1560 the General Assembly had requested that parliament punish him because he caused 'masse daylie to be said, and images holden up, and idolatrie to be maintained within his bounds'. Indeed no effective presentation appears to have been made to this parish between the death of the parson, *c.* 1579, and 22 January 1604 when a minister was appointed to the charge, 'long vacant' since that former incumbent's death.[25]

On the Kirkcudbrightshire side of the Nith, the pattern was very similar. Protestant service was ostensibly achieved in every parish lying within that part of the diocese of Glasgow within the first decade of the Reformation. As the incumbent at one time or another in at least four parishes was, however, Ninian Dalyell, the pre-Reformation schoolmaster of Dumfries and a staunch catholic, the extent of commitment may be seriously questioned. So too in Nithsdale where in August 1575 Peter Watson, minister of Dumfries and commissioner of Nithsdale complained 'that the town of Dumfries in Zuile day last by past, seeing that neither he nor his reader would read or use doctrine upon these days, brought a reader of their own with tabron and whisle, and caused him read prayers; which exercise they used all the days of Zuile.' Four years later in 1579, Watson was accused by the General Assembly of not visiting the bounds committed to him and had to admit 'he had visit only within six miles to Dumfries, the rest of the country being destitut of Ministers through the deposition of many, some be the Generall Assemblie, some be the synodal'.[26]

Amongst those deposed was Ninian Dalyell who held an astonishing number of appointments in the post-Reformation church on both sides of the river Nith. Dalyell's adherence to the reformed cause is more than suspect and in 1579 he was accused:

> That he had privilie professed papistrie, and had corrupted youth with erroneous doctrine in sundrie points, and, namely, that he had alleged that the sacrament cannot be ministred but be a priest, had affirmed the reality of the sacrament, the visibility and succession of the kirk and other like heads.

Dalyell refuted the charges by claiming that 'he had never affirmed such heads and craved only reasoning and conference upon the visibility and succession of the kirk. As to the rest he doubted not.' The disclaimer was questioned and Dalyell's ministry was terminated.[27]

Even such stern action was not immediately effective, and the grievances of the kirk in 1578 still included complaints about the south in general and Dumfries in particular. In addition to condemning the activities of Jesuits and prominent local papists the complaints referred not only to 'no resorting to the hearing of the Word' and lack of discipline but also to 'superstitious dayes keepit be plaine command, and controlling of the deacons of the crafts; all superstitious ryotousnes at Zuile and Pasche; na kirks plantit sufficientlie'. Old beliefs died hard and even as late as 1601 about fifty burgesses of Dumfries, including one of the bailies, a notary and the schoolmaster of the burgh were accused of attending the mass and having 'allurit mony ignorant simple people to schaik of the trew religion'. Many of these difficulties were ascribed to a grave shortage of reformed ministers and as late as 1608 no fewer than seventeen charges in Nithsdale were still vacant.[28]

It was, however, in adjacent Kirkcudbrightshire that catholicism was to make one of its more determined stands. In this area the influence of members of the Maxwell family ensured not only continuance of catholic belief but also continuity of unreformed service for many decades. The abbot of New Abbey, Gilbert Brown, was charged in 1579 with 'enticing the people to papistry' and the high altar still stood there at this date. Brown left Scotland thereafter, but returned in 1589 to conduct a defence of his beliefs against John Welsche, brother-in-law of John Knox. After his arrest in 1603 he was imprisoned at Blackness castle but was permitted to depart for France from which he again returned to New Abbey in 1608. An attempt to arrest him in Dumfries was, however, frustrated by 'a convocation of a great number of rude and ignorant people, armed with stones, muskets and hagbuts in a tumultous and unseemlie manner'. After Brown's subsequent arrest he was lodged in the abbey under suitable sureties, but he appears to have remained a thorn in the side of the reformed church, because in the following year John Spottiswoode, the reformed archbishop of Glasgow, ordered the abbot's chamber door to be broken open. 'A great number of Popish books, copes, chalices, pictures, images and such other Popish trash' were removed, all of which, (except the books, which were handed over to the keeping of Maxwell of Kirkconnell) were publicly burned on a market day in the High Street of Dumfries. Brown then retired to Paris where he died about three years later, and with his departure catholic sympathies appear to have subsided.[29]

The preservation of catholic worship in this area, paralleled to a lesser extent in Aberdeenshire and in Cunningham in Ayrshire, was exceptional. Elsewhere failures in leadership among the ranks of the former hierarchy, and the consequent lack of organization, meant that catholicism – despite its considerable early survival – was left to wither away. Recusant missionary activity, which only became organized after the foundation of a college at Douai in 1576, came too late to change the situation significantly. If, from 1580, the Jesuit mission to England began to have secondary effects in Scotland, its impact by that date was minimized by the entrenched position of the reformed church. A request was made in June 1584 by the exiled archbishop of Glasgow, James Beaton, to Pope Gregory XIII, asking him to persuade the general of the Jesuits to send priests of Scottish birth into Scotland. With some reluctance a few such as Edmund Hay, James Gordon and in the seventeenth century, James Ogilvie, were dispatched but the numbers sent were hopelessly inadequate and at best they could only hope to maintain a flicker of hope in the hearts of a few devout catholics. The old faith was upheld in the last resort only by a handful of important families who were 'characterized not by religious zeal, but by a general conservatism'.[30]

In the course of a century the wheel had turned full circle. The genesis of protestantism in the earlier sixteenth century had lain in the hands of the lairds who had used their chaplains to propagate the reformed faith. The influence of such lairds had in turn extended to several of the burghs in which protestant sympathies were awakened by itinerant preachers. Ultimate victory had been achieved through a combination of political and economic factors and in many localities the committed protestant believers remained for a long time in a decided minority. Time and changing political circumstances, however, allowed that minority to win increasing support by a mixture of persecution and admonition (assisted by the increasing pressures of social conformity). On the catholic side, both before and after the Reformation, a distinct lack of concern both on the part of the papacy and most of the Scottish hierarchy for the welfare of those who sought to retain their catholicism accounts, in part at least, for the reduction in the number of believers to an insignificant minority by the beginning of the seventeenth century.

In its moment of triumph the victorious protestant church was not, however, without its problems. The apparent success achieved by the presbyterians in the 'Golden' Act of 1592 proved to be illusory and the seventeenth century was to witness changing patterns of ecclesiastical government that were only to be resolved by the final presbyterian triumph at the Revolution of 1689/90. Attempts to associate episcopacy with liturgical changes which were almost universally opposed undoubtedly helped the presbyterians in their struggle for ultimate victory but, in this respect equal importance may be attached to the attainment by the end of the sixteenth century of a new relationship between the reformed church and the society in which it operated.

9
Church and Society: Post-reformation

An evaluation of how the Reformed church affected men's lives is not easy. In theory there should have been little change, as both before and after the events of 1559/60, church and society could be seen acting in concert. Nevertheless, the way this partnership worked in post-reformation Scotland was very different from the pre-Reformation era. The most striking aspect of this new relationship was a new religious fervour demonstrated by an unwavering support for Calvinist tenets. If the extent of personal commitment is difficult to assess, inner attitudes were outwardly demonstrated by the device of banding or bonding for religious reasons. Corporate activity or banding was not new and had previously been used to further a variety of causes, but its use to effect religious change in 1559/60 was novel. Success on that occasion had alerted the leaders of ecclesiastical opinion to the strength of the social forces at the disposal of the church, and the device was to be resorted to on many occasions thereafter, initially to maintain the *status quo* against catholicism, but subsequently to oppose religious innovation. In a defence of protestantism the General Assembly of 1572 enacted that 'ane solempnit band and aith may be maid be all thame that professouris of the Evangell within this realme, to joine thameselffis togidder, and be reddie at all occasiouns for resisting the enemis forsaids'. The result was sometimes not a formal banding, but an action taken in unison towards some general end, for example, the move to effect a general moral purge in Elgin in 1593, when it was concluded that:

> Monie of the inhabitantis of the said burghs being convenit within the quair in presens of the minister, baillies and eldaris, they being inquyrit generallis and be thair names particularlie to consent to reformatioun and purgatioun of the said burgh of all and sindrie viked, sclanderous and unprofitabill memberis of the publict veall thairof, eftir inquisitione of the quhilks they all as ane man in ene voce consentit and

aggreit that the said micht be done dilligentlie with exact executioun to the performin whereof they promeist thair concurrence, fortificatione and assistance'.

More often than not the enemies in the sixteenth century were the catholics and banding in subsequent years was directed towards that threat. The Negative Confession of 1581 declared that the subscribers should 'continue in the obedience of the doctrine and discipline of this Kyrke'; this confession already demonstrates something of the introspection which was to become even stronger in the seventeenth century. For if affirmation was made that the only 'true Christione fayth and religion, pleasing God ...' was 'receaved, beleved and defended by manie and sindrie notable Kyrkis and realmes' the rider 'but chiefly by the Kyrk of Scotland', displays a trait which was to become more marked as time went on. Moreover, the refutation of error 'by the worde of God and Kirk of Scotland' argues a partnership in which for some the word of God and that of the kirk were to become synonymous. The general bond of 1590, to which all inhabitants of the kingdom were expected to subscribe, continued this pattern and in this respect the Scottish custom of banding became infused with a new theological concept. In 1596 during a series of public bandings against the popish lords that had been called for by the General Assembly, the term 'covenant' was used to describe such ceremonies for the first time; the idea of a sacred covenant – a compact between the Scottish people and their God – had been born.[1]

The emergence of this concept can also be traced to the strengthening of the participation of the laity in the organization of the church. In some respects the role of the church in society had been greatly reduced because secular forces undertook duties that had previously been the preserve of the church; but within that church itself, lay participation had been maximized. This was immediately obvious in the claim to appointment of ministers of which the first Book of Discipline declared: 'In a church reformed or tending to reformation, none aught to presume either to preach, either yet to minister the sacraments till that orderly they be called to the same. Ordinarie Vocation consisteth in Election, Examination and Admission.'

The right of a congregation to choose its own minister (which was, however, compromised by the continuing exercise of patronage), was also asserted in the second Book of Discipline, which also stressed examination. The means of examination had changed, however, for whereas such duties had earlier been assigned to superintendents or 'failing in open assembly and before the congregation', the second Book assigned the task to 'the judgment of the eldership and consent of the congregatioun'. By eldership was meant an assembly of ministers, doctors and elders drawn from several neighbouring congregations and by 1582 this was interpreted to mean presbyteries. Although the examining body changed, the mode of examination varied little from that laid down in 1561 when the candidate for admission was to be examined 'fyrst privatle upon the cheaf puntis and headis in controversy, and tharefter ane porcion of text assignit to the minister to declar in the pulpiat in the essemble'. Full agreement on these two points existed in both Books, but greater diversity appears to have existed on the question of admission. The first Book of Discipline avoids the use of the term 'ordination' and states instead:

> Other ceremonie than the publict approbatioun of the peple and declaratioun of the chieff minister that the persone thair presented is appoynted to serve that Kirk, we can nott approve for albeit the Apostillis used the impositioun of handis, yet seing the mirakle is ceassed, the using of the ceremonie we juge is nott necessarie.

The second Book, however, defined the ceremony as 'fasting and eirnest prayer and impositioun of handis of the elderschippe.' Nevertheless, it is evident that the ceremony of laying on of hands cannot be attributed solely to the changes of 1578. The General Assembly made no objection to this practice when it endorsed the Helvetic Confession of the Kirk of Zurich in 1566, and its original omission from the first Book seems to have stemmed from a fear that the laying on of hands was still tainted with superstition. As this fear receded, the ceremony again found approval, and the diversity of practice that may have existed even in the 1570s gave way thereafter to ordination by the imposition of hands, although as late as 1597 a conference of ministers belonging to the synod of Fife held at St Andrews answered the question, 'Is he a lawful pastor who wanteth *Impositionem Manuum*' replied: 'Impositioun, or laying on of hands, is not essentiall and necessar, but ceremoniall and indifferent, in admission of a pastor.' This distinction was of theological significance, but may have been of lesser interest to the laity. They were involved with the ministry in a way that had never been possible in the pre-Reformation situation. The involvement of lay society with the church in other respects may have been less, but the overall result was much the same; the church everywhere impinged on the lives of the laity.[2]

This was most obvious in terms of worship, although even in this field certain services previously rendered to society were affected. The place of music in the services of the church and in the life of the people generally was undoubtedly to suffer as a result of the Reformation. Organs were among the first instruments to go; the dean of guild of Edinburgh sold three 'bellices of organs' for six pounds in 1560/1 and in 1574 the kirk session of Aberdeen decreed 'that the organis with al expeditioun, be removit out of the kirk, maid profeit of to the use and support of the pure'. The status of other musical instruments is less certain; and although some of the citizens of Dumfries who held a Christmas service of their own in 1574 brought 'a reader . . . with tabron and whistle, and caused him to read the prayers', this was not a policy countenanced by the established church. Whatever the fate of the organs at the Chapel Royal at Stirling, a chief 'voilar' appears in 1586 and six years later an act of parliament was passed in favour of the musicians of that institution. Nevertheless, it does seem that church music had been dealt a crippling blow by the Reformation.

Hostility to church music did not at first, however, extend to a general disapproval of music as such. Song schools continued to fulfil some of their original functions and in Edinburgh instrumental as well as vocal music was taught. Pre-Reformation musicians contrived to use their talents and were encouraged to co-operate in the making of the Scottish psalter by Thomas Wood (a former monk of Lindores, who later became vicar and then reader at St Andrews), on the grounds that if nothing was done music would perish utterly. One of the servants at St Mary's college, St Andrews, who had attained musical ability in the priory there, taught James Melville 'the Gam, Plean song and monie of the treables of the Psalmes'. At ceremonies held outside the church at which psalms were sung, they were frequently accompanied by musical instruments. When Queen Mary arrived in Scotland she was met, according to Knox, by a 'company of the most honest with instruments of music'; another source records that the instruments were 'mechants violins et petit rebecs', and that the psalms were sung very badly. James VI may have been more fortunate when he made a state entry into Edinburgh in 1579 and was greeted by a company of musicians who sang the 20th psalm, 'others playing upon the viols'. At the baptism of his eldest son in 1594, the 21st psalm was sung 'according to the art of musique', while after the banquet the 128th psalm was sung 'with divers voices and tunes and musical instruments playing'. Organs too appear at secular ceremonies and verses commemorating the entry of Queen Anne into Edinburgh in 1590 record that 'organs and regals there did carp'. Some of this tradition continued privately and musical art persisted in the metrical psalms, but slowly but surely the musical heritage of pre-Reformation Scotland was quietly eroded.[3]

The role of the church in legal affairs also changed considerably after the Reformation. Bishops continued to exercise their consistoral jurisdiction in matrimonial affairs, if only intermittently; their officials and commissaries remained in office, although their activity may have been greatly curtailed. In the eyes of the reformed church any such activity was inappropriate and the courts of the superintendents and that of the kirk session of St Andrews not only sought such consistorial jurisdiction for themselves but also gave judgment in a number of cases. Doubts were certainly felt by the litigants, some of whom went to the court of Session to ensure the legality of their actions. As a result of this confusion and the doubts as to whether the reformed church possessed the personnel or the resources to undertake the task, the privy council resolved on 28 December 1563 that commissaries should be appointed to exercise consistorial jurisdiction. Commissaries of Edinburgh were appointed on 8 February 1564 with a local jurisdiction in all consistorial cases and a general jurisdiction throughout Scotland in cases of divorce and confirmation of testaments. Some church courts may have continued to exercise jurisdiction after this date, but the role of the church in this respect had been much diminished; ecclesiastical courts were now restricted to the enforcement of moral discipline and in this respect could only look to the civil courts for informal assistance, which, however, was frequently forthcoming as bailies were often also elders. The church's role in society had been diminished, but its exclusion from such areas undoubtedly averted the possibility of the slide into secularism that had eventually proved fatal to its predecessor.[4]

The growth of secular attitudes had seriously affected the pre-Reformation tradition of encouraging devotion by means of plays upon religious themes. It was, however, religious scruples that seem to have threatened dramatic art in the post-Reformation era, even if at first a certain latitude appears to have been exercised towards such performances. Knox himself attended a play at St Andrews in July 1571 but then the theme was politically congenial to him. He was at that time a refugee from an Edinburgh, where the castle was held by Kirkcaldy of Grange on behalf of Mary, queen of Scots. In the play 'the castell of Edinbruche was beseiged, takin, and the Captan, with an or twa with him, hangit in effigie'. Performances on religious themes were quite a different matter and although the kirk session of St Andrews gave permission in 1574 for the performance of the 'comede mentionat in Sanct Lucas Evuangel of the forlorn sone [the prodigal son]' on a Sunday, it was on provision that it was approved by a small committee of the kirk and it was 'nocht occasioun to wythtdraw the pepil fra herying of the preaching, at the howre appointed alsweil eftir nune as befoir nune'. In the following year, however, the General Assembly enacted 'that no Clerk playes, comedies or tragedies be made of the Canonicall Scripture, alsweill new as old, neither on the Sabboth day nor worke day'. This total prohibition of the plays based upon canonical parts of scripture was accompanied by a partial ban on all dramatic performances in so far as it was conceded that 'uthir players, comedies, tragedies, and uthers profane players as are not made upon authentick partes of the scripture, may be considderit befor they be proponit publicklie, and they be not playit upon the Sabboth dayes'. The assembly's resolution in this respect was unshakeable for when the burgh of Dunfermline petitioned for permission to stage a performance upon a Sunday afternoon of a play that was not made upon the canonical parts of scripture, the assembly, in accordance with its previous decision, refused permission. Plays associated with former festivals of the church were even more vehemently opposed and at Perth in 1577 the kirk session directed fulminations against those who had 'played Corpus Christi Play upon Thursday the 6th of June last, whilk day was wont to be called *Corpus Christi Day* to the great slander of the Church of God and dishonour of this haill town'. Weekday plays and pageants that lacked religious connotation appear to have been tolerated for some time, for tragedies were played before the king by scholars of Edinburgh High School in 1579, and when he visited St Andrews the following year 'the gentlemen of the country had a guise and a farce to play before the king'. As late as 1589 the kirk session of Perth gave licence to a play on condition that 'neither swearing, banning nor any scurrility be in it', but by this time prohibition was almost complete and the medieval dramatic tradition had been completely extinguished.[5]

The church, however, asserted itself in many other fields. The character of the church was established in the immediate post-Reformation era when political and economic circumstances had forced the victorious reformers to adopt a compassionate attitude towards the representatives of the old faith. Not all members of the old church had expected such an outcome and, at Peebles, for example, a minister of the Holy Cross, on discovering that the local magnates had decided to support the lords of the congregation, not only exchanged his religious habit for a coarse cloth gown and a black bonnet, but also arranged, lest the *status quo* should be restored, to make a deposition before a notary public that he had done so – not from any hatred of his old religion, but for fear of his life. In the event his hopes of counter-Reformation remained unrealized, but so too were his fears. The weakness of the reformers, coupled with the protection offered to the old church by Mary, queen of Scots and magnates of both catholic and protestant persuasion, curtailed any move towards deprivation far less persecution and in this respect the Scottish Reformation was to produce little of the intolerance that characterized the Reformation in England and on the continent. The impracticability of dispossessing existing benefice holders, who were allowed to retain two-thirds of their revenues for life, may have meant comparative security for many priests but others who subsisted on minimum stipends may have experienced financial hardship. Compassion could be exercised in favour of deserving cases and the remission of his third to Johnne Stevinsoun, parson of Furvie, because he was 'ane auld blynd man', was by no means exceptional. Among the secular clergy those most at risk were the parochial chaplains who may have possessed little by way of either security or of permanent endowment. Some escaped from their financial dilemma by joining the reformed church; a few may have suffered impoverishment; others were protected from penury by the compassion of their former employers. At Peebles, for instance, the town officers were instructed by the council to recover all that was owing to Sir James Davidsoun, chaplain of the Holy Rood and the Holy Blood altars in their parish churches because 'the said Sir James is blind and ma nocht work and travell for his lewing'. Friars and canons were equally generously treated; the former were accorded wages, which usually amounted to about sixteen pounds per year, while monks and canons continued to enjoy their chambers and their portions. These arrangements appear to have been honoured. At Kilwinning in Ayrshire the chambers and yards of the monks were only gradually assigned to others as the monks died off; at Crossraguel, where the payments may have become lax because of complex wrangles over its revenues, the last surviving monk of that house, dene John Bryce, successfully sued the earl of Cassillis in 1602 for arrears of his portion amounting to £722.6s.8d. This the court awarded him in consideration of 'the great aige and waikness of the said dene John'. Forty years and more after the Reformation, that aspect of the essential character of the Scottish Reformation remained unaltered.[6]

A policy of moderation has also been claimed for the reformed church in its approach to the material structure of the old church. However, the attitude of the reformers towards existing ecclesiastical holdings varied according to the nature of the foundation; religious houses were less adaptable to the needs of the reformed church than parish churches and in consequence did not need to be maintained. Some religious houses situated in the borders had never recovered from the English attacks of the 1540s, but elsewhere they appear to have been in reasonably good shape. Even Patrick Hepburn, the avaricious commendator of Scone, had embarked on a programme of extensive repairs to the abbey of Scone in 1551 and work was also progressing at Holyrood, Kelso and Newbattle, right up to the eve of the Reformation. The activities of the lords of the congregation, and the 'rascal multitude' that accompanied them, radically affected this apparent stability. The friars whose houses were mainly situated in towns suffered particularly badly. In Edinburgh an attack on the places of the Blackfriars and Greyfriars on 29 June 1559 left them with 'nothing but bare walls; yea, not so much as a door or a window'. This pattern was repeated at Perth, Stirling, St Andrews and Dundee. Elsewhere the picture was more uneven, but at Glasgow, Montrose and even at Banff (where on 20 July 1559 the Carmelites were aroused by intruders 'raising of fire in our said place and kyrk under silens of nicht') many friaries were rendered uninhabitable. Even after the first fury of reformation had passed, the friaries continued to be particularly vulnerable and although the privy council ordered in February 1561/2 that burghs in which the buildings were still 'undemolissit' should consider adapting them to godly purposes as schools and hospitals, little attention was paid to this recommendation, although revenues pertaining to the friaries were often used for this. Only a few in the provinces escaped complete ruin by being turned to secular uses, or as at Peebles and Kirkcudbright, by replacing existing parish churches. By about 1570 the friars, who had been feared by the reformers for their preaching ability (which may account for the violence of the attacks against them) were no longer in occupation of any of their Scottish houses, most of which had physically disappeared.[7]

Monastic houses fared somewhat better in this respect. Some like that at Scone were destroyed almost entirely by the protestant lords, or, as Knox would have it, by 'the rascal multitude'. The Carthusian monastery at Perth suffered likewise, but in most instances the fabric was spared for the time being as long as the interior of the buildings was cleared of all objectionable features. Sometimes as at Lindores this was done by the 'godly brethren' who ordered the community to throw away their monkish habits, overthrew their altars, smashed their statues and burnt their mass books and vestments. On other occasions agreements to achieve such ends were reached privately and in June 1559 Donald Campbell, abbot of Coupar Angus promised that he would forthwith:

> reforme his place of Cowper putting down and birnying oppinlie all Idolis and Imagis and tubernaculis thairin destroying and putting away the altaris. And that na mess be thair done hereaftir nowther privilie nor opinly. And that the superstitiouse habit of his monkis with their ordour ceremonies and service ... be removit. And that na prayers be usit in the kirk but in the English toung. And thair according to the scriptouris of God.

This final stipulation anticipated the recommendation of the first Book of Discipline that whereas the exclusively religious portions of monastic establishments should be suppressed (palaces, mansion houses and dwelling places were excepted), some exceptions might be made when the church or part of it had also been used, as at Coupar Angus, as a parish church. This distinction and an act of the privy council ordering the removal of all places and monuments of idolatry, hastened the process of destruction, which in the west in particular was seen in the burning of Paisley and the 'casting down' of Failford, Kilwinning and part of Crossraguel. At both Paisley and Kilwinning, however, the nave where the parishioners had been accustomed to attend mass continued to be used as the parish church and this was to be the pattern elsewhere. At Dunfermline which was sacked in March 1560 the choir had its roof removed, but even the nave used by parishioners was windowless and its walls cracked; at Holyrood stone from the ruined choir and transepts was used to repair the nave. In the Borders where many of the abbeys had been in a ruinous condition before the Reformation, the situation was even more perilous. At Jedburgh, the nave was used as a parish church, but at Kelso one of the transepts had to suffice. Religious ministrations ceased all together at Dryburgh where the church became a ruin, while at Melrose so much building stone was removed from the church and the conventual buildings by Sir Walter Scott of Branxholm that when the nave was refurbished as a parish church in 1618, it had to be largely re-built. In more remote areas, or in districts where local lords favoured the old faith, as in the south-west where Lord Maxwell upheld the buildings at Sweetheart and Dundrennan, this process was delayed for several decades but demolition or decay was ultimately inevitable. In this respect collegiate churches fared much better; most were modest in construction and already served as parish churches. Kirk of Field, Edinburgh, of which the hospital and prebendaries houses had been burnt by the English in 1544–7, and which had its altars and images burnt in 1559, was sold to the town council in 1563 and in the following year the council purchased the stonework, which was taken either for 'the hospitall or for ane universite to be maid in the said Kirk of Feild'. The General Assembly in 1560 also arranged for the demolition of the collegiate church of Restalrig in 1560, but this was contrary to normal practice and several collegiate churches such as Holy Trinity at Edinburgh were in fact to become parochial after the Reformation.[8]

Cathedrals that had also served as parish churches before the events of 1559/60 were treated in much the same manner as monasteries and only part of their structure preserved for reformed worship; at Aberdeen and Brechin the nave was retained; at Dunblane and Dunkeld it was, however, the choir that survived. Only at Glasgow were both nave and choir to survive and these only after a period of controversy during the course of which it is alleged that the magistrates in 1578 were prevented from destroying the cathedral, or perhaps more accurately part of it, by the crafts of the city. Certainly much discussion between the town council and the deacons of the crafts preceded the ultimate decision by the council on 27 February 1582/3, that it was 'convenient and necessar that the haill kirk be uphaldin and reparit'. At St Andrews, where the cathedral church was monastic and non-parochial, the whole church was unroofed as the parish church of Holy Trinity was quite sufficient for the town's needs; but at Whithorn, which was also monastic but had served as a parish church, the nave continued to be used for this purpose. Size alone militated against the full use of most cathedral churches, but purged of their monuments of idolatry they were quite acceptable to the most ardent of reformers. So it was too with parish churches: the reformers passed from the attack on the parish church of Perth to similar actions at various churches, including Crail, Anstruther and St Andrews, at all of which Knox's preaching incited his hearers to pull down the altars and remove all 'monuments of idolatry'. At Crail the ancient rood which had been an object of pilgrimage was burnt, and wood carvings, paintings and stained glass suffered a similar fate as the congregation, singing psalms and spiritual songs, 'rejoiced that the Lord wrought this happily with them'. The reformers were not, however, wholly negative in their outlook but the requirements of the first Book of Discipline are in stark contrast to the riches of the pre-Reformation church: 'Everie Church must have durris, cloise wyndoes of glass, thak or sclait able to withold raine, a bell to convocat the people together, a pulpite, a basyn for baptisme, and tables for the ministratioun of the Lordis suppar.'

Most parish churches could be readily adapted to meet these simple needs, but the larger burgh churches were too large for the new requirements. Partitioning was the answer; the choir at St Michael's, Linlithgow, or St Giles, Edinburgh and at St Mary's, Dundee were adapted for preaching purposes and the remainder allowed to decay or as at St Giles, used for business purposes. At

St Nicholas church in New Aberdeen a more seemly arrangement was made when the council in 1596 made arrangements for the division of the church into 'tua severall kirkis'.[9]

The utilization of existing churches in this way coupled with the general lack of finance meant that few new parish churches were erected during this period, but one was erected at Eastwood in 1577 and another, characterized by its unusual square shape, was built to the design of a Dutch architect at Burntisland in 1592. Alterations were, however, made to existing structures and the addition of lofts or galleries commenced shortly after 1560. By 1565 there is already reference to the 'loft where the Lordis sittis' in St Giles and a royal loft was added before 1580. In country parishes, lairds began to copy this custom but the oldest of such lairds lofts, which dates from 1602, is that of the Ogilvies in the church of Cullen. In this respect at least the protestant church showed itself to be more class conscious than its catholic predecessor. Seating also began to be provided for at least some of the congregation and in 1560 the Edinburgh town council ordered that 'saittis furmes and stullis for the peple to sitt upon in tyme of sermone and prayeris' were to be made of the timber most convenient for the purpose. At Peebles when the parish church transferred from the old high church of St Andrews to the Cross church of the Trinity friars, it was not only decreed that the burgh treasurer should take down the bells in the old church and 'hing ane of thame in the Croce Kirk to rigne the commoun prayeris', but that he should also 'big with the trap and tymber in the Hie Kirk stepill, settis in the Croce Kirk for eis of the parochinaris'. As women were frequently separated from men in church, such provision was frequently specifically for women; in 1586 in Glasgow the session arranged for old pulpit stones to be laid in 'ranks for women to sit upon'. For various reasons the provision of such seating appears to have caused problems both at Elgin and St Andrews in 1598. At the former the elders ordered 'that all the fixed stools for the women be raised, and put forth out of the kirk'; and at the latter the session specifically decreed that 'the haill weman saittis fixit within the kirk be removit with expeditioun, for eschewing of trubill amongis wemen in the kirk'.[10]

Concern over seating in the kirk was, however, of minor concern compared with the social and educational problems facing the reformed church. On these issues commitment to alleviating the plight of the poor had been expressed by the reformers in one of their earliest manifestations, the Beggars Summons, in which the oppressed poor complained of the friars:

> Quairfore seeing our numbers is sa greate, sa indigent and so heavilie oppressit be your false meanis, that nane take care of oure miserie, and that it is bettir for us to provyde thir our impotent members, quhilk God has gevin us, to oppose to you in plaine contraversie, tha to see you heireftir (as ye have done afoir) steill fra us our lodgeings, and our selfis, in the meintyme to perreis and die for the want of the same.

Despite the raising of such hopes, the immediate effect of the destruction of many of the friaries during the course of the Reformation may have acted against the interests of the poor who were deprived of the dole, however inadequate, which had been provided by friaries and other religious houses. Many hospitals were also closed, although in the larger burghs a considerable amount of continuity was possible. Nevertheless, new solutions had to be devised by the reformed church and concern in this respect is readily apparent in the prominence accorded to poor relief in the first Book of Discipline. Parochial responsibility for the care of the poor was clearly enunciated in the statement that 'every several kirk must provide for the poor within the self'; the widow and fatherless, the aged, impotent and lame were to be sustained but those who made a craft of their begging and might be regarded as 'stubborne and idill beggaris' were to be punished.[11]

The revenues to maintain this ambitious programme were not, however, forthcoming. The revenues of certain friaries were used to meet the needs of the poor, but little else by way of a permanent endowment was available and funds achieved by piecemeal arrangements, which at Peebles involved auctioning the vestments belonging to the parish church and distributing the proceeds to 'pure householdaris', were soon exhausted. Plans to find a more lasting solution were advanced from time to time with little hope of success. On 31 December 1562, John Knox was commissioned by the General Assembly to petition the queen for financial support for the poor; on 7 July 1569 another request was made to the Regent Morton that attention should be paid to setting aside a portion of the teinds for the sustenance of the poor. The response of the state was not, however, to make funds available but rather to pass the responsibility to the parish, while at the same time advocating stern measures against the undeserving poor. In 1574 and again in 1579 acts were passed providing for the punishment of strong and idle beggars. By their terms all such vagrants between the ages of fourteen and seventy were to be arrested and tried. If convicted they were to be scourged and burned through the ear with a hot iron, unless some respectable person would guarantee to keep the offender in his employ for the coming year. The acts included a wide definition of strong and idle beggars, and prohibited the giving of alms to those who were unlicensed. On a more positive note the terms of an act of 1535, which had laid down that all poor people were to return to the parish of their birth, were re-enacted and in 1579 beggars were actually to be licensed to beg their way back to their own parishes. The needs of the poor, and a tax based on an assessment of these needs, were to become the responsibility of elders and headsmen of parishes according to the 1574 act, but the 1579 act transferred this task to provosts and bailies in burghs and 'justices' to be appointed by the king in landward parishes; the condition of hospitals for the aged was also to be examined. Further acts followed and their very frequency indicates difficulties in enforcement. In 1592 it was enacted that ministers, elders and deacons should elect 'justices and commissioners' for the enforcement of the poor law but in 1597 this became the direct responsibility of the kirk sessions who, if already shouldering this burden, thereby became sole statutory administrators of poor relief and partially liable for the administration of laws against vagabonds. In the event, however, voluntary contributions and fines, rather than taxation (which had been authorized 'for the sustenation of the puir' by the General Kirk of Edinburgh on 19 May 1575), became the normal means of providing for the poor.[12]

Thus the vast majority of pecuniary penalties imposed upon those who appeared before the session accused of some moral lapse were devoted to the poor, but collections made by the deacons at the church door appear to have been a more regular source of income. To this end the deacons of the Canongate church were instructed 'till up take the puris silver quhilkis gevin wolintarye be faythful men'. Compulsion was not unknown and at St Andrews in March 1598/9 the session decreed that communion tickets were not to 'be gevin to sic personis as hes nocht payit thair pairt of the contributioun to the puir'. Evasion of payment might result in loss to the poor fund, but it is clear that the revenue collected was sometimes diverted to other purposes and at Aberdeen in 1574 it had to be stressed that 'the pure be nocht defraudit of the almous collectit at the Kirk dure, but the sam to be distributit as is the custom in the uther reformit kirks of this realme'. Once collected, distribution of relief could be complex. To this end kirk sessions usually divided their parishes into districts, to each of which were assigned a number of elders and deacons, whose duties included visiting the sick and the poor and assessing their needs as well as expelling vagabonds who did not belong to the parish. Even the genuine poor had to meet certain requirements before receiving their alms, and at St Andrews the deacons were instructed not to give assistance 'bot to thais that frequentis and cummins to sermoundis, public prayers, examinatioun and wil gyf compt of thair faitht, and can say the Lordis Prayer, Beleve and Commondementis of God, or at the least sal learn the sam wythin one moneth't'. Failure to satisfy the standards of the kirk sessions on any of a number of issues might result in deletion from the register of the poor. Those who collected and distributed alms were also carefully scrutinized and any collector found negligent in his duty would be severely disciplined. Accountability was all important and on 14 August 1565, John Nords was forbidden by the kirk session of the Canongate 'to distribit one pennye' unless he had written authority signed by the minister and elders.[13]

Relief was usually monetary and normally confined to the poor and the chronic sick, but the alleviation of temporary difficulties was possible. In November 1588 the St Andrews kirk session records:

> at the hummill suit of Nicholl Cuik, haifing respect to his gude conversation, honest behavear and tred of lyfe in tymes bigane, and of his present necessite and esteat, has ordanit that thre schillingis four penneis be owklie [weekly] payit and deliverit to him furth of the box of the puir, for the relief of present necessitie . . . and the said Nicholl for that cais promissis to be reddy and obedient to serve at all tymes in sic advis as the sessioun sall charge him within.

A variation on the normal pattern is also provided by the same session, which in December 1597 gave relief to 'Agnes Lockhart and hir son, to hold him at the scole', while in August 1598 Perth kirk session found employment for a poor orphan who had petitioned for their help. As well as keeping a record of the poor, aged and sick, the elders and deacons were also instructed to see to the burial of the poor if their relatives were unable to do this. Care of the poor continued until death, but the needs of the poor might also be remembered at the point of death and in January 1593/4, notaries were requested by the kirk session of St Andrews to bear this in mind when drawing up wills for their clients.[14]

In this manner the reformed church was able in no small way to compensate for its failure to effect the more ambitious plans for poor relief outlined in the first Book of Discipline. So too with education in which very liberal advances in both school and university education had been envisaged. According to the Book of Discipline in country parishes the minister or reader was to provide elementary education for the children; in every town there was to be a schoolmaster able to teach the rudiments and the reading of Latin; and in each of the towns in which superintendents resided there was to be a 'college' with masters qualified to teach 'Logic and Rhetoric and the Tongues'. The extent to which these ideals, which presupposed adequate finance, were effected must remain doubtful. As far as parish schools were concerned the initial programme was relatively modest and although the ideal of a professional schoolmaster in every parish was readily accepted by the church it was not until 1616 that civil legislation to this effect was enacted. The General Assembly had, however, pursued the ideal of at least a school in every parish from a much earlier date. In 1562 it ordered the maintenance of such schools; in the following year it was decreed that instruction should be given only by those of the reformed faith. In the same year commissioners were set up for the planting of schools in Moray, Banff, Inverness, Ross and adjacent counties, but a further commission of 1571 suggests an initial lack of success. The north posed particular problems, but in 1565, John Row, the minister of Perth was commissioned to visit the schools and churches in Ayrshire and remove or suspend any ministers or readers who had proved incapable. By implication, tuition was taking place and this may also be inferred from the appointment of another commission in 1574 to visit schools in Caithness and Sutherland, to appoint masters and to suspend any who had proved incapable. Shortage of personnel and finance certainly made the appointment of independent schoolmasters unlikely in many areas before the early seventeenth century, but this does not mean that the initial ideals of the Book of Discipline were not realized even if by no other means than the adoption of regular catechizing. Private generosity had occasionally come to the rescue as at Fordyce in Banffshire where a school was endowed in 1592, but community action is seen in 1599 in the election of a schoolmaster at Monifieth in Angus. Provision for the payment of his salary was made by ordering that 'everie pleuch occupyed be the ownar to pay zeirlie fortie schillings, and be the fermouair 20 shillings, and everie two merks restrinit to ane pleuch; and sic as has no labouring to paye for everie bairnie x shillings'. The return was, however insufficient and in 1617 the session, because of the 'insufficiencie of ane provisione to the schoolmaister, has thoght expedient that of everie baptism he have two shillings, and of everie marriage fortie pence'.[15]

In towns in which both song schools and grammar schools continued the situation was much more promising, both because of the concern of the burgh authorities and the possibility of diverting some of the revenues of friaries and former prebends to this purpose. To this end the General Assembly in 1565 petitioned the queen that the emoluments of friars, annual rents, altarages and obits of priests should be applied to schools in towns and other places. What little was achieved was not, however, sufficient and complaints by the assembly appear throughout the sixteenth century. In 1575 the regent was implored to provide for schools and men of 'good engine' that they might visit other countries and universities for acquiring more learning; in 1587 the complaint was that youths were not sufficiently instructed in the knowledge necessary 'to come to the true meaning of the will of God'. By 1601 it was averred that the decay of schools caused by the lack of schoolmasters was the cause of defection from the true religion. Despite these complaints, co-operation between burgh councils and the kirk appears to have been quite good. Thus in 1563 when the schoolmaster of Stirling was found guilty of fornication, he was ordered to present his suit in the next General Assembly and abstain from teaching until the church of Stirling made request to the superintendent for him. Such co-operation was formalized in 1567 when parliament enacted that in all schools in burghs and landward no one might instruct youth unless he was examined by a superintendent or visitor of the kirk. In conformity with this act, the council of Haddington in 1576 undertook to appoint a schoolmaster whose life, conversation and doctrine 'tryit be the kirk and conforme to the ordour' should be innocent of any kind of idolatry, while in 1582 the town council of Glasgow 'by advice of the masters of the university, and others having power by act of parliament' chose Mr Peter Blackburne to be master of the grammar school. Changing ecclesiastical organization dictated change of practice from time to time; an act of 1584 required masters of schools and colleges, under pain of deprivation, to conform with all humility to the acts commanding obedience to the bishop as commissioners appointed to have spiritual jurisdiction in the diocese, but in 1594 the presbytery of Jedburgh was commissioned to try a schoolmaster of Dunbar as to whether he could teach in a grammar school. In 1596 the same presbytery ordered all schoolmasters within its bounds to appear before them to show 'how they instruct the youth'. Visitation of schools was also carried out; the first Book of Discipline had proposed that discreet learned and grave men should visit all schools quarterly to examine the progress of scholars in learning, and an act of the General Assembly in 1567 ordered visitors to try masters and doctors in regard to soundness in religion, ability to teach and honesty in conversation. In 1587 the assembly passed another order for inspecting schools and followed this in 1595 by ordering every presbytery within their own bounds to visit and reform grammar schools in towns and deal with magistrates for appointing 'most meet persons' to assist the masters in maintaining discipline. Not all these dictates were followed, but it is clear that in burgh education at least the programme of the first Book of Discipline was in some considerable measure implemented.[16] Lack of information makes it impossible to be too specific about what was done in the field of rural education, but where evidence exists between 1560 and the early seventeenth century, then in the Lowlands at least (unless the parish was very remote, very poor and very small and likely to be suppressed) it is usual to find a schoolmaster or a school or some means of tuition.

The development of the universities whose chief aims were to provide an educated ministry is not dissimilar to that of the burgh schools; some continuity from pre-Reformation practice and planned reforms which were not always implemented. At St Andrews, the first Book of Discipline had anticipated a continuation of the three colleges of St Salvator, St Leonard and St Mary, but had envisaged a closer identification of each college with a separate faculty. The first college was to teach dialectic, mathematics and physics leading to graduation in arts, but was also to be responsible for a five-year course in medicine; the second college was to be responsible for teaching in moral philosophy and in roman and statute law; the third college was to teach Hebrew and Greek and the theological exposition of the scriptures. In 1563 the broad outlines of this plan were retained in the report of a committee established by the privy council. Its most influential member was George Buchanan who proposed in the committee's name that one college should act as a college of humanity; in effect it should be a grammar school in which students would receive a thorough grounding in Latin and Greek before embarking on their university course proper. The second college was to be a college of philosophy in which arts were to predominate, although medicine was also to be taught; while the third college was to concentrate on divinity, but was to include a reader in law. Given limited resources his proposals might have seemed feasible, but in practice they remained unfulfilled. A commission of 1574 achieved no greater success and it was not until 1579 that a new foundation was eventually achieved. Ideas inherent in earlier schemes for reform were still there, but there was a new order, in essence the work of Andrew Melville, who wished to create an 'anti-seminary' of protestant theology as a counterweight to the Jesuit foundations of the counter-Reformation. All teaching was assigned to individual colleges but Melville's seminary, originally planned for St Salvator's was assigned to St Mary's, where he became principal in 1580. Largely due to his influence the idea of professorships was adopted, at least for the time being, although regenting continued at the other colleges. Towards the close of the century Melville's influence began to wane but St Mary's college remained a school of divinity. In contrast the study of law had sadly declined. From comprising one of the higher faculties, it dwindled to a mere 'chair', lingering on for a time after the new foundation at St Salvator, but by the turn of the century it disappeared altogether. Medicine too remained moribund for although the new foundation stipulated that the provost of St Salvator's should be a professor of medicine and lectures in this subject were in fact delivered by him in the late sixteenth century, vitality was non-existent in the faculty. Arts and theology alone prospered in a moderate way and in this respect, the impact of the reformation inhibited more scholarly development.[17]

At Glasgow, on the other hand, although the reformer's proposals for two colleges, one an arts college and the other as a college for the teaching of moral philosophy, roman and statute law, Hebrew and divinity, were never put into effect, the Reformation injected new life into a moribund university, which for lack of endowments had been increasingly threatened in the pre-Reformation era. Even in 1563, however, it could still appear 'rather to be the decay of ane universitie nor ony wyis to be reknit ane establissit fundatioun' but a small number of new endowments granted by Mary, queen of Scots were finally obtained in 1573 and were coupled with the promulgation of a new constitution. It was, however, the arrival of Andrew Melville as principal in 1574 which not only combined leadership with scholarship, but led directly to the *Nova Erectio* of 1577, which re-established the college with a complement of twelve scholars who were to live a collegiate life maintained from the teinds of the wealthy parish of Govan. This endowment was not fulfilled until 1593, long after Melville had departed for St Mary's college at St Andrews. Nevertheless, even in his short spell at Glasgow, his leadership and teaching attracted students to a university of which his nephew James Melville could write that there was: 'Na place in Europe comparable to Glasgow for guid letters, during these years, for a plentiful and guid chepe mercat of all kynd of langages, arts and science.'

The reorganization of the curriculum excluded the study of medicine and law and like St Andrews, Glasgow concentrated on arts and theology. In this respect both might be regarded as nurseries of the church, but no such certainty was immediately evident in post-Reformation Aberdeen.[18]

The effects of the Reformation upon King's college, Aberdeen, which the reformers had intended should have two colleges with forty-eight bursaries, were delayed for almost a decade; the principal and his colleagues remained steadfast opponents of the new regime, and it was not until after the deposition of Mary, queen of Scots, that the General Assembly in 1568 urged that the Regent Morton 'would give commission and authoritie that the currupt office bearers and others be removeit and other qualified persons placed in their roumes so that the youth be instructed in godliness and good letters'. In 1569 Principal Anderson and his colleagues were summoned before the commissioners. They refused to subscribe to the Confession of Faith, and were summarily dismissed. The new principal was Alexander Arbuthnot of whom it was written that he was 'in all sciences expert, a good poet, mathematician philosopher, theologian, lawyer and in medicine skilful'. To the reformers his prime importance lay in the fact that he was a protestant divine, but if in consequence changes had been hoped for, these hopes were quickly dashed as Arbuthnot and Andrew Melville were still discussing proposed reforms in 1575. In 1578, a new foundation which proposed the abolition of the teaching of canon law and medicine was accepted but little change was evident and the college continued to train at least canonists. Only the briefest of reports survives from an ecclesiastical visitation of 1583 and this simply records that it had been found 'that travels had been taken therein and ane order set down which is in the Principall's hands'. Problems certainly existed and plans for a new constitution appear to have encountered opposition; this inertia rather than the continuance of any hostility towards the reformed faith may have been the reason why the earl Marischal founded a new college in 1593; where teaching was to be conducted by specialist teachers, with an emphasis upon languages, including Hebrew and Syriac. Not until 1597 was a new constitution for King's college at last forthcoming, but the controversy that it engendered continued well into the seventeenth century. Of the three medieval universities that the reformers had hoped to revitalize in such a way that those who studied therein would 'profit the Church or commonwealth, be it in the lawes, physick or divinity', Aberdeen proved the least amenable. Students at King's college probably never numbered more than thirty in any academic year. Yet it was not all misspent enthusiasm; an educated ministry was gradually to materialize, and while many of these ministers were laird's sons, the tradition of the poor scholar was also maintained. Thus when Andrew Stevin approached the kirk session of Aberdeen and asked for support 'to help his intertenement at the college during his four years cours' the session 'seeing he is a native born townis barne, and hes not the moyen to mak his intertenement, being fatherless' ordered their collector to give Andrew the sum of five marks 'till a better help be providit for him heirefter'. If the kirk session of Aberdeen could respond in this manner, it suggests that other parish churches might have reacted in a similar fashion, particularly if the student was a native born 'townis barne'.[19]

Although the reformers' hopes for the development of these three universities had met with a somewhat mixed success, the advantage of inheriting such institutions from their predecessors had obviously enabled their plans to be at least partially fulfilled. The programme of the first Book of Discipline had not been content with merely preserving the *status quo*, but had in fact envisaged that every 'notable town, specially the town of the superintendent' should have an arts college and a sufficient number of masters to teach 'Logic and Rhetoric and the Tongues'. In order to have fulfilled this ambitious plan, finance, which was simply not available, would have to have been forthcoming. In some towns the grammar schools went some way to meet this ideal by extending their curricula; the foundation of Marischal college in New Aberdeen may also owe its inception to such a development and so too, in part at least, does the foundation of the university of Edinburgh. The antecedents of such a college actually appear before the Reformation with the teaching of law and Greek from 1556. Without endowment the opportunities for erecting a college in the immediate pre-Reformation era might have remained bleak, but for a legacy of 8000 merks bequeathed in 1558 by Robert Reid, bishop of Orkney, for the purchase of lands in Edinburgh with a view to the foundation of a college there. Plans for its foundation began in 1561, and a site was purchased in 1563, but not until twenty-one years later were the funds finally made available by the privy council. Building had in fact already commenced and the nucleus of a library existed in the form of a bequest from an Edinburgh lawyer, Clement Little, to the ministers of Edinburgh. In consequence the college was functioning under the principalship of Robert Rollock by the autumn of 1583. If its weakness lay in the close supervision exercised by the town council, as exemplified in an act of 14 January 1595/6 which ordered the dean of guild 'to caus mak ane loft in the eist end of the kirk of the Trinity College for the students and regents of the tounes colledge', its strength perhaps lay in its largely non-residential character, which resulted from the outset in a large number of students studying arts and theology.[20]

The need for the provision of an educated ministry had been stressed from the earliest days of the Reformation movement and although formal education was to provide the basis from which this ideal might be realized, emphasis was also placed upon continuing education. In this respect superintendents were 'to take count what bookes every minister has in store in the tyme of their visitation, and how the said minister, and every one of them does profite from tyme to tyme in reiding and studying the samein'. This was not an idle dream for ministers not only presented books but supplemented their stocks by borrowing from and lending to other clergymen. When Thomas Cranston, minister of Tranent died in 1569 his testament reveals that he had on loan from other ministers 'ane volume of Johnne Colvyne upone the lesser prophettis and utheris twa lyttil volumes' and 'Musculus upone Mathew and upone Johnne', while he in turn had lent to them, 'ane volume of Harie Bullinger aganis the Anabaptists' and 'Johne Calvyne upone the Actis of the Apostiles'.[21]

Ministers were not only expected to maintain a high educational standard, but were also expected in both their personal lives and that of their families to preserve a high standard of morality. Even unseemly dress could be cause for complaint. In 1574 the General Assembly found it necessary to bann all kind of embroidery, piping, sticking with silks; all kind of costly sewing of silk pieces, all kind of light hews in clothing, velvet breeches, gilt swords and silk hats. They and their wives were instead to dress in grave colours such as black, russet, sad grey, sad brown or such like. Those who transgressed might be suspended or even dismissed. In 1562 Paul Methven, who had played a prominent part in the making of the Reformation was dismissed as parish minister of Jedburgh because of his adultery; John Knox himself had been sent by the General Assembly to investigate the slander upon him. On 31 December 1563 Alexander Jardine, minister of Inchture, Kilspindie and Rait was suspended from office for fornication, but resumed office thereafter. So too, Alexander Forrester, minister of Tranent who had been suspended for baptizing a child in a private house, but who had had this suspension lifted by the General Assembly after acknowledging his offence, on condition that he made public repentance in the kirk of Tranent. In the early years following the Reformation ministers could also be taken to task by their congregations during the superintendent's visitation. For amongst the many enquiries made at the superintendent's congregational meetings was the standard question put to the congregation (after the minister had been removed), as to whether they had anything to lay to his charge either in life or doctrine. In 1566 the parishioners of the Canongate had no complaint to make 'but prissis God, requiring God to increase his giftis in him'. With the disappearance of superintendents, the sessions appear to have discharged this duty themselves and could censure when required. Thus at St Andrews in 1596 although one of the ministers, David Blak, had no objections raised against him, his colleague, Robert Wallace was reminded that he should be 'mair diligent and cairfull over the maneris of the people, and in visiting of the seik'. The reader Robert Zwill was also admonished 'of multiplicatione of wordis in his doctrine, and that his nottis be in few wordis that the people may be maur edifiit'. Ministers were obviously aware of their highly critical audiences and at Elgin in 1601 the minister at one meeting of the session inquired 'gif thair wes any of the session that culd find fault with his doctrein on Sunday last let them declair and tell it now, for he is redie to answer for himself, and all being severallie speirit [asked] at answert in ane voce they found nane, quhairupon the minister desyrit a not thereof be registrat'.[22]

In this instance theory had been translated into practice, with laity and ministry inter-relating and thus far at least visibly demonstrating not only the unity of church and society but also the practicality of the covenant ideal. Given the opportunity, such concepts could prove to be the means by which religious enthusiasm could be utilized to effect the changes that some sections of society believed would herald the Apocalypse. At a more practical level these attitudes nurtured a preference for presbyterianism, which, at moments of crisis, seemed to be the only form of church government to guarantee the freedom of the church against encroachment by the state. In the ensuing conflicts the laity were destined to play as decisive a role in the ecclesiastical fluctuations of the seventeenth century as they had initially played at the Reformation.[23]

Notes

I RELIGIOUS AND SECULAR INFLUENCES IN PRE-REFORMATION SCOTLAND

1. I. B. Cowan, 'Church and Society' in *Scottish Society in the Fifteenth Century*, ed. Jennifer M. Brown (London, 1977), pp. 122–35, examines this relationship at an earlier period.
2. *Aberdeen Breviarium*, Pars Estiva, pp. iii–xxvii.
3. D. McKay, 'Parish Life in Scotland, 1500–1560', in *Essays on the Scottish Reformation*, ed. D. Roberts (Glasgow, 1962), pp. 98–100.
4. W. McMillan, *Worship of the Scottish Reformed Church, 1550–1638* (London, 1931), pp. 249–52, 291; J. Dowden, *The Medieval Church in Scotland* (Glasgow, 1910), pp. 251–71; *Protocol Book of Mark Carruthers*, ed. R. C. Reid (Scottish Record Society, 1950), nos. 106, 135; *The Acts of the Parliament of Scotland*, eds. T. Thomson and C. Innes (Edinburgh, 1814–75), p. 245.
5. D. Patrick, ed. *Statutes of the Scottish Church*, pp. 77, 139; Anna J. Mill, *Medieval Plays in Scotland* (Edinburgh, 1927), pp. 247–53; Anna J. Mill, 'The Perth Hammermen's Play' in *Scottish Historical Review*, xlix, (1970), pp. 146–53; *Aberdeen Council Register of the Burgh of Aberdeen* (Spalding Club, 1846–8), i, pp. 448–51; *The Hammermen of Edinburgh and their Altar in St Giles*, ed. J. Smith (Edinburgh, 1906), pp. xxxviii–xlvii; McKay in *Essays on the Scottish Reformation*, p. 107–8.
6. D. McRoberts, 'Scottish Pilgrims to the Holy Land' in *Innes Review*, xx, (1968), pp. 80–106; D. McKay in *Essays on the Scottish Reformation*, pp. 108–9.
7. *PSAS*, 2nd series, iii, p. 168; *Registra Supplicationum* in Vatican Archives 433, fo. 43v; Lindsay, *The Works of Sir David Lindsay*, i, pp. 278–9.
8. D. McGibbon and T. Ross, *The Ecclesiastical Architecture of Scotland*, iii, pp. 195–8; J. H. Cockburn, 'The Ochiltree Stalls and other

Medieval Carvings in Dunblane Cathedral' in *The Society of Friends of Dunblane Cathedral*, viii, (1961, pp. 102–8, 142–5; M.R. Apted and W.N. Robertson, 'Late Fifteenth-Century Church Paintings from Guthrie and Foulis Easter', *PSAS*, xcv, (1961–2) pp. 262–79; *Report of the Royal Commission on Ancient and Historical Monuments* (Edinburgh, 1951), pp. 38–40; D. McRoberts, 'A Sixteenth-century Portrait of Saint Bartholomew from Perth' in *Innes Review*, x, (1959), pp. 281–6.

9. A. Oldham, 'Scottish Polyphonic Music' in *Innes Review*, xiii (1962), pp. 54–61; Cowan and Easson, *Scottish Religious Houses*, pp. 97–8; *Records of the Earldom of Orkney*, pp. 365–6; *Aberdeen Registrum*, ii, pp. 113–21; A. Myln, *Vitae Dunkeldensis Ecclesiae Episcoporum* (Bannatyne Club, 1831), pp. 19–20, 24; a translation of this work covering the years 1483–1516 is printed *Dunkeld Rentale*, pp. 302–34; *History of the Chapel Royal of Scotland*, ed. C. Rogers (Grampian Club, 1882), liii; *Essays on the Scottish Reformation*, pp. 91–2, 99–102, 149–50, 224.
10. *Treasurers Accounts*, iv, p. 338; *Edinburgh Burgh Records, 1557–71*, 10; A. Oldham, in *Innes Review*, xiii, p. 56.
11. J. Durkan, 'Education in the Century of the Reformation', in *Essays on the Scottish Reformation*, pp. 145–68; *Aberdeen, St. Nich. Cart.*, ii, p. 342.
12. *Records of the Earldom of Orkney*, pp. 368–9; Durkan, *Essays on the Scottish Reformation*, pp. 148–9, 158–9.
13. *Registrum de Panmure*, ed. J. Stuart (Edinburgh, 1874), ii, p. 266; *St. Andrews Formulare*, ii, pp. 185–7; *APS*, ii, p. 238.
14. I.B. Cowan and D.E. Easson, *Medieval Religious Houses, Scotland* (London, 1976), pp. 232–4.
15. *St. Andrews Acta*, pp. liii, lxxiii, cliv, clviii.
16. J. Durkan and J. Kirk, *The University of Glasgow*, pp. 174–5; Cowan and Easson, *Medieval Religious Houses, Scotland*, p. 232; *APS*, ii, p. 238.
17. *St. Andrews Acta*, pp. liii, lxxiii, cliv, clviii; Durkan and Kirk, *The University of Glasgow*, pp. 114–15, 131, 174, 216, 285.
18. G. Donaldson, 'The Church Courts', in *An Introduction to Scottish Legal History* (Stair Soc., 1958), pp. 363–73.
19. An examination of the archives of the Rota is at present being conducted on behalf of the universities of Dundee and Glasgow and is the source of this information; Myln, Vitae, *Dunkeld Rentale*, p. 326.

20. W. Angus, 'Notarial Protocol Books, 1469–1700' in *Sources and Literature of Scots Law* (Stair Soc., 1936), pp. 289–300.
21. M. Sanderson, 'Kirkmen and their Tenants in the era of the Reformation' in *RSCHS*, xviii, pp. 26–42.
22. Sanderson, in *RSCHS*, p. 29.
23. Cowan and Easson, *Medieval Religious Houses, Scotland*, pp. 168–9, 172, 175–6, 178–80, 182, 185–7, 192, 195; *Protocol Books Glasgow*, ed. R. Renwick (Glasgow, 1894–1900), ii, pp. 103–110.
24. Cowan and Easson, *Medieval Religious Houses, Scotland*, pp. 175, 178–9.
25. Perth Kirk Session Records in *Blast and Counterblast*, p. 36; 'The Beggars' Summons' in Dickinson *et al.*, *Source Book of Scottish History*, ii, pp. 168–9.
26. R.K. Hannay, *The College of Justice* (Edinburgh, 1933), pp. 1–78; *Aberdeen Registrum*, ii, p. 323.

2 THE MONASTIC IDEAL

1. Cowan and Easson, *Medieval Religious Houses, Scotland*, pp. 61, 84–5, 89–90; G. Stell, 'Architecture: the changing needs of society' in *Scottish Society in the Fifteenth Century*, pp. 175–7; *Hist. Mon. Comm. (Roxburghshire)*, (1956), pp. 194–209.
2. G.C. Coulton, *Scottish Abbeys and Social Life* (Cambridge, 1933), pp. 232–3.
3. *Prot. Book of James Young* (Scottish Record Society, 1932) no. 859; A. Ross, 'Notes on the Religious Orders in Pre-Reformation Scotland' in *Essays on the Scottish Reformation*, pp. 215–17.
4. J. Herkless and R.K. Hannay, *Archbishops of St. Andrews* (Edinburgh, 1907–15), i, pp. 157–8.
5. Herkless and Hannay, *Archbishops of St. Andrews*, p. 158; Dowden, *Bishops*, pp. 78–80, 329–31; Eubel, *Hierarchia Catholica Medii Aevi*, iii, p. 108; *James V Letters*, pp. 12–19, 23–4, 31, 36–7, 41, 71–2, 127; Watt, *Fasti*, pp. 296–8; *APS*, ii, pp. 309–10; R. Keith, *History of Affairs of Church and State*, 3 vols, Spottiswoode Society, (1844–50), i, pp. 461–4.
6. *James IV Letters*, pp. 48–51, 91–2, 311, 335; Reg. Supp., 917, fo. 169v; 929, fo. 13v. 931, fo. 286; 953, fo. 222v. 958, fos 299r and v.
7. Herkless and Hannay, *Archbishops of St. Andrews*, i, pp. 157–8; *Ayr – Galloway Coll.*, pp. 180–3; *James IV Letters*, no. 504; *Prot. Bk.*

Simon, ii, no. 621, 630–1; 'The Flodden Death Roll' in *Scottish Antiquary*, xiii, (1899), p. 105; *James V Letters*, pp. 28, 85–6; Fraser, *The Douglas Book*, iv, pp. 79–82; D.E.R. Watt, *Fasti Ecclesiae* (SRS, 1969), p. 298; Arm. Miscellanea (Vatican Archives), 7, fos., 99 and v, 126v–127, fos., 155, 163v; the documentation relating to the bailiary of Kilwinning is found in the Eglinton Muniments deposited in the Scottish Record Office, GD3/1/689 *et seq.*; Eglinton Muniments GD3/1/728–730, 732–4; Fraser, *Eglinton*, ii, p. 136.

8. *James V Letters*, pp. 3, 13, 36–7, 41, 48–9, 70–5, 80, 84, 153–4, 161–2, 246–7; *Acts of Council (Public Affairs)*, pp. 10, 22, 34, 67–8; *Statuta Capitularum Generalium Ordinis Cisterciansii, 1116–1786*, ed. J. Canivez (1933) 1518 no. 84; *Wigtownshire Charters* ed. R.C. Reid (SHS, 1960), pp. 44–6, 95–8; *Ayr – Galloway Coll.*, i, pp. 180–3; *Charters of the Abbey of Crossraquel*, i, no. 4, Watt, *Fasti*, p. 149; Reg. Supp., 1820, fos. 202 and v; 1850, fos. 235 and v; 1980, fos. 203v; 2086, fos. 244 and v; Reg. Vat. 1403, fos. 137–140.
9. *James V Letters*, pp. 246–7, 380, 392–3, 398; Reg. Supp., 2029, fos. 137v–138; 2049, fos. 244 and v; 2157; fos. 73 and v, 2354, fos. 212 and v; Reg. Vat., 1694 fos. 244 and v; *Reg. Lat.*, 1730, fos. 16–21v.
10. Reg. Supp., 1139, fos. 126, 183–4; 1815, fos. 218 ord v; 2013, fo. 94; fos. 289 and v, 2047, fos. 280 and v; 2054, fos. 50; 2065, fos. 253 and v; 2079, fos. 30–1, 2130, fos. 94 and v, 2132, fos. 94 and v; 2524, fo. 188v; 2940, fos. 105; 2941 fos. 59 and v; 2963, fos. 94 and v; *James V Letters*, pp. 315, 317, 334–5; A.I. Cameron (ed.), *The Apostolic Camera and Scottish Benefices, 1418–88* (Oxford, 1934), pp. 104, 110, 170.
11. Cowan and Easson, *Medieval Religious Houses, Scotland*, pp. 70, 74, 86–7.
12. Ferrerius, *Historia*, pp. 35–8, 57–84; Ross, *Essays on the Scottish Reformation*, p. 214.
13. Reg. Supp. 1955, fos. 92v–93v; *Kinloss Recs.*, 11; *CR*, pp. 49–50; Ferrerius, *Historia*, pp. 46–53.
14. Ferrerius, *Historia*, p. 40; Cowan and Easson, *Medieval Religious Houses*, p. 80; *Beauly Chrs.*, p. 105 and *n*, 177–81, 236–7, 257, 268; *LP Henry VIII*, 1^2, 1522; Ferrerius, *Historia*, pp. 47–9.
15. *Melrose Records*, iii, pp. 176–7; D. McRoberts in *Essays on the Scottish Reformation*, pp. 421–5; Cowan and Easson, *Medieval Religious Houses*, pp. 89, 90, 95.
16. G. Donaldson, *The Scottish Reformation* (Cambridge, 1960), p. 2; *Coulton, Scottish Abbeys and Social Life*, pp. 243–4.

17. *James V Letters*, pp. 187, 202, 210–11; Cowan and Easson, *Medieval Religious Houses, Scotland*, p. 26.
18. Cowan and Easson, *Medieval Religious Houses, Scotland*, pp. 26–7; *James IV Letters*, no. 107; *Coupar Angus Chrs.*, lxiii–lxv.
19. *Melrose Records*, iii, pp. 176–7; Donaldson, *The Scottish Reformation*, p. 4; Ferrerius, *Historia*, 35–8, 47–9, 57–84; Cowan and Easson, *Medieval Religious Houses, Scotland*, p, 76; Coulton, *Scottish Abbeys and Social Life*, p. 240; Durkan, 'Paisley Abbey in the Sixteenth Century' in *Innes Review*, xxvii, (1976), pp. 12–13.
20. Cowan and Easson, *Medieval Religious Houses, Scotland*, pp. 58, 67–8, 70, 73–4, 76–7, 90, 96.
21. Cowan and Easson, *Medieval Religious Houses, Scotland*, pp. 77–8, 83–4, 89, 94, 101–2; *Prot. Bk. Cristisone*, nos. 144–7.
22. McRoberts in *Essays on the Scottish Reformation*, pp. 427–8.
23. Cowan and Easson, *Medieval Religious Houses, Scotland*, pp. 143–55; *James V Letters*, pp. 232–3, 301; Lindsay, *Works*, ii, pp. 281, 317; Coulton, *Scottish Abbeys and Life*, pp. 232–3; Ross in *Essays on the Scottish Reformation*, p. 225.
24. *Arbroath Liber.*, ii, p. 245; D. Patrick, ed., *Statutes of the Scottish Church, 1225–1559* (SHS, 1907), pp. 106–7, 135–6, 176; Ferrerius, *Historia*, 80; Ross in *Essays on the Scottish Reformation*, p. 217; *Munimenta Alme Universitatis Glasquensis* (Maitland Club, 1954) ii, pp. 55, 68, 73, 136.
25. Ross in *Essays on the Scottish Reformation*, pp. 215–16, 225; *Kinloss Recs.*, pp. 2–13; *Ayr Burgh Accounts*, pp. 28, 112; J. Durkan, 'St. Andrews in the John Law Chronicle' in *Innes Review*, xxv, (1971), pp. 49–62; Oldham in *Innes Review*, xiii, (1962), pp. 57–8.
26. Ross in *Essays on the Scottish Reformation*, p. 225; Coulton, *Scottish Abbeys and Social Life*, pp. 232–3; *Crossraquel Charters*, i, p. 55; Fraser, *Eglinton*, ii, p. 132; Donaldson, *The Scottish Reformation*, p. 6; Haws, *Scottish Parish Clergy*, i, p. 322.
27. Cowan and Easson, *Medieval Religious Houses, Scotland*, pp. 116–21, 124–7, 129–33, 135–8, 140–1.
28. Fraser, *Eglinton*, ii, pp. 132, 195–6; *Charters of the Friar Preachers of Ayr* (Archaeological and Historical Collections relating to the Counties of Ayr and Wigton, 1881), pp. 66–75; W.M. Bryce, *The Scottish Grey Friars*, 2 vols. (Edinburgh, 1909), i, pp. 474, 476; *TA*, viii, p. 461.
29. Bryce, *Grey Friars*, i, pp. 130–1.
30. *Ayr Friars*, pp. 87–8; Bryce, *Grey Friars*, i, p. 373.

31. Bryce, *Grey Friars*, i, p. 373, ii, pp. 103–17; *Prot. Bk. Carruthers*, nos. 25, 42, 52.
32. *Dunkeld Rentale*, p. 304; Bryce, *Grey Friars*, i, pp. 95, 102, 337–8; A. Ross, 'Libraries of the Scottish Blackfriars, 1481–1560' in *Innes Review*, xx (1969), pp. 3–36; I.B. Cowan, *Regional Aspects of the Scottish Reformation* (Historical Association, 1978), pp. 12, 15.
33. D. Laing, ed., *The Works of John Knox* (Edinburgh, 1846), i, pp. 321–3.

3 THE SECULAR CLERGY

1. Watt, *Fasti*, pp. 3–4, 60–1, 77–8, 132, 204–5, 253–4, 269–70, 296; J. Dowden, *The Bishops of Scotland* (Glasgow, 1912), pp. 35–8, 129–43, 139–41, 222–30, 247–50, 263–8, 290–3, 370–5.
2. Watt, *Fasti*, pp. 216–17; Dowden, *Bishops*, pp. 163–72.
3. Watt, *Fasti*, pp. 49–50, 149–50, 296–8; Dowden, *Bishops*, pp. 38–44, 331–52.
4. Watt, *Fasti*, pp. 27, 41; Dowden, *Bishops*, pp. 189–91, 387–91.
5. M. Mahoney, 'The Scottish Hierarchy, 1513–1565' in *Essays on the Scottish Reformation*, pp. 45–51.
6. Mahoney in *Essays on the Scottish Reformation*, pp. 51–4.
7. Cowan and Easson, *Medieval Religious Houses, Scotland*, pp. 203–7, 210–11.
8. Cowan and Easson, *Medieval Religious Houses, Scotland*, pp. 203–5, 207–9.
9. Watt, *Fasti*, pp. 21–3, 36–7, 91, 122–4, 138–9, 179–87, 211–12, 242–3, 263, 287, 314–22; *Dunkeld Rentale*, p. 304.
10. McKay, 'Parish Life in Scotland', in *Essays on the Scottish Reformation*, p. 98; *Dunkeld Rentale*, p. 328; Myln, *Vitae*, pp. 66–7.
11. Watt, *Fasti*, pp. 24–5, 57, 73–4, 92–3, 125–6, 141–2, 191–6, 213, 245–6, 265, 288, 328–32.
12. Myln, *Vitae*, pp. 60–1; *Dunkeld Rentale*, p. 324.
13. Dowden, *Medieval Church in Scotland*, pp. 76–80; *Glasgow Registrum*, ii, pp. 341–57, 611–12; *Aberdeen Registrum*, ii, p. 75.
14. *Dunkeld Rentale*, pp. 320–29; Myln, *Vitae*, pp. 56–69; Durkan and Kirk, *The University of Glasgow*, pp. 168–9.
15. Dowden, *Medieval Church in Scotland*, pp. 66–71; I.B. Cowan, *St Machars Cathedral in the Early Middle Ages* (1980), p. 12.
16. *Dunkeld Rentale*, pp. 329–31.

17. Cowan and Easson, *Medieval Religious Houses, Scotland*, pp. 213–28; *SRO*, Gordon Castle Muniments, GD 44/15/3/1.
18. Durkan, 'Education in the Century of the Reformation' in *Essays on the Scottish Reformation*, pp. 148–52.
19. McKay in *Essays on the Scottish Reformation*, pp. 97–8; A. Maxwell, *of Old Dundee prior to the Reformation* (Edinburgh and Dundee, 1891), pp. 123–31; *Edinburgh Burgh Records, 1528–1557*, pp. 348, 358; *Ayr Burgh Records*, p. 123.
20. *Prot. Bk. Carruthers*, nos. 16, 123, 138, 151, 182, 190, 197.
21. *Prot. Bk. Carruthers*, nos. 16, 138, 151.
22. *Prot. Bk. Carruthers*, no. 60.
23. Laing, *Lindores*, p. 196; *Elgin Records*, i, p. 87; *Inverness Records*, i, p. 7.
24. *Prot. Bk. Carruthers*, no. 119.
25. *Prot. Bk. Carruthers*, no. 129.
26. I.B. Cowan, 'Some Aspects of the Appropriation of Parish Churches in Medieval Scotland', in *RSCHS*, xiii, pp. 203–22.
27. Quintin Kennedy, 'Ane Compendius Tractive' in *Wodrow Society Miscellany* (Edinburgh, 1944), pp. 151–2.
28. G. Mollett, *Lettres Communes de Jean XXII (1316–33)* (Paris, 1921), pp. 9–17; *St. Andrews Copiale*, pp. 89, 435; *St. Andrews Formulare*, i, no. 193.
29. *APS*, ii, pp. 5, 144, 146, 237–8; *RSS*, i, nos. 999, 2273, 4087.
30. *Prot. Bk. Simon*, i, pp. 314–19, 331, 336, 353–4; J.J. Robertson, 'The Development of the Law' in *Scottish Society in the Fifteenth Century*, pp. 151–2.
31. Scottish entries from the Vatican archives series of Resignationes et Consensus on a study of which these entries are based, are held on microfilm in the Department of Scottish History, University of Glasgow.
32. I.B. Cowan, 'Vicarages and the Cure of Souls in Medieval Scotland' in *RSCHS*, xvi, pp. 111–24.
33. Cowan in *RSCHS*, xvi, pp. 124–5; Patrick, *Statutes*, pp. 111–12, 169–70.
34. Cowan in *RSCHS*, xvi, pp. 126–7.
35. Cowan in *RSCHS*, xvi, p. 127.
36. Prot. Bk. of Sir John Crawford (SRO), fo. 41 (a); *Dunkeld Rentale*, p. 259.
37. *Gude and Godlie Ballates*, ed. D. Laing (1868), p. 205.
38. *Dunkeld Rentale*, pp. 327–9; Patrick, *Statutes*, 146; *Moray Registrum*, v–vi.

4 REFORM FROM WITHIN

The best analysis of attempts at reform from within the pre-Reformation church are to be found in three articles in *Essays on the Scottish Reformation*: 'The Popular Literature of the Scottish Reformation' by Brother Kenneth, 'The Conflicting Doctrines of the Scottish Reformation' by Maurice Taylor and 'Church Courts in Sixteenth-Century Scotland' by Thomas Winning.

1. Lindsay, *Works*, i, pp. 83, 142, ii, pp. 51, 89, 281, 315, 317, 349.
2. Lindsay, *Works*, ii, pp. 259–63, 269, 273, 349.
3. Lindsay, *Works*, ii, p. 129.
4. Lindsay, *Works*, ii, p. 275; Ferrerius, *Historia*, p. 80; *Records of the Earldom of Orkney*, 365; Durkan, 'Education in the Century of the Reformation' in *Essays on the Scottish Reformation*, pp. 160–1; G. Hill, 'The Sermons of John Watson, canon of Aberdeen' in *Innes Review*, x, (1959), pp. 3–34, 104–5; *Essays on the Scottish Reformation*, pp. 234, 369–70; J. Durken, 'Robert Wauchope, Archbishop of Armagh' in *Innes Review*, i, (1950), pp. 48–65.
5. Patrick, *Statutes*, pp. 97–8, 115–16, 128–31, 137–8, 141–2, 177–83.
6. Patrick, *Statutes*, pp. 178–9, 181–2, 185–6.
7. Patrick, *Statutes*, pp. 89–114, 118, 135–6, 163–9, 171–2; *Essays on the Scottish Reformation*, pp. 161, 351.
8. Patrick, *Statutes*, pp. 127–8, 138–9, 146, 184.
9. Patrick, *Statutes*, pp. 143–8.
10. *Essays on the Scottish Reformation*, pp. 64–6, 252–5, 301–2, 326–9, 344–5, 367–8.
11. *Essays on the Scottish Reformation*, pp. 66, 253–5.
12. Patrick, *Statutes*, pp. 167, 172–3.
13. Patrick, *Statutes*, pp. 175–6, 188–90; *Essays on the Scottish Reformation*, pp. 359–61.
14. *Essays on the Scottish Reformation*, pp. 259–60; C.A. Kuipers, *Quintin Kennedy (1520–1564): Two Eucharistic Tracts* (Nijmegen, 1964), pp. 25–32.
15. Kuipers, *Two Eucharistic Tracts*, pp. 49–51; Quintin Kennedy, 'Ane Compendius Tractive', in *Wodrow Society Miscellany*, pp. 151–2; *Essays on the Scottish Reformation*, pp. 260–2, 264–5; Knox, *History*, i, pp. 266–7; Knox, *Works*, iv, pp. 465–520.
16. *Melrose Records*, iii, pp. 167–86; *Spalding Club Miscellany*, iv, pp. 57–8; *BUK*, i, p. 163.

5 TOWARDS PROTESTANTISM: THE 1540S AND 1550S

The information contained in this chapter on the spread of protestant opinion is mainly drawn from the most important contemporary source – John Knox's *History of the Reformation in Scotland*, ed. W.C. Dickinson, 2 vols. (Edinburgh, 1949). Knox derived much of his material from Foxe's *Book of Martyrs* (London, 1877), and the pre-Reformation information contained in both was in turn utilized by the seventeenth-century historian David Calderwood in his *History of the Church of Scotland*, ed. T. Thomson and D. Laing, 8 vols. (Woodrow Society, 1842–9). However, Calderwood contains some additional material derived from other, now lost, contemporary sources. As both Calderwood and Knox were strongly partisan they are unlikely to have minimized protestant advance in the pre-Reformation period and to this extent they must be considered unreliable. References for evidence for the pre-Reformation situation derived from either of these sources, other than direct quotations, have not been specifically cited.

1. *St. Andrews Copiale*, pp. 136, 383–4, 460; *APS*, ii, pp. 7, 295; *St. Andrews Acta*, i, p. 11.
2. *APS*, ii, pp. 341–2, 370–1.
3. *Irvine Muniments*, p. 157; *Glasgow Rental*, i, no. 539; *Ayr Friars Chrs. passim.*
4. R. Pitcairn, ed., *Ancient Criminal Trials in Scotland* (Bannatyne Club, 1829), i, pp. 287, 335; *St. Andrews Formulare*, ii, p. 59; D. Shaw, 'John Willock' in *Reformation and Revolution* (Edinburgh, 1967), p. 46; J. Durkan, 'Paisley Abbey in the Sixteenth Century' in *Innes Review*, xxvii, pp. 121–2.
5. *Aberdeen Council Register*, i, pp. 98, 107–8, 110; Pitcairn, *Trials*, i, p. 221; Calderwood, *History*, i, pp. 107; G. Donaldson, 'Aberdeen University and the Reformation' in *Northern Scotland*, i, p. 133; *Acts of Council (Public Affairs)*, p. 371–2.
6. Brother Kenneth, 'Popular Literature of the Scottish Reformation' in *Essays on the Scottish Reformation*, p. 170; *Acts of Council (Public Affairs)*, p. 423.
7. *St. Andrews Acta*, i, pp. lvii–lviii, lix–lxi.
8. Calderwood, *History*, i, pp. 142–3; *Gude and Godlie Ballatis*, pp. 10, 72, 167–8; Pitcairn, *Trials*, i, pp. 252, 286.
9. *Diurnal of Occurrents*, p. 15; Pitcairn, *Trials*, i, pp. 217, 252.
10. Calderwood, *History*, i, pp. 124, 127; Pitcairn, *Trials*, i, p. 216.
11. Taylor, 'Conflicting Doctrines of the Scottish Reformation' in *Essays on the Scottish Reformation*, pp. 246–7.

12. *APS*, ii, pp. 370–1, 415, 425.
13. Fittis, *Ecclesiastical Annals of Perth to the period of the Reformation* (Edinburgh, 1885), p. 189; Calderwood, *History*, i, pp. 171–2; Pitcairn, *Trials*, i, p. 335.
14. *Aberdeen Council Register*, i, pp. 206, 211–12; *Diurnal of Occurrents*, p. 29; *Aberdeen Registrum*, ii, p. 317; *RSS*, iii, no. 820.
15. A. Maxwell, *History of Old Dundee* (Edinburgh and Dundee, 1884), p. 395.
16. Calderwood, *History*, i, pp. 176, 190; *St. Andrews Rentale*, p. 200.
17. Calderwood, *History*, i, p. 226; Knox, *History*, i, p. 93; *LP Henry VIII*, xvii, pt. ii, no. 128.
18. *Hamilton Papers*, ii, p. 15; Pitcairn, *Trials*, i, p. 330; Calderwood, *History*, i, p. 156; Knox, *History*, i, p. 43; Moir Bryce, 'Burgh Recs of Edinburgh' in *Old Edinburgh Book*, iii, p. 56; *Mary of Lorraine Correspondence*, pp. 68–9, 132–3, 240–1.
19. *Ayr Burgh Accounts*, pp. 90, 96–7; Knox, *History*, i, p. 61.
20. *Reg. Privy Council*, i, pp. 28–9, 61, 63.
21. Taylor in *Essays on the Scottish Reformation*, pp. 249–51.
22. *Mary of Lorraine Correspondence*, p. 368.
23. Pitcairn, *Trials*, i, pp. 352–3; Knox, *Works*, i, pp. 544–8.
24. Patrick, *Statutes*, pp. 84, 127; M. Sanderson, 'Aspects of the Church in Scottish Society', in *RSCHS*, xvii, p. 95.
25. *Woodrow Society Miscellany*, i, p. 54.
26. Calderwood, *History*, i, pp. 303–4; Knox, *History*, i, pp. 120–2; Robertson, *Concilia*, ii, p. 295; *Edinburgh Burgh Records, 1528–1557*, pp. 251–2.
27. Taylor, 'Conflicting Doctrines of the Scottish Reformation' in *Essays on the Scottish Reformation*, pp. 256–7.
28. Knox, *History*, i, p. 121; Calderwood, *History*, i, pp. 307, 320, 333.
29. G. Donaldson, *James V–James VII, The Edinburgh History of Scotland* (Edinburgh, 1965), iii, pp. 88–90.
30. Calderwood, *History*, i, pp. 333, 347; Pitcairn, *Trials*, i, pp. 406–7.
31. *Wodrow Miscellany*, i, p. 54; Knox, *History*, i, pp. 181–2; Pitscottie, *History*, ii, p. 137.
32. Sanderson in *RSCHS*, p. 93, *Ayr Burgh Accounts*, pp. 128–30; Ayr Burgh Court Book (MS B6/12/3, Scottish Record Office), fos. 23v.
33. Calderwood, *History*, i, p. 343; *Miscellany of the Spalding Club* (Aberdeen, 1849), iv, pp. 57–8; *Peebles Charters*, pp. 242, 253.
34. Knox, *Works*, vi, p. 78.

6 THE TRIUMPH OF PROTESTANTISM

Information, other than direct quotations, derived from Knox, *History of the Reformation in Scotland* and Calderwood, *History of the Church of Scotland*, has not normally been cited. For further information about the politics outlined in the First and Second Books of Discipline, reference should be made to the standard editions by J.K. Cameron and James Kirk to whose scholarly introductions the present writer acknowledges a deep debt of gratitude. It should be noted, however, that the interpretation of events leading to the compilation of the Second Book of Discipline are a matter of controversy. In this respect the views of Dr Kirk, which are further exemplified in his article 'The Polities of the Best Reformed Kirks: the Scottish achievements and English aspirations in church government after the Reformation' in *SHR*, lix (1980), pp. 22–53, are markedly at variance with those expressed by Professor Gordon Donaldson, *The Scottish Reformation* (1960).

1. Knox, *Works*, vi, p. 78; Knox, *History*, i, pp. 160, 163, 181–2; C. Haws, 'Scottish Clergy at the Reformation' (Glasgow Ph.D., thesis).
2. J.H. Baxter, *Dundee and the Reformation* (Abertay Historical Society, 1960), p. 23; Ayr Burgh Court Book (MS B6/12/3 Scottish Record Office), fo. 56v; W. Motherwell, *Memorabilia of Glasgow* (Glasgow, 1835), pp. 3–4, 7–8, 13–14; Pitcairn, *Trials*, i, p. 407; Knox, *History*, i, pp. 48, 178, *Peebles Charters*, p. 258.
3. Knox, *History*, i, pp. 264–5; vi, p. 78; B. Maclennan, 'The Reformation in the Burgh of Aberdeen' in *Northern Scotland*, ii, p. 128 ff.; G. Donaldson in *Northern Scotland*, i, pp. 129–42; C.H. Haws, *Scottish Parish Clergy at the Reformation* (SRS, 1972), p. 3.
4. 'Histoire of the Estate of Scotland' in *Wodrow Soc. Misc.*, p. 67.
5. *APS*, ii, pp. 525–6; P. McNeill and R. Nicholson, eds., *Historical Atlas of Scotland* (St Andrews, 1975), pp. 84–5, 196–7.
6. J.K. Cameron, *The First Book of Discipline* (Edinburgh, 1972), pp. 3–75.
7. Donaldson, *Thirds of Benefices*, vii–xxxv; J. Kirk, *The Second Book of Discipline* (Edinburgh, 1980), pp. 3–35.
8. Kirk, *Second Book of Discipline*, pp. 35–42; *Diary of James Melville*, ed. R. Pitcairn (Edinburgh, 1842), p. 24; *BUK*, pp. 238, 244–9, 349.
9. Kirk, *Second Book of Discipline*, pp. 57–130.
10. Kirk, *Second Book of Discipline*, pp. 57–64; Calderwood, *History*, iii, p. 158; Cameron, *First Book of Discipline*, pp. 99, 103, 120, 127, 164,

200; Donaldson, *The Scottish Reformation*, pp. 130–48; Knox, *Works*, ii, p. 118, v, pp. 324, 443, 490.

11. Kirk, *Second Book of Discipline*, pp. 11–12; Calderwood, *History*, pp. 156–62.
12. D. Shaw, *The General Assemblies of the Church of Scotland* (Edinburgh, 1963), pp. 17–20, 71–4, 107–12; *BUK*, i, pp. 10, 38, 44, 60–1, 71, 83, 124, 164–5, iii, 947–8; Calderwood, *History*, v, p. 86.
13. Shaw, *The General Assemblies of the Church of Scotland*, pp. 102–6, 113–15.
14. Shaw, *The General Assemblies of the Church of Scotland*, pp. 75–94, 116–23; *BUK*, i, p. 124, iii, pp. 935–47.
15. Kirk, *Second Book of Discipline*, pp. 116–21, 169, 204; *St. Andrews Kirk Session*, i, pp. 2, 4, 5.
16. Kirk, *Second Book of Discipline*, pp. 74–84, 176, 222; Cameron, *First Book of Discipline*, p. 115; Donaldson, *The Scottish Reformation*, pp. 102–29; *St. Andrews Kirk Session Reg.*, i, pp. 74–5; Calderwood, *History*, iii, p. 160.
17. Donaldson, *The Scottish Reformation*, pp. 122–4; Kirk, 'Polities of the Best Reformed Kirks', in *SHR*, lix (1980), pp.29–30.
18. Kirk, *Second Book of Discipline*, pp. 35–42; Donaldson, *The Scottish Reformation*, pp. 183–202.
19. Kirk, *Second Book of Discipline*, pp. 102–107, 199; *BUK*, ii, p. 439; Donaldson, *The Scottish Reformation*, pp. 203–9.
20. Kirk, *Second Book of Discipline*, pp. 107–114, 130–54; Donaldson, *The Scottish Reformation*, pp. 209–220.
21. Kirk, *Second Book of Discipline*, pp. 88–100, 192, 204, 207–8; Cameron, *First Book of Discipline*, pp. 175, 178–9; W.H Makey, 'The Elders of Stow, Liberton, Canongate and St. Cuthberts in the mid-seventeenth century' in *RSCHS*, xvii (1970), pp. 155–7; *St. Andrews Kirk Session Reg.*, pp. 805, 821, 884, 926, 932.
22. Kirk, *Second Book of Discipline*, p. 231; *St. Andrews Kirk Session Reg.*, pp. xxiv–xxv, xcvi–xcvii, 453–4, 487, 511, 608, 650; Alexander Carstares was one of the few who in turn served as deacon, elder and bailie (*St. Andrews Kirk Session Reg.*, pp. 369, 427).
23. Makey, *RSCHS*, xvii, pp. 157–67; *St. Andrews Kirk Session Reg.*, pp. 412, 427, 760, 801–2; *Elgin Records*, ii, p. 32.
24. *St. Andrews Kirk Session Reg.*, p. 866; *Elgin Records*, ii, p. 4.
25. *St. Andrews Kirk Session Reg.*, pp. 815–7; 822; *Buik of the Kirk of the Canagait*, p. 62; *Aberdeen Ecclesiastical Records*, p. 16.
26. *St. Andrews Kirk Session Reg.*, pp. 141, 324, 819; *Elgin Records*, ii, p. 90.

7 WORSHIP

The standard works on worship during this period are W. McMillan, *The Worship of the Scottish Reformed Church, 1550–1638* (London, 1950) and G.B. Burnet, *The Holy Communion in the Reformed Church of Scotland, 1560–1960* (Edinburgh, 1960). References for evidence from either of these standard works, other than direct quotations, have not been cited.

1. *St. Andrews Kirk Session Reg.*, ii, pp. 504, 829–30; *Elgin Records*, ii, p. 71.
2. *St. Andrews Kirk Session Reg.*, ii, pp. 828–9; *Spottiswoode Misc.*, ii, pp. 257–8.
3. *Spottiswoode Misc.*, ii, p. 256; *St. Andrews Kirk Session Reg.*, ii, p. 856.
4. Knox, *Works*, ii, pp. 238–9.
5. *APS*, iii, p. 139; *Elgin Records*, ii, p. 17; *RPC*, ii, p. 545; *BUK*, pp. 125–6.
6. *Maitland Club Misc.*, i, pp. 67–8, ii, pp. 317–18; *St. Andrews Kirk Session Reg.*, ii, lxx–lxxiii, pp. 771, 887, 923, 925; *Elgin Records*, ii, pp. 26–7; *Spottiswoode Misc.*, ii, p. 271.
7. Lee, *Lectures on the History of the Church of Scotland* (Edinburgh, 1860), i, pp. 391, 402; *Elgin Records*, ii, p. 17.
8. *Maitland Club Misc.*, ii, p. 98.
9. Cameron, *First Book of Discipline*, p. 92.
10. Lee, *Lectures*, i, pp. 395, 402; *St. Andrews Kirk Session Reg.*, ii, pp. 815, 884; *Maitland Club Misc.*, ii, p. 67.
11. Winzet in Hewison, J.K., ed., *Certain Tractates* (STS, 1888–90), i, p. 84; McMillan, *Worship*, p. 201; *Edinburgh Dean of Guild Accounts*, pp. 133, 137–8; J.B. Paul, 'The Post-Reformation Elder' in *SHR* (1912), ix, p. 261.
12. *Maitland Club Misc.*, i, pp. 129–30; Patrick, *Statutes*, pp. 189–90.
13. *RPC*, 1st series, i, p. 492; *Edinburgh Burgh Records*, iii, p. 70; Winzet, *Certain Tractates*, i, p. 84.
14. *St. Andrews Kirk Session Reg.*, ii, pp. 809, 884; *BUK*, p. 192.
15. *St. Andrews Kirk Session Reg.*, i, p. 379, ii, p. 505; *Elgin Records*, ii, p. 121.
16. *St. Andrews Kirk Session Reg.*, i, pp. 204–5; *Elgin Records*, ii, p. 40; *Aberdeen Ecclesiastical Records*, i, p. 33.
17. Winzet, *Certain Tractates*, i, p. 89; *BUK*, ii, pp. 465, 524–5.
18. *St. Andrews Kirk Session Reg.*, ii, p. 830; *APS*, iii, p. 221; *Perth Kirk Session Recs.*, cited Cowan, *Blast and Counterblast*, p. 65; McMillan, *Worship*, pp. 257–60.

19. Knox, *Works*, i, p. 197.
20. Winzet, *Certain Tractates*, i, pp. 83–4; *St. Andrews Kirk Session Reg.*, ii, p. 533; *Aberdeen Ecclesiastical Records*, i, pp. 108–9.
21. *Records of Elgin*, ii, p. 232.
22. *BUK*, i, p. 43.
23. *St. Andrews Kirk Session Reg.*, i, p. 341; *Maitland Club Misc.*, i, p. 104.
24. *St. Andrews Kirk Session*, i, p. 241.
25. *BUK*, i, p. 6.
26. Knox, *Works*, ii, pp. 185–6; *BUK*, i, p. 90.
27. *St. Andrews Kirk Session Reg.*, i, p. 389; *Aberdeen Ecclesiastical Records*, i, p. 18; *Elgin Records*, ii, p. 76; *Chronicle of Perth*, pp. 52–3; *RPC*, 1st series, i, p. 200; Lord Herries, *Memoirs* (Abbotsford Club, 1836), p. 67; Calderwood, *History*, iii, p. 477; *Aberdeen Council Register*, i, p. 459.
28. M.S. Perth Kirk Session Records, cited Cowan, *Blast and Counter-blast*, p. 56; *Chronicle of Perth*, p. 51; *Bannatyne Club Misc.*, i, p. 234; Calderwood, *History*, viii, p. 226.

8 CONSOLIDATION AND RECUSANCY

The best account of the survival of Catholicism in post-Reformation Scotland is found in Margaret H.B. Sanderson, 'Catholic Recusancy in Scotland in the Sixteenth Century' in *Innes Review*, xxi, pp. 87–107, to which the present writer acknowledges his indebtedness and to which reference should be made for all documentation that is otherwise unspecified. The details relating to the consolidation of the protestant ministry are based upon an analysis of Charles H. Haws, *Scottish Parish Clergy at the Reformation, 1540–1574* (Scottish Records Society, 1972), to which reference should be made for details relating to individual parishes.

1. J.H. Pollen, *Papal Negotiations with Mary Queen of Scots* (SHS, 1901), p. 137; *APS*, ii, pp. 534–5; *BUK*, i, p. 6.
2. Pitcairn, *Trials*, i, p. 30; *BUK*, i, p. 10.
3. *BUK*, i, p. 46.
4. *St. Andrews Kirk Session Reg.*, i, pp. 106–7, 333, 376, ii, p. 808.
5. *Spalding Club Misc.*, iv, pp. 120–2; *BUK*, i, pp. 25, 33.
6. Calderwood, *Kirk of the Canagait*, p. 109; *Spottiswoode Club Misc.*, i, pp. 235, 249; *BUK*, ii, p. 784.
7. See also John Todd, 'Pre-Reformation Cure of Souls in Dunblane Diocese' in *Innes Review*, xxvi (1975), pp. 27–62.

8. *St. Andrews Kirk Session Reg.*, i, p. 226; *BUK*, i, p. 43, ii, p. 451.
9. *St. Andrews Kirk Session Reg.*, i, 40, 163, ii, 720.
10. *BUK*, i, p. 33; *Diurnal of Occurrents*, p. 69; Sanderson in *Innes Review*, p. 88; Pitcairn, *Trials*, i, p. 433.
11. *BUK*, i, p. 6; G. Donaldson, 'Galloway Clergy at the Reformation' in *Dumfriesshire Trans.*, 3rd series, xxx (1951–2), p. 38 ff.
12. N. Napier, *Memoir of John Napier of Merchiston* (Edinburgh, 1834), p. 69; G. Donaldson, 'Adam Bothwell and the Reformation in Orkney', *RSCHS*, xiii (1959), p. 85 ff.
13. D.E. Meek and J. Kirk, 'John Carswell, Superintendent of Argyll: a reassessment', *RSCHS*, xix (1975), pp. 1–22.
14. C. Giblin, *The Irish Franciscan Mission to Scotland, 1619–1646* (Dublin, 1964), vii–viii.
15. *BUK*, i, pp. 27, 34; *Elgin Records*, ii, pp. 5–7, 18, 35, 379.
16. *BUK*, ii, p. 718.
17. *BUK*, ii, p. 718.
18. *BUK*, ii, p. 190; *Aberdeen Ecclesiastical Records*, p. 20; *Ellon Presbytery Records*, pp. 11–12, 27, 42; G. Donaldson, 'Aberdeen University and the Reformation' in *Northern Scotland*, i, pp. 137–42.
19. *RPC*, iii, p. 273; *BUK*, ii, p. 722.
20. *BUK*, ii, p. 721.
21. *RPC*, i, p. 615; *BUK*, ii, p. 722.
22. *BUK*, i, p. 364, ii, p. 720.
23. *BUK*, iii, p. 997.
24. *BUK*, iii, pp. 1053, 1061.
25. *BUK*, i, p. 6; *RSS* (SRO), lxxiv, fo. 128.
26. *BUK*, i, p. 334, ii, p. 429.
27. *BUK*, ii, p. 431.
28. *BUK*, ii, p. 716, iii, p. 1053; *RPC*, vi, pp. 312, 326–7.
29. *BUK*, ii, p. 429; J.S. Richardson, *The Abbey of Sweetheart* (HMSO, 1951), pp. 6–7.
30. W.J. Anderson, 'Rome and Scotland, 1513–1625' in *Essays on the Scottish Reformation*, p. 478.

9 CHURCH AND SOCIETY: POST-REFORMATION

1. S.A. Burrell, 'The apocalyptic Vision of the Covenanters' in *SHR*, xliii (1964), pp. 12–13; *Elgin Records*, ii, p. 33; *BUK*, i, p. 254, ii, pp. 515–18, 862.

2. Cameron, *First Book of Discipline*, pp. 96–7, 102; Kirk, *Second Book of Discipline*, pp. 65–73, 178–80; *St. Andrews Kirk Session Regs.*, i, p. 75–6; Knox, *Works*, ii, pp. 192–3; Calderwood, *History*, v, p. 586.
3. Edinburgh, *Dean of Guild Accounts*, p. 117; *Aberdeen Ecclesiastical Records*, p. 19; *BUK*, i, p. 334; Rogers, *History of the Chapel Royal* (Grampian Club, 1882), p. c; *APS*, iv, p. 75; McMillan, *Worship*, pp. 79–80; *Diary of James Melville*, pp. 23–4.
4. Donaldson in *An Introduction to Scottish Legal History*, pp. 363–73.
5. *Diary of James Melville*, pp. 22, 81; *St. Andrews Kirk Session Reg.*, i, p. 396; *BUK*, i, pp. 322–3, 375; *Spottiswoode Soc. Misc.*, ii, pp. 233, 264; *Edinburgh Burgh Records*, iv, pp. 114–15.
6. *Peebles Burgh Records*, pp. 259, 300; Donaldson, *Thirds of Benefices* (SHS, 1949), pp. 89, 97; Sir James Fergusson, 'The Last Monks of Crossraguel' in *The White Hind* (London, 1963), pp. 59–60.
7. *Prot. Book of Robert Rollok* (SRS, 1931), no. 99; Knox, *History*, 192; *Scottish Notes and Queries* (Edinburgh, 1887–1935), 4th series, vi, p. 521; *BUK*, p. 51; *Peebles Burgh Records*, p. 264; see in general D. McRoberts; 'Material Disruption caused by the Scottish Reformation' in *Essays on the Scottish Reformation*, pp. 415–62.
8. Knox, *Works*, vi, p. 21; 'Two Papers from the Argyll Charter Chest' in *SHR*, xxi (1924), pp. 140–3; Cameron, *First Book of Discipline*, p. 94; *Edinburgh Burgh Records*, 1557–71, p. 182, *BUK*, i, p. 5.
9. McRoberts in *Essays on the Scottish Reformation*, pp. 429–31, 442–5, 451–2; Cameron, *First Book of Discipline*, pp. 202–3.
10. McMillan, *Worship*, pp. 155, 362–3; *Peebles Burgh Recs.*, p. 288; *Elgin Records*, ii, pp. 63, 79.
11. W.C. Dickinson *et al*, *Source Book of Scottish History*, 3 vols. (Edinburgh, 1952–4), ii, pp. 168–9; Cameron, *First Book of Discipline*, p. 112.
12. *Peebles Burgh Records*, p. 277; *BUK*, i, pp. 30, 146; *APS*, ii, pp. 347–8, iii, pp. 86–8, 139–42, 576, iv, p. 140.
13. *St. Andrews Kirk Session Reg.*, pp. 340–1, ii, 884; Calderwood, *Kirk of the Canagait*, pp. 5, 26, 43; *Aberdeen Ecclesiastical Records*, pp. 19–20.
14. Cameron, *First Book of Discipline*, pp. 130–1; *St. Andrews Kirk Session Reg.*, ii, pp. 629, 776, 845; *Spottiswoode Soc. Misc.*, ii, p. 277.
15. Cameron, *First Book of Discipline*, pp. 129–36; *BUK*, i, pp. 17, 34, 239, 311; *Monifieth Kirk Session Registers*, cited J.E. Jessop, *Education in Angus* (London, 1931), pp. 47–8; J. Scotland, *The History of Scottish Education* (London, 1969), p. 51.

16. *BUK*, i, pp. 44, 60, 127, 253, 339, 415, ii, pp. 723, 856, 965; *APS*, iii, pp. 24, 38, 347; Glasgow Burgh Records and Haddington Presbytery Records cited by J. Grant, *History of the Burgh Schools in Scotland* (Glasgow, 1876), pp. 85–6.
17. Cameron, *First Book of Discipline*, pp. 137–43; P.H. Brown, ed., *The Vernacular Writings of George Buchanan* (STS, 1892) pp. 6–17; R.G. Cant, *Short History of the University of St. Andrews* (Edinburgh, 1972), pp. 45–58; Cant, *The College of St. Salvator* (Edinburgh, 1950), pp. 167–74.
18. Durkan and Kirk, *History of the University of Glasgow*, pp. 300–46.
19. Donaldson, in *Northern Scotland*, i, pp. 136–42; *Aberdeen Ecclesiastical Records*, i, p. 26; G.D. Henderson, *The Founding of Marischal College, Aberdeen* (Aberdeen, 1946), pp. 12–18.
20. D.B. Horn, *Short History of the University of Edinburgh* (Edinburgh, 1967), p. 1 ff; *Edinburgh Burgh Records, 1589–1603*, p. 149.
21. *BUK*, i, p. 15; Edinburgh Testaments, 20 Oct. 1569 cited in Cowan, *Blast and Counterblast*, p. 31.
22. *BUK*, i, pp. 29, 45, 335, 524–5; Calderwood, *Kirk of the Canagait*, p. 62; *St. Andrews Kirk Session Reg.*, pp. 815–17; *Elgin Records*, ii, p. 95.
23. See Ian B. Cowan, *The Scottish Covenanters, 1660–88* (London, 1976).

Bibliography and References

References, unless otherwise stated are standardized to conform to the 'List of Abbreviated Titles of the Printed Sources of Scottish History to 1560' in *Scottish Historical Review*, vol. xlii (October, 1963) in which full bibliographical details of works not noted below will be found.

Aberdeen Council Register: Extracts from the Council Register of the Burgh of Aberdeen (Spalding Club, 1844–8).

Aberdeen Ecclesiastical Records: Selections from Ecclesiastical Records of Aberdeen, ed. J. Stuart (Spalding Club, 1846).

APS: The Acts of the Parliament of Scotland, eds. T. Thomson and C. Innes, 12 vols. (Edinburgh, 1814–75).

Baxter, J.H. *Dundee and the Reformation* (Abertay Historical Society, 1960).

Buchanan, *Vernacular Writings*; Brown, P.H., ed., *The Vernacular Writings of George Buchanan* (STS, 1892).

BUK: The Booke of the Universall Kirk, Acts and Proceedings of the General Assemblies of the Kirk of Scotland, 1560–1618, Bannatyne and Maitland Clubs, 3 vols., and Appendix vol. (Edinburgh, 1839–45).

Burnet, G.B., *The Holy Communion in the Reformed Church of Scotland, 1560–1960* (Edinburgh, 1960).

Calderwood, *Kirk of the Canagait:* Calderwood, A.B., ed., *The Buik of the Kirk of the Canagait, 1564–1567* (SRS, 1961).

Calderwood, *History*: Thomson, T., ed., *The History of the Kirk of Scotland by Mr. David Calderwood*, 8 vols. (The Wodrow Society, 1842).

Cameron, J.K., *The First Book of Discipline* (Edinburgh, 1972).

Cant, R.G., *The College of St. Salvator*, St Andrews University Publications, no. 47 (Edinburgh, 1950).

Cant, R.G., *The University of St. Andrews: a short history* (Edinburgh, 1972).

Chronicle of Perth: The Chronicle of Perth (Maitland Club, 1831).

Coulton, G. C., *Scottish Abbeys and Social Life* (Cambridge, 1933).

Cowan, I.B., *Blast and Counterblast: Contemporary Writings on the Scottish Reformation* (Edinburgh, 1960).

Cowan, I.B., 'Church and Society in Post-Reformation Scotland' in *RSCHS*, xvii (1971), pp. 185–201.

Cowan, I.B. and Easson, D.E., *Medieval Religious Houses, Scotland* (London, 1976).

Cowan, I.B., *Regional Aspects of the Scottish Reformation* (Historical Association, 1978).

Cowan, I.B., 'Some Aspects of the Appropriation of Parish Churches in Medieval Scotland' in *RSCHS*, xiii (1959), pp. 203–22.

Cowan, I.B., 'The Five Articles of Perth' in D. Shaw, ed., *Reformation and Revolution* (Edinburgh, 1967).

Cowan, I.B., 'The Medieval Church in Argyll and the Isles' in *RSCHS*, xx (1978), pp. 15–29.

Cowan, I.B., 'The Medieval Church in the diocese of Aberdeen in *Northern Scotland*, i (1972), pp. 19–48.

Cowan, I.B., 'Vicarages and the Cure of Souls in Medieval Scotland' in *RSCHS*, xvi, pp. 111–27.

Diurnal of Occurrents: A Diurnal of Remarkable Occurrents that have passed within the Country of Scotland since the death of King James the fourth till the year MDLXXV (Bannatyne Club, 1875).

Donaldson, G., 'Aberdeen University and the Reformation' in *Northern Scotland*, i (1973), pp. 129–42.

Donaldson, G., 'Alexander Gordon, Bishop of Galloway (1559–1575) and his work in the Reformed Church', *Dumfriesshire Trans.*, 3rd series, xxiv (1965–6), pp. 111–28.

Donaldson, G., 'Bishop Adam Bothwell and the Reformation in Orkney' in *RSCHS*, xiii (1959), pp. 85–100.

Donaldson, G., 'The Church Courts' in *An Introduction to Scottish Legal History*, The Stair Society, vol. xx (1958), pp. 363–73.

Donaldson, G., *James V to James VII*, The Edinburgh History of Scotland, 3 (Edinburgh, 1965).

Donaldson, G., 'The Polity of the Scottish Church 1560–1600' in *RSCHS*, xi (1955), pp. 212–26.

Donaldson, G., *The Scottish Reformation* (Cambridge, 1960).

Donaldson, G., *Thirds of Benefices*: Donaldson, G., *Account of the Collectors of Thirds of Benefices 1561–1572* (SHS, 1949).

Dowden, J., *The Medieval Church in Scotland* (Glasgow, 1910).

Dumfriesshire Trans.: *Transactions of the Dumfriesshire and Galloway Natural History and Antiquarian Society*.

Dunlop, A.I., 'The Polity of the Scottish Church 1600–1638' in *RSCHS*, xii (1956), p. 161.

Durkan, J., 'Care of the Poor: Pre-Reformation Hospitals' in D. McRoberts, ed., *Essays on the Scottish Reformation, 1513–1625* (Glasgow, 1962), pp. 116–28.

Durkan, J., 'Chaplains in Late Medieval Scotland' in *RSCHS*, xx (1979), pp. 91–117.

Durkan, J. and Ross, A., *Early Scottish Libraries* (Glasgow, 1961).

Durkan, J., 'Education in the century of the Reformation' in D. McRoberts, ed., *Essays on the Scottish Reformation, 1513–1625* (Glasgow, 1962), pp. 145–68.

Durkan, J., 'Paisley Abbey in the Sixteenth Century' in *Innes Review*, xxvii (1976), pp. 110–26.

Durkan, J. and Kirk, J., *The University of Glasgow* (Glasgow, 1977).

Edinburgh Burgh Records: Extracts from the Records of the Burghs of Edinburgh, The Scottish Burgh Records Society (Edinburgh, 1869–72).

Edinburgh Dean of Guild Accounts: City of Edinburgh Old Accounts, ii, Dean of Guild Accounts, 1552–67, ed. R. Adam (Edinburgh, 1899).

Elgin Records: The Records of Elgin, 1234–1800, ed. W. Cramond and S. Ree, 2 vols. (New Spalding Club, 1903–8).

Ellon Presbytery Records: Mair, T., ed., *Narratives and extracts from the records of the presbytery of Ellon, 1597–1800*.

'Extracts from the Kirk Session Register of Perth', *The Spottiswoode Miscellany*, ii, pp. 225–311 (Edinburgh, 1846).

Fittis, R.S., *The Ecclesiastical annals of Perth to the period of the Reformation* (Edinburgh, 1885).

Foster, W.R., *The Church before the Covenants* (Edinburgh, 1975).

Grant, J., *History of the Burgh Schools of Scotland* (Glasgow, 1876).

Gude and Godlie Ballatis, ed. A.F. Mitchell (STS, 1897).

Haws, *Scottish Parish Clergy*: C.H. Haws, *Scottish Parish Clergy at the Reformation* (SRS, 1972).

Hay, G., *The Architecture of Scottish Post-Reformation Churches, 1560–1843* (Oxford, 1957).

Herkless, John and R.K. Hannay, *The Archbishops of St. Andrews*, 5 vols. (Edinburgh, 1907–15).

Herkless, John and R.K. Hannay, *The College of St. Leonard* (Edinburgh, 1905).

Historical Atlas of Scotland: P. McNeill and R. Nicholson, eds., *An Historical Atlas of Scotland* (St. Andrews, 1975).

Horn, D.B., *A Short History of the University of Edinburgh, 1556–1889* (Edinburgh, 1967).

James IV Letters, The Letters of James the Fourth, ed. R.K. Hannay and R.L. Mackie (SHS, 1953).

James V Letters, The Letters of James the Fifth, ed. R.K. Hannay and D. *VIII*, ed. J.S. Brewer and others (London, 1864–1932).

Kenneth, Brother, 'The Popular Literature of the Scottish Reformation' in D. McRoberts, ed., *Essays on the Scottish Reformation, 1513–1625* (Glasgow, 1962), pp. 169–84.

Kerr, J., *Scottish Education, School and University from Early times to 1908* (Cambridge, 1910).

Kirk, J., 'The Influence of Calvinism on the Scottish Reformation', *RSCHS*, xviii (1974), pp. 157–79.

Kirk, J., *The Second Book of Discipline* (Edinburgh, 1980).

Knox, *History*: Dickinson, W.C., ed., *John Knox's History of the Reformation in Scotland* (Edinburgh, 1949).

Knox, *Works*: Laing, D., ed., *The Works of John Knox*, 6 vols. (Edinburgh, 1846).

Kuipers, C.A., *Quintin Kennedy (1520–1564): Two Eucharistic Tracts* (Nijmegen, 1964).

Laing, A., *Lindores Abbey* (Edinburgh, 1876).

Law, T.G., *The Catechism of John Hamilton ... 1552* (Oxford, 1884).

Lee, J., *Lectures on the History of the Church of Scotland from the Reformation to the Revolution Settlement*, 2 vols (Edinburgh, 1860).

Lee, M., *James Stewart, Earl of Moray: a political study of the Reformation in Scotland* (New York, 1953).

Lindsay, *Works: The Works of Sir David Lindsay, 1490–1555*, ed. D. Hamer, 4 vols. (STS, 1931–36).

LP Henry VIII : Letters and Papers, foreign and domestic of the reign of Henry VIII, ed. J.S. Brewer and others (London, 1864–1932).

MacGibbon, D. and Ross, T., *The Ecclesiastical Architecture of Scotland*, 3 vols. (Edinburgh, 1897).

MacGregor, J., *The Scottish Presbyterian Polity* (Edinburgh, 1926).

McKay, D., 'Parish Life in Scotland, 1500–1560' in D. McRoberts, ed., *Essays on the Scottish Reformation, 1513–1625* (Glasgow, 1962), pp. 85–113.

McLennan, B., 'The Reformation in the burgh of Aberdeen' in *Northern Scotland*, ii (1976–7), pp. 119–44.

McMillan, *Worship*; McMillan, W., *The Worship of the Scottish Reformed Church, 1550–1638* (London, 1931).

McRoberts, D., ed., *Essays on the Scottish Reformation, 1513–1625* (Glasgow, 1962).

McRoberts, D., 'Material Destruction caused by the Scottish Reformation' in D. McRoberts, ed., *Essays on the Scottish Reformation, 1513–1625* (Glasgow, 1962), pp. 415–62.

McRoberts, D., 'Scottish Pilgrims to the Holy Land' in *Innes Review*, xx (1969), pp. 80–106.

Mahoney, M., 'The Scottish Hierarchy, 1513–65' in D. McRoberts, ed., *Essays on the Scottish Reformation, 1513–1625* (Glasgow, 1962), pp. 39–84.

Makey, W.H., 'The Elders of Stow, Liberton, Canongate and St. Cuthbert's in the mid-seventeenth century' in *RSCHS*, xvii (1970) pp. 155–67.

Maxwell, A., *Old Dundee prior to the Reformation* (Edinburgh and Dundee, 1891).

Meek, D.E. and Kirk, J., 'John Carswell, Superintendent of Argyll: a reassessment' in *RSCHS*, xix (1975), pp. 1–22.

Melville, *Diary*: Pitcairn, R., ed., *The Autobiography and Diary of Mr. James Melvill* (The Wodrow Society, 1842).

Munimenta Alme Universitatis Glasguensis, 1450–1727, 2 vols. (Maitland Club, 1854).

Oldham, A., 'Scottish Polyphonic Music' in *Innes Review*, xiii (1962), pp. 54–61.

Original Letters relating to the Ecclesiastical Affairs of Scotland, ed. D. Laing, 2 vols. (Bannatyne Club, 1851).

Patrick, *Statutes*: Patrick, D., ed., *Statutes of the Scottish Church, 1225–1559* (SHS, 1907).

Pitcairn, *Trials: Ancient Criminal Trials in Scotland*, ed. R. Pitcairn, 3 vols. (Bannatyne Club, 1829–33).

Pryde, G.S., ed., *Ayr Burgh Accounts, 1534–1624* (SHS, 1937).

PSAS: Proceedings of the Antiquaries of Scotland.

Rait, R.S., *The Universities of Aberdeen* (Aberdeen, 1895).

Reg. Lat.: Registra Lateranensa in Vatican Archives.

Reg. Supp.: Registra Supplicationum in Vatican Archives.

Reg. Vat.: Registra Vaticana in Vatican Archives.

Ross, A., 'Reformation and Repression' in D. McRoberts, ed., *Essays on the Scottish Reformation, 1513–1625* (Glasgow, 1962), pp. 371–414.

Ross, A., 'Some Notes on the Religious Orders in Pre-Reformation

Scotland' in D. McRoberts, ed., *Essays on the Scottish Reformation, 1513–1625* (Glasgow, 1962), pp. 185–244.

RPC: The Register of the Privy Council of Scotland, ed. J.H. Burton and others (Edinburgh, 1877).

RSCHS: Records of the Scottish Church History Society.

RSS: Registrum Secreti sigilli Regum Scotorum, ed. M. Livingstone and others (Edinburgh, 1908).

St. Andrews Acta: Acta Facultatis Artium Universitatis Sancti Andree, 1413–1588, ed. A.I. Dunlop, 2 vols. (SHS, 1964).

St. Andrews Kirk Session Register: Fleming, D.H., ed., *Register of the Minister, Elders and Deacons of the Christian Congregation of St. Andrews 1559–1600*, 2 vols. (SHS, 1889–90).

Sanderson, M., 'Catholic Recusancy in Scotland in the Sixteenth Century' in *Innes Review*, xxi (1970), pp. 87–107.

Sanderson, M., 'Kirkmen and their tenants in the era of the Reformation' in *RSCHS*, xviii (1972), pp. 26–42.

Sanderson, M., 'Some Aspects of the Church in Scottish Society in the Era of the Reformation' in *RSCHS*, xvii (1970), pp. 81–98.

Shaw, D., 'John Willock' in D. Shaw, ed., *Reformation and Revolution* (Edinburgh, 1967), pp. 42–69.

Shaw, D., *The General Assemblies of the Church of Scotland 1560–1600* (Edinburgh, 1963).

Shaw, D., 'The Inauguration of Ministers in Scotland 1560–1620' in *RSCHS*, xvi (1966), pp. 35–62.

SHR: Scottish Historical Society.

SHS: Scottish History Society.

SRO: Scottish Record Office.

Spalding Club Miscellany: Miscellany of the Spalding Club, iv (Aberdeen, 1849).

SRS: Scottish Record Society.

STS: Scottish Text Society.

Taylor, M., 'The Conflicting Doctrines of the Scottish Reformation' in D. McRoberts, ed., *Essays on the Scottish Reformation, 1513–1625* (Glasgow, 1962), pp. 245–73.

Watt, *Fasti*: Watt, D.E.R., *Fasti Ecclesiae Scoticanae Medii Aevi ad annum 1638* (SRS, 1969).

Winning, T., 'Church Councils in Sixteenth-Century Scotland' in D. McRoberts, ed., *Essays on the Scottish Reformation, 1513–1625* (Glasgow, 1962), pp. 332–58.

Winzet, *Certane Tractates*: Hewison, J.K., ed., *Certane Tractates together with the Book of Four Score Three Questions*, by Ninian Winzet (STS, 1888–90).

Wodrow Soc. Misc.: D. Laing, ed., *Miscellany of the Wodrow Society*, i (Edinburgh, 1844).

Index